DEMOCRACY AND HUMAN RIGHTS

DEMOCRACY AND HUMAN RIGHTS

Surinder Khanna

SWASTIK PUBLICATIONS
Delhi-110094 (India)

DEMOCRACY AND HUMAN RIGHTS

First Published, 2012

ISBN 978-93-81084-47-2

Published in India by

SWASTIK PUBLICATIONS

31, Gali No. 1, A-Block, Pocket-5,
CRP Water Tank, Sonia Vihar,
Delhi-110094 (INDIA)
Mob. 9968482939, 9899462604
E-mail : swastik_books@yahoo.com.

Printed at : Deepak Offset Press, Delhi.

Preface

Democracy and human rights are distinct yet interrelated concepts, with democracy referring to government by the people, and human rights referring to universal rights that apply to all individuals in all societies. This book examines the interdependence of human rights and democracy, with a specific focus on the application of these concepts in the Palestinian Territories. The book first discusses the conceptualisation of democracy in terms of mechanisms, institutions, civil society and citizen rights, then discusses the conceptualisation of human rights with specific focus on the human security perspective. It also examines human rights and democracy in Palestine with regards to elections, political parties, separation of powers, judiciary reform, security, and civil society.

Human rights and democracy have historically been viewed as separate, albeit parallel, concepts. However, understandings of both human rights and democracy are dynamic and varied, and recent re-conceptualisations of both ideas have led to the emergence of a discourse that recognises their interdependence. Specifically, definitions of democracy have expanded from the traditional procedural democracy to encompass the ideals of a substantive, liberal democracy. Likewise, the human rights framework has begun to further develop conceptions of social, economic, and cultural rights, in addition to civil and political rights, thus expanding the notion of human rights to include human security, and extending human rights to the collective as well as the individual level. These renewed definitions present opportunities for recognising the convergence of the theories and fields related to human rights and democracy.

This book begins with a theoretical discussion of the principles of democracy, distinguishing between substantive and procedural democracy and identifying key elements and institutions inherent in a liberal democracy. It examines the emerging re-conceptualisation of the human rights framework, including the human security perspective, which has enhanced the complementarity between human rights and democracy. The present book discusses the convergence of the democracy and human rights fields and theories, and concludes that the two concepts are not only complementary, but are indeed interdependent. This book focuses on the application of this theory in the case of Palestine by analysing past and present experiences with democracy and human rights in the Occupied Territories, including obstacles and points of progress, and discussing recommendations for future implementation.

The book has been divided into nine chapters and each chapter deals with a different topic. A large number of problems have been included in those chapters which are more common in the syllabii of different Indian universities. The solutions to the problems have been written in a manner that they can be easily grasped by the students. In some problems the solutions were not the requirement. The book will be of use for the students of sociology and political science in degree classes of Indian universities.

I am thankful to all my colleagues and friends, whose invaluable suggestion were helpful to give the book in its present form. I also thanks to Swastik Publications for bringing out the book in such a short-time.

Author

Contents

1

Introduction

Human rights and democracy have historically been viewed as separate, albeit parallel, concepts. However, understandings of both human rights and democracy are dynamic and varied, and recent re-conceptualisations of both ideas have led to the emergence of a discourse that recognises their interdependence. Specifically, definitions of democracy have expanded from the traditional procedural democracy to encompass the ideals of a substantive, liberal democracy. Likewise, the human rights framework has begun to further develop conceptions of social, economic, and cultural rights, in addition to civil and political rights, thus expanding the notion of human rights to include human security, and extending human rights to the collective as well as the individual level. These renewed definitions present opportunities for recognising the convergence of the theories and fields related to human rights and democracy.

The necessity of acknowledging the interdependence of democracy and human rights is becoming especially important in emerging democracies such as Palestine. In these cases, in which the development and reform of democratic institutions is starting to take place, it is imperative to ensure that such institutions are built on foundations of both human rights and democracy if they are to be sustainable. To be sure, previous attempts at democracy by the Palestinian Authority (PA) in the 1990s proved to be ephemeral, largely due to the absence of protection for human rights. Likewise, human rights advocates have found it difficult to affect systemic change in the absence of a legitimate democracy. Thus, as Palestine looks ahead to new opportunities for democracy in the future, it is necessary to integrate the broadened human rights framework, including human security, with the ideals and institutions of a liberal, participatory democracy.

This chapter begins with a theoretical discussion of the principles of democracy, distinguishing between substantive and procedural democracy and identifying key elements and institutions inherent in a liberal democracy. The next section examines the emerging re-conceptualisation of the human rights framework, including the human security perspective, which has enhanced the complementarity between human rights and democracy. The following section discusses the convergence of the democracy and human rights fields and theories, and concludes that the two concepts are not only complementary, but are indeed interdependent. The second half of the chapter focuses on the application of this theory in the case of Palestine by analysing past and present experiences with democracy and human rights in the Occupied Territories, including obstacles and points of progress, and discussing recommendations for future implementation.

Human Rights and Democracy: Theoretical Analysis

The idea of democracy has been understood and applied in different ways, both temporally and culturally, with democracy taking various forms in different societies. From a historical perspective, the direct democracy of ancient Athens has been transformed into the representative democracy that is common today. Likewise, former restrictions on the political participation of women and other marginalised groups have been challenged in modern times to allow for more inclusive democracies. Most recently, both theorists and practitioners of democracy are starting to further articulate differences between procedural democracies and substantive, liberal democracies. However, all of these forms of democracy are based to some extent on the original Greek notion of *demokratia*, that is, "government by the people," from the words *demos*(people) and *kratos* (rule or power). This core concept still forms the crux of modern definitions of democracy, including the 1993 Vienna Declaration's statement that "democracy is based on the freely expressed will of the people to determine their own political, economic, social and cultural systems and their full participation in all aspects of their lives."[1] From this starting point, it is possible to identify several key principles and institutions that are inherent to a sustainable democracy.

While historically there has been more emphasis on the political institutions and procedures that comprise democracy, namely elections, political parties, and governmental bodies, increased attention has recently been given to the ideals and principles that underscore those mechanisms. As stated by David Beetham, Director of the Centre for Democratisation Studies at the University of Leeds, "to define democracy simply in institutional terms is to elevate means into ends, and to concentrate on the forms without the substance."[2] Jack Donnelly, Professor of International Studies at the University of Denver, agrees, noting that "pure procedural democracy can easily denigrate into non-democratic or even anti-democratic formalism," thus, "substantive conceptions rightly insist that we not lose sight of the core values of popular authority and control over government."[3] However, Donnelly also notes that purely substantive approaches fail to recognise the "idea of the people *ruling* rather than just benefiting... The term 'democratic' easily slides into an essentially superfluous synonym for 'egalitarian.'"[4] That is, government *for* the people is not synonymous with government *by* the people, and therefore may or may not be democratic. To be sure, substantive conceptions risk being susceptible to normative associations that identify any positive sociopolitical elements as indicators of democracy.

This chapter takes the position that neither "substantive" nor "procedural" conceptions of democracy should be considered more important than the other; indeed, it is questionable if the two notions can even be separated. Instead, substantive and procedural elements should be viewed as complementary and in fact essential to each other. The principles that underscore substantive democracy will only remain theoretical ideals unless mechanisms are present for translating those ideals into reality, while procedural institutions, however democratic in form, are meaningless if they do not yield ends that reflect democratic values. For the remainder of this paper, the term "substantive democracy" will refer to democracies that embody both the principles *and* the institutions that form the foundation of democracy, in contrast to "electoral democracies," which may be democratic in name and form but not in practice.

The basic elements of a substantive democracy, according to Beetham, "are that the people have a right to a controlling influence over public decisions and decision makers, and that they should be treated with equal respect and as of equal worth in the context of such decisions."[5] Beetham refers to these concepts as *popular control* and *popular equality*, both of which contribute to the foundation of the principles and institutions that inform democracy. These primary elements, in conjunction with the rule of law, open government, and public participation, form the core of substantive democracies, as reflected in their mechanisms and institutions, and the presence of civil society and citizen rights.

Mechanisms

The primary indicator of democracy is the presence of popular elections. According to Beetham, "popular authorisation is achieved through regular competitive elections according to universal secret ballot, which ensures voters a choice of candidates and policies and gives them the opportunity to dismiss politicians who no longer command their confidence."[6] As Shadrack Gutto, Director of the

Centre for Applied Legal Studies at the University of Witwatersrand in Johannesburg, states however, "for elections to be substantially 'free and fair,' it is imperative that enabling principles and rights be observed," including "the rights to or freedom of association, opinion, expression, and assembly."[7] Gutto also notes the importance of available and adequate material and human resources to educate voters, register voters, monitor the voting process, count election results, and reconcile disputes. Indeed, the democratic nature of an electoral process should be assessed by "the reach, inclusiveness, independence, integrity, and impartiality of elections, as well as how equally the electoral process treats citizens, how much effective choice it offers them, how far the government actually fulfills the electoral choices made, and how many people in practice exercise the right to vote."[8] In addition, political parties function as a mechanism within electoral systems by organising different policies into cohesive programmes, nominating appropriate candidates, and advocating for the implementation of decisions supported by the electorate.

Institutions

As Beetham articulates, "although elections form a key mechanism for the popular control of government, they are of limited effectiveness on their own without institutions that secure a government's continuous accountability to the public."[9] Gutto agrees, noting how "elected representatives can play a democratic role only to the extent that enabling institutions of governance with clear systems and procedures that are secured by a normative framework and laws exist."[10] Open and accountable political institutions depend primarily on the decentralisation of governance and the separation of powers between the executive, legislative, and judiciary spheres. These branches should be monitored through a system of checks and balances by each other, through horizontal accountability, and also be answerable to the people as a whole through vertical accountability. These institutions' specific roles and functions can be best understood and implemented when articulated in a constitution or equivalent "rule of law." The constitution should also articulate the financial responsibilities of the legislature, as well as allow for a system of regional and local government.

Civil Society

As Gutto notes, "however effective public institutions and accountability processes may be in any society aspiring to democracy, their effectiveness and impact would nevertheless be diminished in the absence of a vibrant and activist civil society."[11] Civil society, sometimes referred to as "democratic society," creates opportunities for active citizenship and direct involvement in the functioning of a democracy. The key elements of civil society include an independent media, sources of policy expertise independent of the state, and associations that may include organisations dedicated to social services, development, health, education, human rights, women's empowerment, or other issues. An active civil society has the additional benefit of fostering respect for the rights of other citizens by creating environments of diversity and dialogue.

Citizen Rights

Democracy also includes the presence of political and civil rights for citizens, especially freedom of expression, association, and assembly, which require the guarantee of due legal process and liberty and security of person to be effective. There has been recent debate on the necessity of economic, social, and cultural rights as conditions of democracy, however, it is becoming more widely accepted that "for civil and political rights and freedoms to have any value, citizens must possess the capacity to exercise them."[12] The majority of political, civil, economic, social, and cultural rights at the national level relate directly or indirectly to the international human rights framework, as will be discussed further.

The Dynamism of Democracy

It should be noted that, despite these common elements (mechanisms, institutions, civil society, and citizen rights), democracy can take a variety of forms; there is no "one size fits all" democracy. As Beetham explains, "different societies and diverse circumstances require different arrangements if democratic principles are to be effectively realised."[13] Abdul Aziz Said, Professor of International Peace and Conflict Resolution at American University, agrees, noting that "the form of democracy is always cast in the mold of the culture of a people;" he thus urges a "more democratic theory of democracy" that recognises its potential for variation and dynamism.[14] Relatedly, Said specifically emphasises that "democracy is not a western product." As noted above, the principles and institutions that inform substantive democracy are based on tenets that transcend national and political ideologies; thus, democracy is not exclusive to the West. This point has several implications. First, it implies that there is no fundamental incompatibility between democracy and the Arab world, nor between democracy and Islam. As Said notes, "the lack of democracy in the Middle East is due more to a lack of preparation for it than to a lack of religious and cultural foundations."[15] Secondly, the idea that democracy is not exclusive to the West can serve to caution superpowers to avoid imposing their models of democracy on other societies, and encourage them to instead assume a supportive role in developing democracy in local contexts. Likewise, superpowers should be cautious of pursuing national interests under the guise of democracy to prevent the association of democracy with western imperialism. At the same time, local democracy advocates are called upon to consider how their social mechanisms, values, and contexts can inform culturally sustainable democracies.

Defining Human Rights: The Human Security Perspective

As Donnelly summarises, "human rights are, literally, the rights that one has simply as a human being. As such they are equal rights, because we are all equally human beings. They are also inalienable rights, because no matter how inhumanely we act or are treated we cannot become other than human beings."[16] Human rights are defined in several key documents, namely, the Universal Declaration of Human Rights (UDHR), adopted by the United Nations General Assembly in 1948; the International Covenant on Civil and Political Rights (ICCPR), adopted in 1966; and the International Covenant on Economic, Social, and Cultural Rights, also adopted in 1966. The Vienna Declaration, adopted at the World Conference on Human Rights in 1993, further expanded the meaning of human rights.

Originally, human rights were developed to outline a set of individual rights that states were required to respect or provide for their citizens. The framework not only included the *prohibition* of certain acts, but also the "imposition of *the duty to perform* certain obligations in order to promote and protect the enjoyment of certain rights."[17] In other words, abuse of human rights can take the form of both violations and denials. While the full realisation of human rights is still an ideal, much has been achieved in the name of human rights. According to Anthony Langlois, Professor of International Relations at Flinders University in Adelaide, Australia, achievements include "international recognition of human rights as the basic set of norms of human behavior, the internationalisation of human rights institutions of various types, and the development of International Human Rights Law."[18]

The notion of human rights has begun to be broadened in recent years. First, the responsibility of ensuring human rights has been expanded beyond only state governments to include individuals, groups of people, and other non-state actors. Secondly, the common association of human rights law with peacetime (and, in turn, the association of international humanitarian law (IHL) with wartime) has given way to the widespread recognition that human rights law applies in conflict situations, just as it does in periods of stability. Finally, and perhaps most importantly for the context of this paper, the past ten years have seen increased acknowledgment of the interdependence and indivisibility of human rights. While this has always been true in theory, in the past the two separate Covenants suggested divisions between political and civil rights and economic, social, and cultural rights. While some divisions still exist, the gaps between the two fields of rights were largely bridged in 1993 at Vienna, where it was declared that "human rights are universal, indivisible and interdependent and interrelated" and that the international community "must treat human rights globally in a fair and equal manner."[19]

In other words, the notion of human rights is expanding to include the concept of human security in a more conscious and deliberate manner. According to the United Nations Development Report of 1994, "human security can be said to have two main aspects. It means, first, safety from such chronic threats as hunger, disease and repression. And second, it means protection from sudden and hurtful disruptions in the patterns of daily life—whether in homes, in jobs or in communities."[20] This renewed interest in human security and development has accordingly placed increased emphasis on economic and social rights, thus contributing to the re-conceptualisation of the human rights framework. As Beetham summarises:

> The idea of economic and social rights as human rights expresses the moral intuition that, in a world rich in resources and the accumulation of human knowledge, everyone ought to be guaranteed the basic means for sustaining life, and that those denied these are victims of a fundamental injustice. Expressing this intuition in the form of human rights both gives the deprived the strongest possible claim to that of which they are deprived and emphasises the duty of responsible parties to uphold or help them meet their entitlement.[21]

Democracy and Human Rights

Democracy and human rights are clearly different notions; "they are distinct enough for them to be viewed as discreet and differentiated political concepts."[22] Whereas democracy aims to empower "the people" collectively, human rights aims to empower individuals. Similarly, human rights is directly associated with the how of ruling, and not just the who, which may be the case in an electoral democracy, though not in a substantive democracy. Thus, "democracies" exist that do not necessarily protect human rights, while some non-democratic states are able to ensure some, though not all, human rights. On another level, the international acceptance, institutionalisation, and legal aspects of human rights mentioned above do not apply to democracy.

These distinctions have influenced the traditional separation of the theories and fields of human rights and democracy. From the human rights perspective, many have adhered to the separationist theory, which argues that "democracy is not immediately needed for the observation of human rights and that the maintenance of an essential link between human rights and democracy may well have the effect of delaying the implementation of human rights norms in various states."[23] A recent corollary of the separationist theory is the "democracy as neo-imperialism" notion that charges that "democracy is a 'Western-centric' approach to government that is not found indigenously in all societies and is not desirable for all peoples."[24]

These arguments are subject to several key counter arguments that illustrate the interdependence of human rights and democracy. First, in terms of the neo-imperialist argument, it is certainly true that Western superpowers should not impose their particular forms of democracy on other societies and expect them to be accepted and sustainable, as noted above. However, it is equally culturally insensitive to claim that democracy is only an option in the West, or that it is incompatible with other cultures. Secondly, in reference to the separationist theory, while it would be unwise to "wait" for democracy to start promoting human rights, it must also be recognised that some human rights are intrinsically linked with institutions and principles of democracy. Furthermore, separating human rights from democracy undermines opportunities for implementation, in that it reduces human rights to standards or norms; as Langlois states, "human rights amount to little more than charity if they are not functioning in a democratic framework."[25]

Essentially, the inclination to separate human rights from democracy is rooted in the acceptance of their traditional definitions. An electoral democracy that lacks the other institutions and principles of a substantive democracy can function without necessarily guaranteeing human rights, just as some narrowly defined human rights can still be realised in the absence of democracy. However, the re-conceptualisation of democracy as substantive, and of human rights as being more far-reaching and inclusive, underscores the necessity of linking the two. This interdependence occurs on the levels of principle, enforcement, and specific rights.

On the conceptual level, as Langlois notes, "both contemporary liberal democracy and human rights are derived from and express the assumptions of liberalism,"[26] which include individualism, egalitarianism, and universalism. Furthermore, both democracy and human rights pursue a common agenda, and it is "only within a democracy that human rights standards or norms [are] transcended such that the values articulated by these norms or standards are genuine rights."[27] In addition, it is only in a well-functioning democracy that individual citizens have access to mechanisms to ensure the implementation of their rights.

The relationship between human rights and democracy is perhaps most clear through an examination of civil and political rights, especially those articulated in Article 21 of the UDHR and

Article 25 of the ICCPR, both of which ensure citizen participation in government through free and fair elections and through direct service and participation. These rights are related to the rights of expression, association, assembly, and movement, which are also interdependent with democracy, as well as the rights to liberty, security of person, and the guarantee of due process of the law.

Economic, social, and cultural rights are also being increasingly recognised as being mutually dependent, if not integral, with democracy. As Gutto writes, "the pursuit of the right to development and socio-economic rights is strongly associated with the social democracy vision of poverty eradication and the equitable distribution of ownership, control, and the benefits of wealth."[28] Indeed, political and civil rights can best (and perhaps only) be realised by citizens who meet a basic level of physical security in terms of access to shelter, water, sanitation, and food, as well as education, healthcare, and employment or income. Socially, democracy is interrelated with rights to equality and non-discrimination, especially for marginalised groups including women and minorities. Culturally, the respect for diversity and pluralism inherent to democracy is linked to the protection of rights related to language, religion, or ethnicity.

It is thus clear that human rights and democracy are interdependent, especially when defined in the broader conceptualisations of democracy as substantive democracy, and human rights as civil, political, economic, social, and cultural rights. These different kinds of rights cannot be realised in a non-democratic system, and likewise, no democracy is sustainable without the presence of these rights. While this relationship is evident in theory, it is perhaps more useful to consider the interdependence of human rights and democracy through the case study of an emerging democracy.

Human Rights and Democracy in Palestine

The status of democracy in Palestine is somewhat open to

interpretation. Many democracy advocates agree that Palestine is moving in the direction of becoming a substantive democracy, but that it still has ways to go. Specifically, the will of the people reflects a keen desire for democracy, but that has yet to translate into viable democratic institutions and principles. As Nathan J. Brown of the Carnegie Endowment for International Peace states, "Palestine is… a model liberal democracy. Its most significant flaw is that it does not exist."[29] That is, democracy in Palestine is evident in theory, but it has not been able to fully manifest itself in practice.

Obstacles to realising both human rights and democracy are rooted in both external and internal factors. In terms of external factors, the Israeli occupation and the protracted Israeli-Palestinian conflict have posed obvious challenges to the development of democracy and human rights in Palestine. To start with democracy, political reform is difficult in the midst of any ongoing violent conflict.[30] In the case of Israel-Palestine, the challenge of political reform is further exacerbated by the nature of the occupation, which creates a complicated system of dual authority between Israel and the PA. Indeed, according to democracy advocates interviewed for this report,[31] the occupation remains the most prominent obstacle to Palestinian democracy.

Challenges resulting from the external influence of the occupation are interrelated with internal factors as well, most notably corruption in the executive branch of the PA under Arafat and the failure of the security services to be effective. Indeed, the Oslo Accords "were predicated on the ability of the PA to enhance Israeli security and thus focused on enabling the executive and placing few fetters on the security services in internal matters."[32] In addition to, and perhaps, because of the fact that the PA lacked sovereignty, it also lacked legitimacy. This problem emerged not only from the external fact of the occupation however, but also from internal shortcomings such as centralisation of power, lack of accountability and transparency, corruption, and human rights violations.

To be sure, human rights, like democracy, have suffered from both internal and external factors. On the one hand, numerous human rights violations by Israel against Palestinians have been cited, including targeted assassinations, restrictions on movement, collective punishment, and home demolitions. On the other hand, Palestinian security forces under the PA have also been guilty of numerous human rights violations, including detention without trial and/or specific charges, improper trials, torture, maltreatment, and use of the death penalty.[33]

Both human rights and democracy have also been hindered by poverty and the lack of human security in many communities in Palestine. As George Giacaman of Muwatin (the Palestinian Institute for the Study of Democracy) stated, "the democratic system is not sustainable with rampant poverty. Democracy requires a more equitable economic system based on a fair distribution of wealth."[34] Khalid Nassif of the Civic Forum Institute agreed, noting that democracy regresses in the absence of economic and social rights that ensure human security. According to Nassif, "when the economy improves, people have a greater sense of freedom and safety, and they can give more time and attention to joining parties and organisations and taking an interest in democracy."[35]

Clearly then, both human rights and democracy in Palestine have been hindered by both internal and external factors, primarily, the conflict with Israel and the limitations of the PA, and also by regional and international influences. Nevertheless, the will for both democracy and human rights in Palestine is strong on both individual and collective levels, and in fact, both exist to some extent in theory and on paper. The current key issue before Palestinians at this time is to translate those conceptualisations into realised practices and institutions, which can only be possible through an integrative approach that recognises the interdependence of human rights and democracy. At the same time, Israel and the international community must acknowledge that a democratic state in Palestine requires the existence of a state, as well as democracy. The next section of this chapter examines the institutions and elements of a substantive democracy that are necessary for bringing the ideals of human rights and democracy in Palestine to fruition.

Elections

The presidential elections of January 2005 were a major step towards procedural democracy. The elections followed the death of president Yasser Arafat, who had been elected in January 1996, and provided an opportunity for new leaders and parties to emerge. Though the election of Mahmoud Abbas (Abu Mazen) was predicted, the elections saw widespread participation, with 71 percent of registered voters casting ballots,[36] and were declared free and fair by local and international monitors. To refer to Beetham's standards for democratic electoral processes, the January elections were deemed successful in terms of their reach, inclusiveness, independence, integrity, and impartiality. The Central Elections Commission (CEC) was credited with making laudable efforts in registering voters, coordinating the monitoring of the voting process, and counting and implementing results. While the process was far from flawless, it was considered to be an overall success, and resulted in a smooth transfer of power and authority. The success of the election was largely made possible by pressure on both Israeli and Palestinian officials to protect rights to association, assembly, and expression, and the process itself underscored the procedural rights defined in Article 21 of the UDHR and Article 25 of the ICCPR.

The municipal elections of May 2005 were likewise considered to be successful overall. In addition to being another step towards procedural democracy, these elections also affirmed support in the electoral system and thus contributed to the strengthening of substantive democracy. As journalist Bakr Abu Bakr wrote in the Palestinian daily Al-Hayat Al-Jadidah:

> It is important…to point out what these elections represent[ed] to a Palestinian people still struggling to be free, still fighting Israeli occupation, and exercising democracy… They represented: first, an assertion of a course and a way of life chosen by the Palestinian people exemplified by freedom, dignity, dialogue, responsibility, and respect for the will of the people; second, the will and aspiration of many popular leaderships to serve the people…; third, a demonstration of Palestinian solidarity…; fourth, the continuity of Palestinian political struggle towards common goals; fifth, a renewal of societal leaderships.[37]

Clearly, the elections represented more than simply a procedure; they were a tangible expression of democratic ideals and principles. These ideals were intertwined with human rights, including the rights to dignity, freedom, and political participation. Furthermore, the electoral process, while reflecting human rights, also served to facilitate human rights by functioning as an expression of Palestinian unity.

The next phase of elections, for the Palestinian Legislative Council (PLC), were originally scheduled for July 2005 but were postponed to allow more time to formalise amendments to the proposed new electoral law. While most democracy advocates support the adoption of the new law and recognise the need for giving ample time for its passage, most view the indefinite postponement as a setback to democratic processes and momentum. Furthermore, the postponement was interpreted by many as an attempt by Fatah to consolidate its support to secure a victory over Hamas in particular. This widely accepted theory, regardless of its veracity, has unfortunately undermined the apparent commitment to democratic procedures established in the presidential and municipal elections.

Political Parties

Political parties are a mechanism that can facilitate free and fair elections, and thus contribute significantly to a sustainable procedural democracy. Likewise they provide opportunities for citizen participation and expression, and thus contribute to the development of a substantive, liberal democracy as well. As Giacaman stated, "a multi-party system is essential for establishing a sustainable democracy."[38]

In Palestine, there exists some foundation for a pluralist party structure. Although Fatah has remained the dominant party for some time, and has at times been difficult to distinguish from the PLO and the PA, other political parties have always remained in existence, and Islamist parties like Hamas in particular have gained considerable support in the past ten years. Thus, it is clear that "there is a plurality of parties; the parties are based on ideological differences but still operate within a national consensus; and they generally accept one another's legitimacy. Missing, of course, are the democratic institutions that would induce existing parties to channel their energies toward electioneering and governance."[39] That is, while various groups have long existed in Palestine, until recently they have lacked the electoral processes within which to operate.

To be sure, the majority of parties in Palestine have traditionally considered themselves "movements" or "fronts," and thus focus their attention on activities not necessarily related to electoral processes. In addition, the historical dominance of Fatah, and more recently, Hamas, have created challenges for the development of electoral parties in that "Fatah is too indistinguishable from the PA and Hamas too removed from it."[40] Indeed, while Fatah has traditionally identified itself as the primary force for Palestinian liberation, its loose cohesion has suffered from various fractions, due both to its position as the central party of the PA and to its handling of the second intifada. In contrast, Hamas has distanced itself from the PA, identifying itself as an "alternative to the status quo" and "the main opposition to Fatah and the PA."[41] This contrast was not only established on the conceptual level but on the direct level as well, as Hamas provided numerous social services to communities that Fatah and the PA had been unable to supply. Also, Hamas has distinguished itself from Fatah by intentionally using religious rhetoric, in contrast to Fatah's secular nature. In the past six months however, the nature of Hamas's political involvement has been shifting from that of an independent movement to a perhaps viable party in that members participated for the first time in municipal elections and plan to participate in PLC elections.

Many democracy advocates are now calling for a "third movement" that would provide an alternative to the so-called "old guard" of Fatah and the PA, and to fundamentalist groups like Hamas. As Mustafa Barghouthi, Director of the Health, Development, Information, and Policy Institute on Palestine commented, "Palestinians do not have to choose between autocracy and fundamentalism. There is a democratic alternative. Palestine could be a state that is independent and sovereign."[42] Dr. Lily Feidy of MIFTAH (Palestinian Initiative for the Promotion of Global Dialogue and Democracy) agreed, advocating for a third movement that is secular and democratic. According to Nassif, who has observed numerous town meetings through the work of the Civic Forum Institute, it is evident that "people want change, and want more participation by political parties. They want real democracy, and they want political parties to function as a fundamental part of that democracy."[43]

It should be noted that electoral party systems can take many forms, and in fact, a strictly organised party system could actually be detrimental in Palestine since many active reformists in the PLC have functioned essentially as independents, in practice at least if not in name. However, it is clear that the development of institutions to support electoral parties is becoming a necessity. Brown suggests three minimal steps to further democratic transition in the area of electoral parties. First, Fatah must be disentangled from the PA, for "when politicisation of official positions runs deeply throughout the bureaucracy, and where there is a conflation of roles and ruling bodies… mechanisms of horizontal and vertical accountability begin to break down."[44] Secondly, parties need to develop clear structures of internal governance and take "significant organisational steps, such as determining their membership, internal procedures, selection of candidates, and decision-making structures."[45] Third, organisations need to re-orient themselves to function in electoral competition, that is, groups need to consciously decide if they are primarily violent movements or if they are electoral parties.

In order for these steps to take place, certain human rights must be ensured. The rights to assembly and movement are inherent to political party organisation, and the rights to opinion and expression are necessary for allowing diverse parties to develop and mature. These rights must be protected by both the PA and by Israel. As Barghouthi stated, "[Israeli] suppression of secular democratic forces in Palestine will lead to a polarisation… between Hamas fundamentalists and the PA."[46] Indeed, the protection of human rights are essential for the emergence of a third movement.

Separation of Powers

As Hussein Sirriyeh, Professor of Arabic and Middle Eastern Studies at the University of Leeds, writes, "the definition of democracy should not merely be restricted to the narrower sense of free elections and a multi-party system. It should also encompass a broader spectrum of ingredients, including government by consent and accountability…"[47] To be sure, in order for political parties to function in effective institutions, especially the legislature, there needs to be a clear separation of power between the executive, legislative, and judiciary branches, with a viable system of checks and balances between them, articulated in a Constitution. This is necessary for ensuring transparency and accountability, and for enabling the different branches to fulfill their respective duties.

In Palestine, power was largely concentrated in the executive branch under the leadership of Arafat, who developed a highly personalised system of authority. Under this system, Arafat managed to bypass the majority of institutions to extend his personal influence. While this strategy was arguably motivated by Arafat's attempt to unite various factions of Palestinians with different opinions and interests, and to bolster his status as the unifying symbol of Palestine, the centralisation of power proved detrimental and only further crippled the already limited legitimacy of the PA.

This centralisation manifested itself in various ways. The most measurable indication was evident in the PA budget, in which over one quarter of the PA revenues were placed under the direct and unaccountable control of Arafat by 1997. The executive's domination was also felt strongly by the legislative and judiciary branches. While the PLC had the authority to draft and pass laws, it had no mechanism to ensure that the president would approve them. Thus, numerous bills and laws that were passed by the PLC, including the Basic Law, were subject to interminable waiting for Arafat's approval. Similarly, the executive responded to many court orders from the judiciary by simply ignoring them.

Sirriyeh proposes several theses to explain the authoritarian nature of the PA under Arafat. Some of these reasons include the desire of the PA to make an impression on the Israelis by suppressing anti-Oslo opposition, the issue of internalised PNA insecurity, the "outsider" status of the original PA leadership, the lack of political experience of the PA, and the desire to promote national unity by subordinating divisions within Palestine. Whatever the reason, the failure to separate powers, compounded by widespread corruption within the PA, resulted in a system that lacked transparency, accountability, and ultimately, legitimacy. This crippled the development of democratic institutions in their early stages, and it is only recently that the new PA leadership under Abu Mazen has begun to confront the process of de-centralising authority.

Judiciary

The branch of government that perhaps requires the most immediate attention is the judiciary. The judiciary was virtually nonexistent during the majority of the post-Oslo period, and it was only in 2002 with the passing of the judicial organisational law that the judiciary began to be managed by an independent judicial council. However, to date the council has consisted of judges who, while inexperienced in administrative matters, are intent on preserving their autonomy, thus causing them to lose the support of the bar association. The judiciary has also been embroiled in rivalries with the PLC and the executive branch's Ministry of Justice, with disputes occurring most recently over a draft judicial law for reform introduced by a special committee under Abu Mazen and currently referred to the legislature. Despite these challenges, the fact that an independent judiciary council does exist provides a foundation for starting judicial reform.

Although building a strong judiciary is a long, complex process, it is imperative for several reasons. On the conceptual level, judicial reform is symbolically significant because it can address the general lawlessness that directly affected many Palestinian communities during the second intifada and can thus restore confidence in the PA. To be sure, an effective court system has the potential to restore order and thus serve as an indicator to Palestinians of the authenticity of reforms.

Furthermore, "judicial reform is a logical priority because it can be a genuine tool—not simply a symbolic one—in addressing the corruption that is perhaps one of the most corrosive issues for

Palestinian governance."[48] Although laws exist regarding hiring for government positions, disclosing personal finances, and monitoring public funds, there have been no mechanisms for implementing them or prosecuting corrupt officials. This problem can be addressed by focusing initial reform efforts on the office of public prosecution.

A strong judiciary can serve other important functions as well, including being a leading force in constitutional reform and the development and application of the Basic Law. It also can function as a key body for placing checks and balances on the executive and legislative branches. Indeed, according to Hamdi Shaqqura of the Palestinian Centre for Human Rights (PCHR), the empowerment of a strong and independent judiciary can alleviate current debates regarding concern over the popularity of Hamas as a political party. Shaqqura suggests that any hypothetical attempts by elected Hamas officials to "Islamicise" the system or re-introduce violence as an acceptable policy would be countered by the judiciary.

Finally, a strong, independent judiciary is necessary for preserving human rights. First, it would provide a legitimate institution for prosecuting cases of human rights abuses. According to Lamis Alami of the Palestinian Independent Commission for Citizens' Rights (PICCR), ombudsmen and monitoring groups like PICCR can document human rights violations, but they currently lack effective institutions for addressing them.[49] Furthermore, an effective judiciary branch is necessary for protecting rights to fair and public hearings and trials, as articulated in Articles 10 and 11 of the UDHR.

Security

Closely related to the topic of judicial reform is the issue of security. Indeed, in order to ensure due process and avoid violations such as arbitrary arrests or torture, it is necessary that an effective security apparatus, including a police force, operates with legitimacy. Viable security services are necessary for preserving the rule of law, which is essential in a sustainable democracy. The issue of security is particularly important in Palestine, as security continues to play a vital role in many aspects of the Israeli-Palestinian conflict. To be sure, "for some external actors—especially Israel—security forms the basic logic of the reform process,"[50] and many of Israel's actions and policies are justified by concern for security. In the post-Oslo period however, many Palestinians perceived that the thrust of the so-called security reforms in the Occupied Territories was to protect Israeli security at the expense of Palestinian security. Inside Palestine, security concerns were not only associated with Israel but with internal elements as well, as the security services came to be associated with authoritarianism, corruption, and human rights violations against fellow Palestinians, including illegal detentions, improper trials, torture, and executions.[51]

The failure of the Palestinian security services after Oslo is largely attributable to other flaws within the PA. Primarily, "the absence of an effective control by an identifiable institution led to the excessive manipulation of responsibilities by members and leaders of these organisations."[52] To be sure, "the security services effectively answered to the president regardless of the content of the Basic Law. When Arafat was president, he encouraged multiple security services but declined to draw clear divisions of responsibilities among them."[53] This resulted in a lack of order and organisation, lack of mandate, lack of professionalism, and consequently, lack of legitimacy. Indeed, over a dozen security organisations were operating under Arafat, and none of them proved effective in providing either internal or external security.

As Brown suggests, "the myriad layers of overlapping forces and command structures need to be replaced with a consolidated and transparent organisation with clear lines of command to a democratically accountable official or set of officials."[54] The president should still have some involvement, but other executive branch officials should include members of the Ministry of the Interior. Furthermore, the PLC should be involved by finishing the draft of the legal framework for the security services' operation, as well as by examining the security budget.

In addition to these top-down measures, reforms need to occur directly within the security services, first through consolidation and re-organisation, and also through improved trainings. Specifically, security personnel trainings should be infused with human rights training, and ideally, should take place in conjunction with local human rights organisations. This model is helpful for facilitating a professional ethos within the security services; that is, "their training should focus not only on developing technical expertise but also on fostering a sense of what security services should not do."[55] Steps should also be taken to establish a multi-level system of monitoring and accountability, including:

- A system for security personnel and officers to report human rights abuses and violations;
- A procedure for families to appeal for investigations;
- A joint investigative body at the local level consisting of senior and junior security officers, human rights activists, and jurists to review cases of abuse allegations;
- A stronger Committee on Human Rights within the PLC;
- A stronger PICCR or similar ombudsman institution. Some reforms have already taken place under Abu Mazen, but the process of security reform will inevitably be long and complex. Nevertheless, "Palestinian reform will clearly be moving forward if the Ministry of Interior exercises real oversight, if the PLC passes (and monitors compliance with) a set of laws governing security forces, and if the regular reporting of human rights groups and

other NGOs suggests that the security forces are more respectful of the limits to their authority."[56]

Civil Society

As discussed above, democracy depends largely on the presence of a vibrant civil society. In Palestine, the presence of a strong civil society can be considered one of the most promising assets for the development of a sustainable democracy. Numerous civil organisations have existed since the early years of the occupation, essentially "keeping the country going before the PA, and still very active" after Oslo and during the present period.[57] Dajani notes that, in Palestine, "in the absence of a state and central government, and without any formal, centrally organised political socialisation via schools, the media, religion, friends or family, people began to organise themselves in civil groups—which subsequently became known as NGOs—and took over the role of a government."[58] These organisations have assumed a variety of roles and duties, including the provision of social services, political activism, human rights monitoring, education and advocacy, media and outreach, and others. Civil society groups have thus taken a number of forms, such as women's groups, media outlets, trade unions, human rights groups, religious groups, etc. While duplication, and at times, competition, are inevitable, many civil society organisations collaborate with each other and complement each others' work, and over 90 organisations belong to the Palestinian NGO Network (PNGO), an umbrella group that seeks to support, strengthen, and consolidate Palestinian civil society.

Organisations that focus on women's rights and empowerment are especially important for ensuring the viability of a sustainable democracy. As Feidy explains, a strong Palestinian women's movement has existed since the 1920s, and women have been active in civil society throughout Palestinian history. However, women have been largely marginalised under the PA, with the old guard seeking to limit the participation of both women and youth.[59]

According to Alami, the women's agenda has lagged at times because many active women believe that political activism against the occupation deserves more attention than the women's movement, although one cannot really separate one agenda from the other. Indeed, if women are to have an impact politically, they need to have the rights and access to participation. As Giacaman stated, "Equality is central to democracy."[60]

In addition to political marginalisation, women also face challenges related to employment, education, violence, early marriage, and inheritance rights.[61] Many Palestinian Muslim women also confront unique issues related to certain interpretations of Islam. The range of challenges related to women has resulted in a variety of responses by different civil society groups. Some focus on advocating for legal reform, such as the establishment of a quota to ensure a certain percentage of local or PLC seats are reserved for women, while others focus more on assisting female candidates and encouraging women to run for office or to vote for candidates who are female or who support women's rights. Other groups focus on making women aware of their civil and political rights through trainings, workshops, and conferences. As Mu'alim explains of his work with PCPD, "We are not speaking for people; rather, we empower people to speak on behalf of themselves. People have listened too long. They need to use their own voices now."[62] This approach is especially important for women's empowerment.

An obvious institution for channeling these voices is the media, and indeed, newspapers and media outlets are important institutions within Palestinian civil society. A strong foundation exists in Palestine for a free press; according to Brown, "the basis for independent media that can facilitate reform [in Palestine] is solid."[63] To be sure, the majority of media outlets in Palestine are privately owned, in contrast to the state-controlled media that dominates in some other parts of the Arab world and elsewhere.

Similarly, despite noted attempts by some PA officials to constrict discourse on certain topics such as Islamist parties, or certain stories, such as internal discord, the PA never fully stifled public expression. Nevertheless, there is still much room for improvement. Palestinian journalists should thus continue to build on their sound foundation of free media institutions to ensure that the media can function as a viable institution in a substantive democracy.

Journalists and media outlets are not the only groups focusing on media concerns. Many organisations that advocate for democracy and reform are embracing media issues, as well as women's rights, as key areas of concentration for their work, under the larger goal of promoting democracy and working towards the development of sustainable institutions. Some of the leading democracy organisations include MIFTAH, which focuses on democracy, human rights, gender equity, and participatory governance; Muwatin, which initiates intellectual debate on democratic issues and options; PCPD, which promotes human rights, tolerance, participation, accountability, empowerment, and rule of law; and Civic Forum Institute, which aims to increase citizens' awareness of democratic concepts and institutions and develop civil society institutions. This list is not intended to be exhaustive, but rather is meant to provide brief insight into the types of organisations that currently exist in the area of democracy advocacy.

Civil society is just one vital aspect of a participatory democracy, in which citizens are active participants in their government and communities, rather than just passive recipients. It should be noted that democratic participation can take many forms, including voting, holding public office, volunteering a service, writing letters to officials and/or newspapers, participating in marches, protests, and other forms of direct activism, and countless others. It is not the objective of this chapter to evaluate the impact of various forms of participation; rather, it is to recognise the importance of citizen agency. Perhaps the best indication of the potential for participatory democracy in Palestine was the early years of the first intifada, which saw widespread popular participation of different forms. Though the nonviolent "people power" strategies employed during that time have yet to be duplicated on the same scale, the spirit of that period is evident in the willingness of the people to express their opinions and voice their criticisms of both the PA and Israel.

Participatory democracy, and thus civil society, are both inputs and outputs of human rights. First of all, as an output, the emergence of civil society depends on the rights to freedom of thought, opinion, and expression (Articles 18 & 19), the right to assembly and association (Article 20), and the right to participation and service in government or country (Article 21). As an input, many civil society groups adopt missions that help to ensure economic, social, and cultural rights such as access to social services like food, clothing, housing, and medical care (Article 25), education (Article 26), and human security (Article 22); and others focus on securing civil and political rights. In addition, human rights organisations in particular, as a part of civil society, play an important role in monitoring and documenting human rights violations and advocating for the protection of rights.

Assessment of Democracy and Human Rights in Palestine

Foundations clearly exist in Palestine for the emergence of a substantive democracy, but the process still has far to go. A helpful way of conceptualising Palestine's current level of democracy is the transition theory, advocated by Dankwart Rustow. According to this theory, democratic development occurs in four main stages: "a stage when a national unity is being established; a preparatory phase of prolonged and inconclusive political struggle; a decision phase when a historical movement of choosing a democratic path is taken; and a habituation phase witnessing a consolidation of democracy."[64] In the case of Palestine, a national unity has long been established, and one might consider the post-Oslo period and second intifada to be periods of prolonged struggle. It is possible that, at present, Palestine is transitioning into the third stage, embarking upon a path of decision to work deliberately towards democracy. Most democracy advocates interviewed agreed, suggesting that Palestine is in a middle stage, on the way to democracy.

It is thus important at this stage to identify obstacles that prevent Palestine from fully realising a substantive democracy. First, it should be noted that any transition to democracy is a long, slow process. In the case of Palestine, there have also been additional setbacks in the form of clashes in reform visions, both internally and between internal and external actors. Another obstacle is the persistence of the old guard, who continue to occupy many key positions. The past six months have seen hope for progress in both of these areas however, with the election of Abu Mazen. The new president has committed himself to reform, and in doing so has reconciled differences between international and domestic agendas, and has opened up the PA and Fatah to be more transparent and accountable.

As Brown notes however, "the primary obstacle to further Palestinian reform lies in the international context: Political reform is difficult in the midst of an ongoing conflict."[65] Specifically, it is not possible to establish a substantive democracy under occupation. Unfortunately, international actors like the United States have to date have "approached diplomacy and reform as sequential rather than interdependent… [though] it is precisely the mutual dependence of reform and peace that make both so difficult achieve."[66] To be sure, the "peace now, democracy later" philosophy of Oslo proved to be ineffectual and perhaps even detrimental, and it is doubtful that the current logic of "democracy now, peace later" will be any different. As Brown notes, it is futile to build "public institutions that are expected to establish authority and accountability while placing them in a context of extremely limited autonomy."[67]

Perhaps a better way to conceptualise the peace and democracy equation is to integrate the variable of human rights. As has been discussed in this paper, democracy is necessary for human rights, and human rights are necessary for democracy. Likewise, a real just peace cannot exist unless peace is integrated with the protection of human rights. Because human rights is thus a common variable to both peace and democracy, it makes sense to focus on the human rights framework when pursuing both diplomacy and institution-building. Only when human rights and democracy are pursued simultaneously will either be achieved, and it is only then that a just peace will be possible.

Conclusion

Human rights and liberal democracy are not merely complementary, rather, they are interdependent. A democracy that is substantive as well as procedural cannot function without human rights, just as human rights, meaning civil, political, economic, social, and cultural rights, cannot be ensured in the absence of democracy.

In the case of Palestine, a foundation exists for both the realisation of human rights and the development of a substantive democracy, but both internal and external factors have hindered the building of viable institutions to actualise those ideals. Greater attention thus needs to be given to the development of mechanisms such as elections, political parties, and separation of powers, and the restructuring of institutions including the judiciary branch and security sector.

Despite the absence of these institutions to date, the will and perseverance of the Palestinian people, through both civil society and direct participation, has continued to push forward the democracy and human rights movements. Thus, attention must be given to these bottom-up efforts of popular participation, in addition to the top-down efforts of institution-building, if a liberal democracy is to be established. To be sure, no amount of institutional reform will be sustainable if it does not develop in tandem with popular will and public participation. For this reason, it is necessary for civil society organisations and actors to continue to facilitate political participation and raise public awareness, and it is imperative that individuals and communities seize opportunities to demonstrate their will. Media institutions in particular can play a key role in this process by serving as a means of popular communication, education, and mobilisation. The human rights framework can be helpful for developing direction and coordination for these efforts, and can integrate the distinct yet interdependent ideals of peace and justice, and human rights and democracy.

A summary of specific recommendations thus includes:

- The continuation of fair and free elections, including the scheduling of the PLC elections, currently postponed indefinitely;
- Political party reform and the development of a pluralist party structure;
- Separation of power and the establishment of a system of checks and balances between the executive, legislative, and judiciary branches of the PA;
- Security sector reform through consolidation, re-organisation, and the infusion of human rights training;
- The strengthening of the Committee on Human Rights within the PLC and the PICCR as an independent ombudsman.

Bottom-up community participation initiatives

- Strengthening of PNGO and improved coordination between civil society organisations;

- Increased opportunities for community meetings and civic forums;
- Empowerment of women, youth, and other marginalised groups;
- Humanitarian aid and sustainable development initiatives;
- Utilisation of a free and independent media;
- Human rights education and training;

Increased opportunities for direct public participation and nonviolent activism.

In addition to these initiatives, the success of both top-down and bottom-up efforts for the development of democracy depends also on the deliberate removal of internal and external obstacles. Under Abu Mazen, it appears that some of the internal problems that plagued the PA under Arafat are beginning to be addressed. Yet these reforms will prove ineffectual if the perpetuating issue of the occupation is not acknowledged. It is thus now imperative for both domestic and international actors to recognise the legitimacy of the public will for democracy in Palestine and support the establishment of an independent Palestinian state built on the foundations of democracy and human rights.

REFERENCES

1. Vienna Declaration and Programme of Action. United Nations GAOR. World Conference on Human Rights, 48th Sess., 22d plen. Mtg. Part I, Paragraph 8.
2. Beetham, David. "Democracy and Human Rights: Contrast and Convergence." Seminar on the Interdependence Between Democracy and Human Rights. United Nations. Office of the High Commissioner for Human Rights. Geneva: 25-26 November 2002. 3.
3. Donnelly, Jack. "Human Rights, Democracy, and Development." Human Rights Quarterly 21.3 (1999): 608-632. 612.

4. Ibid.
5. Beetham, David. "Democracy and Human Rights: Contrast and Convergence." Seminar on the Interdependence Between Democracy and Human Rights. United Nations. Office of the High Commissioner for Human Rights.Geneva: 25-26 November 2002. 2.
6. Ibid. 5.
7. Gutto, Shadrack. "Current Concepts, Core Principles, Dimensions, Processes and Institutions of Democracy and the Inter-Relationship Between Democracy and Modern Human Rights." Seminar on the Interdependence Between Democracy and Human Rights. United Nations. Office of the High Commissioner for Human Rights. Geneva: 25-26 November 2002. 5.
8. Beetham, David. Democracy and Human Rights. Cambridge: Polity Press, 2000. 163.
9. Beetham, David. "Democracy and Human Rights: Contrast and Convergence." Seminar on the Interdependence Between Democracy and Human Rights. United Nations. Office of the High Commissioner for Human Rights. Geneva: 25-26 November 2002. 5.
10. Gutto, Shadrack. "Current Concepts, Core Principles, Dimensions, Processes and Institutions of Democracy and the Inter-Relationship Between Democracy and Modern Human Rights." Seminar on the Interdependence Between Democracy and Human Rights. United Nations. Office of the High Commissioner for Human Rights. Geneva: 25-26 November 2002. 6.
11. Ibid. 10.
12. Beetham, David. "Democracy and Human Rights: Contrast and Convergence." Seminar on the Interdependence Between Democracy and Human Rights. United Nations. Office of the High Commissioner for Human Rights. Geneva: 25-26 November 2002. 4.

13. Ibid. 9.

14. Said, Abdul Aziz. "Let Us Be Democratic About Democracy." Al-Hayat 27 June 2004.

15. Ibid.

16. Donnelly, Jack. "Human Rights, Democracy, and Development." Human Rights Quarterly 21.3 (1999): 608-632. 612.

17. Gutto, Shadrack. "Current Concepts, Core Principles, Dimensions, Processes and Institutions of Democracy and the Inter-Relationship Between Democracy and Modern Human Rights." Seminar on the Interdependence Between Democracy and Human Rights. United Nations. Office of the High Commissioner for Human Rights. Geneva: 25-26 November 2002. 13.

18. Langlois, Anthony J. "Human Rights Without Democracy? A Critique of the Separationist Thesis." Human Rights Quarterly25.4 (2003): 990-1019. 997.

19. Vienna Declaration and Programme of Action. United Nations GAOR. World Conference on Human Rights, 48th Sess., 22d plen. Mtg. Paragraph 1(5).

20. United Nations Development Programme. Human Development Report, 1994. New York: Oxford University Press, 1994. 22.

21. Beetham, David. Democracy and Human Rights. Cambridge: Polity Press, 2000. 119.

22. Langlois, Anthony J. "Human Rights Without Democracy? A Critique of the Separationist Thesis." Human Rights Quarterly25.4 (2003): 990-1019. 999.

23. Ibid. 1000.

24. Ibid. 1001.

25. Ibid. 1004.

26. Ibid. 1010.

27. Ibid. 1014.
28. Gutto, Shadrack. "Current Concepts, Core Principles, Dimensions, Processes and Institutions of Democracy and the Inter-Relationship Between Democracy and Modern Human Rights." Seminar on the Interdependence Between Democracy and Human Rights. United Nations. Office of the High Commissioner for Human Rights. Geneva: 25-26 November 2002. 4.
29. Brown, Nathan J. "Evaluating Palestinian Reform." Carnegie Papers Middle East Series. Democracy & Rule of Law Project No. 59 (June 2005). 3.
30. Ibid. 21.
31. Interviews were conducted from May-June 2005 with representatives from MIFTAH (The Palestinian Initiative for the Promotion of Global Dialogue & Democracy), Muwatin (Palestinian Institute for the Study of Democracy), Palestinian Center for Peace and Democracy (PCPD), the Jerusalem Center for Social and Economic Rights (JCSER), Civic Forum Institute, Middle East Nonviolence and Democracy (MEND), the Palestinian Independent Commission for Citizens' Rights (PICCR), the Palestinian Centre for Human Rights (PCHR), the Al Mezan Center for Human Rights, and the PNA Ministry of the Interior.
32. Ibid. 3.
33. Sirriyeh, Hussein. "Democratisation and the Palestinian National Authority: From State-in-the- Making to Statehood." Israel Affairs 7.1 (August 2000): 49-62. 51.
34. Giacaman, George. Personal interview. 26 May 2005.
35. Nassif, Khalid. Personal interview. 1 June 2005.
36. Source: Central Elections Commission (CEC)
37. Abu Bakr, Bakr. Commentary. Al-Hayat Al-Jadidah 13 May 2005: 2.
38. Giacaman, George. Personal interview. 26 May 2005.

39. Brown, Nathan J. "Evaluating Palestinian Reform." Carnegie Papers Middle East Series. Democracy & Rule of Law Project No. 59 (June 2005). 14.

40. Ibid.

41. Abu Bakr, Bakr. Commentary. Al-Hayat Al-Jadidah 13 May 2005: 3.

42. Swift, Richard. "Towards a Democratic Palestine: Interview with Mustafa Barghouthi." New Internationalist 348 (August 2002): 1.

43. Nassif, Khalid. Personal interview. 1 June 2005.

44. Brown, Nathan J. "Evaluating Palestinian Reform." Carnegie Papers Middle East Series. Democracy & Rule of Law Project No. 59 (June 2005). 15.

45. Ibid.

46. Swift, Richard. "Towards a Democratic Palestine: Interview with Mustafa Barghouthi." New Internationalist 348 (August 2002): 2.

47. Sirriyeh, Hussein. "Democratisation and the Palestinian National Authority: From State-in-the- Making to Statehood." Israel Affairs 7.1 (August 2000): 49-62. 49.

48. Brown, Nathan J. "Evaluating Palestinian Reform." Carnegie Papers Middle East Series. Democracy & Rule of Law Project No. 59 (June 2005). 18.

49. Alami, Lamis. Personal interview. 7 June 2005.

50. Brown, Nathan J. "Evaluating Palestinian Reform." Carnegie Papers Middle East Series. Democracy & Rule of Law Project No. 59 (June 2005). 16.

51. Sirriyeh, Hussein. "Democratisation and the Palestinian National Authority: From State-in-the- Making to Statehood." Israel Affairs 7.1 (August 2000): 49-62. 51.

52. Ibid.

53. Brown, Nathan J. "Evaluating Palestinian Reform." Carnegie Papers Middle East Series. Democracy & Rule of Law Project No. 59 (June 2005). 16.
54. Ibid. 17.
55. Ibid.
56. Ibid.
57. Feidy, Lily. Personal interview. 26 May 2005.
58. Dajani, Munther. The Concept of Civil Society. Jerusalem: PASSIA, 1997. 2.
59. Feidy, Lily. Personal interview. 26 May 2005.
60. Giacaman, George. Personal interview. 26 May 2005.
61. Nassif, Khalid. Personal interview. June 1, 2005.
62. Mu'alim, Naseef. Personal interview. 27 May 2005.
63. Brown, Nathan J. "Evaluating Palestinian Reform." Carnegie Papers Middle East Series. Democracy & Rule of Law Project No. 59 (June 2005). 19.
64. Sirriyeh, Hussein. "Democratisation and the Palestinian National Authority: From State-in-the- Making to Statehood." Israel Affairs 7.1 (August 2000): 49-62. 61.
65. Brown, Nathan J. "Evaluating Palestinian Reform." Carnegie Papers Middle East Series. Democracy & Rule of Law Project No. 59 (June 2005). 21.
66. Ibid.
67. Ibid. 22.

2

Development of Human Rights and Democracy

Introduction

Apart from being a subject of global concern, the topic: "Human Rights, Democracy and development" is particularly sensitive to the present socio-economic and political circumstances of our time. The topic is essentially appropriate at present when the search for democracy and political transition from one civilian government to another has become more paramount in the affairs of many freedom-loving Nigerians.

Divergent theories, hypotheses and legal opinions have been put forward on the concepts of human rights, democracy and development. The overall purpose of this article is to relate these intellectual postulations to the present-day socio-economic and political needs of Nigeria with a view to ascertaining the authenticity of such postulations. Edmund Burke was right when he said that:

> "I do not vilify theory and speculation because that would be to vilify reason itself. Whenever I speak against theory, I mean always a weak, erroneous, fallacious, unfounded or imperfect theory and one of the ways of discovering that it is a false theory is by comparing it with practice."[1]

This article examines the philosophical concepts of Human

Rights, Democracy and Development. It attempts to place the meaning and scope of these constitutional and political terminologies in the perspective of modern internationally accepted standard with the Nigeria experience in focus. Is there any relationship between human rights, democracy and development? Can the three concepts exists independently of one another? Should there be a *nexus* between them? Which, out of the concepts of human rights, democracy and development is primarily fundamental? Of what importance is the promotion of human rights to democracy and development? What is the status of human rights in the schemes of democracy and development? What are the major problems besetting effective realization of human rights, democracy and development in Nigeria? The above problematic questions, among others, are meant to be raised in this article while efforts will be made to give some suggestions and recommendations with a view to charting a new outlook for Nigeria in her tortuous journey towards an enduring democracy and reliable governance.

Human Rights

The whole theory of human rights have a very remote and chequered history. Over the years, divergent opinions have been expressed by various schools of thought about the concept, nature, legality and philosophy of human rights[2] The subject of 'right' and 'human rights' have always received correlative and comparative intellectual considerations from scholars of different socio-economic, cultural and political backgrounds.[3] One fact that stands out clear is that human rights relate to human beings who constitute members of a group, community, society or a state. The origin of human rights can be held to be traceable to the creation of man and the right to life accorded him by God while the inherent nature of these rights is one of the many qualities that God has given to man.

Fundamental human rights have been defined as moral rights which every human being everywhere, at all times, ought to have simply because he is rational and moral in contradistinction with other beings.[4] Lois Henkin defines human rights as those liberties, immunities and benefits which, by accepted contemporary values, all human beings should be able to claim as of right in the society in which they live.[5] Human rights have also been held elsewhere[6] to represent demands or claims which individuals or groups make on society, some of which are protected by law and have become part of *lex lata* while others remain aspirations to be attained in the future. Umozurike[7] contends that the fact that such rights are denied or violated does not detract from their status since the rights are supposed to be claims, invariably supported by ethics and so, should be by law, made on the individuals or groups on the basis of their humanity.

Human rights were thus initially believed to be natural rights of every individual and as such, those rights had a distinct anthropological quality. In other words, basic human rights and fundamental freedoms were determined by their author's perception of the nature and essential characteristics of the human person. The particular rights and freedoms that were thus thought to be natural *concomitants* of being human were identified by contemplating the condition of an individual person in a stateless society. By eliminating all conditions that might be conditioned by a person's station in life as a member of a political society, philosophers attempted to penetrate the true essence of the human being and sought to translate that vital modality of being human into rights talk.[8]

With the emergence of positivism towards the middle of the 18th Century, the doctrine of natural law, of which the theory of natural rights was a distinct variety, lost much of its appeal. A tendency accordingly emerged of placing human rights into three generations. The first generation consists of the civil and political rights which are rights and freedoms that are pertinent to safeguarding the person and citizen's basic liberties *vis-à-vis* governmental authority and requiring of the state to permit or endure those entitlements.[9]

The second generation of rights refers to economic, social and cultural rights which had their origin in the Constitution of Mexico, 1917. Economic, social and cultural rights were subsequently included in the USSR Constitution 1904 as the right to work, to leisure, to maintenance in old age and sickness, right to education and freedom of association. The notion of such rights found its way into the Universal Declaration of Human Rights, 1948 and constituted the subject-matter of the International Covenant on Economic, Social and Cultural Rights, 1966. Economic, social and cultural rights were also incorporated, as (non-justiciable), "Directive Principles of State Policy" first, in the Constitution of Spain 1932, Constitution of Irish Republic 1937, the 1948 Constitutions of Burma and India, the 1950 Constitution of Indonesia, the 1960 Constitution of Ghana and lately, the 1979 and 1999 Constitutions of the Federal Republic of Nigeria. The "Directive Principles of State Policy" which still remain as non-justiciable rights in most countries in Africa have been entrenched as enforceable rights in the enterprising Basic Law of the Federal Republic of Germany.[10]

During the last two decades, a new category of rights emerged, which is commonly referred to as "third generation rights" and which was first conceptionalised by Karel Vasak in his inaugural address to the Tenth Study Session of the international Institute of Human Rights in Strasbourg, France in 1979. These rights include the right to peace, the right to development of disadvantaged sections of political community or, in the international context, of developing countries, the right to nature conservation and to a clean and healthy environment, the right to share in the common heritage of humankind and so on.[11] The third generation rights have the following attributes among others: First, the beneficiaries of these rights are no longer confined to individuals. The rights are now collectively perceived, either in the sense of humanity as a whole, a particular political community or a distinct section of the population within the body politic. Second, the third generation rights cannot be adequately protected within the confines of municipal bills of rights and their effective implementation consequently requires international cooperation. For instance, pollution cannot, in all instances, be contained within national borders.[12]

In the case of Nigeria, provisions of human rights were first introduced into the 1960 Independence Constitution as a result of the report submitted by the Henry Willink Minorities Commission to the effect that such constitutional provisions would assist in allaying the fears of minority groups in Nigeria.[13] The rights also appeared in the 1963 Republican Constitution.[14] The Constitutions of the Federal Republic of Nigeria 1979 and 1999 also contain, in Chapter IV, bills of fundamental human rights to life, dignity of human person, personal liberty, fair hearing, private and family life, freedom of thought, conscience and religion, freedom of expression and the press, peaceful assembly and association, freedom of movement, freedom from discrimination and right to property.[15]

It is also interesting to find the second generation of rights which are often known as "Fundamental Objectives and Direction Principles of state Policy" in Chapter II of the 1979 and 1999 Constitutions of Nigeria. The chapter comprises of sections 13-21 and 13-24 respectively, to make provisions for Political Objective, Economic Objective, Social Objective, Educational Objective, Foreign Policy Objective, Environmental Objective, Directive on Nigerian Culture, Obligation of the Mass Media, National Ethic and duties of the citizens.

For instance, Section 16 of both the 1979 and 1999 Constitutions on Economic Objective provides that:

(1) The State shall, within the context of the ideals and objectives for which provisions are made in this Constitution—

(a) Control the national economy in such manner as to secure the maximum welfare, freedom and happiness of every citizen on the basis of social justice and equality of status and opportunity..

In the same vein, section 17 of the same Constitutions on Social Objective provides that:

Unfortunately, judicial pronouncements from some Nigerian courts of law in certain cases have shown that provisions on Fundamental Objectives and Directive Principles of State Policy are not justiceable in Nigerian courts of law. For instance, in Archbishop Anthony Olubunmi Okogie & Ors. V. The Attorney-General of Lagos State, the Court of Appeal had held that:

> "The arbiter for any breach of the objectives and Directive Principles of State Policy is the legislature itself or the electorate."

From theoretical and practical points of view, it should be noted that the second and third generations of rights as enumerated earlier, appear to be more relevant in streamlining the political relationship between citizens and the state in the sense that by the expression of these rights, both the state and citizens have correlative obligations to protect the rights of one another. Hence, the citizens have every right to protest and to seek redress whenever the State or any authority violates any of their rights. A state of persistent violation of citizens' fundamental rights is not an attribute of effective democracy and good governance. No doubt, democracy and good governance are inevitably prerequisites to the overall development of a nation.

Democracy

In the world of today, democracy has become a popular

concept in every contemporary discourse. It is now a word that resonates in people's minds and springs from their lips as they struggle for freedom and for a better way of life. In its Greek understanding, the term democracy originally referred to the right of the citizens of the Greek City states to participate directly in the act of governance.[18] The word 'democracy' is known to have been coined from two Creek words: demos (the people) and Kratos (rule) which simply means people's rule.[19] It is an institution of governance which envisages a popular government as practiced in ancient Greece.

Although the conditions *in a modern State* make direct participation of all the people in the government of the state impossible, the concept of democracy still emphasizes the rule of the people, in that sovereign power is exercised by the people but now indirectly through a system of representation. The people chose their representatives who then govern in their name. In a democracy, power resides in the people and belongs to the people. In a democracy, the people own the government, and not government owning the people. A democracy is thus distinguished from a Monarchy (the rule of a Monarch) or Aristocracy (the rule of a privileged class) or an Oligarchy (the rule of a junta). While making a comparative examination of the three perverted forms of government (Democracy, Oligarchy and Tyrany), Aristotle described democracy as the most tolerable in contrast to oligarchy and tyranny.

Two great political philosophers, Pericles of Athens and Abraham Lincoln of America had made theoretical and practical demonstrations for an effective understanding of the concept of democracy in the political affairs of Man. A thorough analysis of their various postulations will reveal that democracy has some unique political connotations rooted in the following axes:

(a) Obedience to law and respect for constituted authority: According to Pericles:

"While we are thus unconstrained in our private intercourse, a spirit of reverence pervades our public acts; we are prevented from doing wrong by respect for the authorities and for the laws ... [21]

In other words, the culture of obedience to laws including lawful orders of our various courts and obedience to the unwritten laws, the conventions of the democratic process are equally important for the inner life and survival of the institution of democracy. Experience over the ages has shown that the activities of the City State can only be successfully carried on with the voluntary co-operation of the citizens, and the main instrumentality of this cooperation lies in the free and full discussion of government policies in all their aspects by the people. Pericles observed again that:

"The greatest impediment to action is, in our opinion, not discussion .... For we have a peculiar power of thinking before we act and of acting too, whereas, other men are courageous from ignorance but hesitate upon r election. " [22]

(b) Obedience to democratic process: The foundation of all democracy is the right to vote. The people must be allowed to elect their representatives, express their choices and make their preference at the polls. It is absolutely necessary that such polling should be fair and free i.e. free from force or fraud; free from intimidation and corrupt or undue influences. Citizens must be given the opportunity to cast their votes without any form of intimidation. Once the people have voted, made their choices, the candidates and their political parties should accept and respect the verdict of the electorate.

(c) Respect for human rights and fundamental freedom. Modern democracy envisages a new notion conceived in liberty and dedicated to the proposition that all men are created equal. As boldly affirmed by Franklin Roosevelt:

"In the future days which we seek to make secure, we look forward to a world founded upon four essential human freedoms, the first is freedom of speech. The second is freedom of every person to worship God in his own way .... The Third is freedom from want .... The fourth is freedom from fear or oppression[23]

Without these four necessary freedoms, no government will deserve to be called a democracy. Clara Smith was thus right when she described "freedom" as "man's birth right, a sacred, living rampart, a pulsebeat of humanity, the throb of a nation's heart."[24]

(d) Index of good governance and development: Where the government of a State is founded on the principles of obedience to law, democratic process and respect for human rights, there is every possibility that the State's legal order will be good and just. It will be a state where leaders will have respect for citizens' fundamental rights and basic freedoms. This quality will obviously place the citizens, who constitute the human resources of the nation in a pedestal to love their nation and struggle to contribute to its socio-economic, cultural and political development.

Concept of Development

By concept of development is meant a gradual advance or growth through progressive changes. It is a gradual differentiation of an ecological community[25] Within the context of this article, the term 'development' is a conscious acceleration of economic, political, social, educational and technological growth of Nigeria through effecting, consistent, progressive and enduring policies of the government. It is conceived in this article that such effective policies of government that are capable of effective progressive development in all spheres of our national life must curiously evolve from a truly democratic political system in which adequate value is placed on protection and promotion of human rights and fundamental freedoms. It is also believed in this piece that the overall development of Nigeria cannot be realized in an environment which is characterized by lack of respect for democratic process and fundamental rights of citizens. The need for a nexus between the concepts of human rights, democracy and development will be examined later in this article.

Human Rights, Democracy and Development in International Perspective

Adherence to the concepts of human rights and democracy had since been recognized as a veritable means of achieving peace, stability and development in the world. At present, efforts are being intensified by various individuals, regional and international organizations as well as non-governmental bodies to internationalise and globalise the campaigns for promotion of human rights and democracy with a view to eradicating all forms of oppressive regimes in all human societies.

For instance, a one-time Chief Justice of Japan once said that "fundamental human rights were not created by the State but are external and universal institutions common to all mankind and antedating the State and founded upon natural law."[26] This position has been given judicial approval by the Chief Justice of India, Justice Chandrachund, who described fundamental rights as *transcendental,* inalienable, primordial and that they constitute the *ark* of the Constitution. About a century earlier in the United States of America, Thomas Jefferson, in one of his letters to James Madison dated December 21, 1891 had said:

> "Let me add that a bill of rights is what the people are entitled to against every government on earth, general or particular and what no just government should refuse or rest on interfere.[28]

The need to internationalise the promotion of human rights could be traced to various dehumanizing events, gross violation of human rights and wanton destruction of lives and property during the Second World War (1939-1945) which compelled most nations of the World to adopt the Charter of the United Nations at San Francisco City in 1945 with the following preamble which reads in part as follows:

> "We the peoples of the United Nations determined to reaffirm our faith in fundamental human rights, in the dignity and worth of human person, in the equal rights of men and women and the nations, large and small, and to establish conditions under which justice and respect for the obligations arising from treaties and other sources of international law cad be maintained, and to promote social progress and better standards of life in larger freedom"

Long before the adoption of the United Nations Charter in 1945, various exploitative and oppressive regimes in many nations had caused violent revolutions which formed the roots of many human rights declarations which were formulated into different bills of rights such as the English Bill of Rights 1688, the American Declaration of Rights of Man 1776 and the French Declaration of Independence, 1789. Specifically, the American Declaration of Rights of Man provides in part that:

> "we hold these truths to be self evident that all men are created equal; that they are endowed by their creator with certain inablienable rights, that among these are life, liberty and pursuit of happiness."

Also, the glaring dangers of racial prejudice and the increasing awareness that unless checked; tyranny and oppression would dominate the world and the dignity of man rendered meaningless, were factors which pressed on the United Nations to adopt the Universal Declaration of Human Rights 1948 which perambulates as follows:

> "Whereas, recognition of the inherent dignity and of the equal and inalienable rights of all members of the human family is the foundation of freedom, justice and peace in the world; whereas, disregard and contempt to human rights have resulted in barbarous acts which have outraged the conscience of mankind that human rights should be protected by the rule of law...."

This Universal Declaration of Human Rights was followed by the adoption of two important International Covenants namely: Civil and Political Rights (adopted by the general assembly of the United Nations in 1966) and the International Covenant on Economic, Social and Cultural rights (adopted also in 1966) both of which recognize:

> " the inherent dignity and the equal and inalienable rights of all members of the human family as the foundations of freedom, justice and peace in the world."

This truism has since formed the focal point around which the constitutions of virtually all countries revolve and thus provides international standard against which such Constitutions are tested for legitimacy and, or validity.

Other international and regional conventions designed to internationalise the protection and promotion of human rights include; the Genocide Convention (UN) 1964, the Untied Nations Convention on the Elimination of Racial discrimination 1965, Convention on the Elimination of All Forms of Discrimination Against Women 1979, Convention against Discrimination in Education and the Convention on the Rights of the Child 1989; the European Convention on Human Rights, the Inter-American convention on Human Rights 1969, African charter on Human and Peoples' Rights, 1981 etc.

While giving his opinion on the need to internationalsie the protection of fundamental human rights, Professor Bolaji Akinyemi, a one-time Nigerian Minister of External Affairs once remarked:

"Treatment of one's citizens is no longer a matter of demostic concern alone and there should be no place in the world community for governments who behave in a barbarious fashion towards their own citizens."

It is our contention in this piece that this internationalisation of human rights is, without equivocation, the greatest single achievement of the world community. By this step, the world community may be seen to have contributed immensely to the evolution of democratic governments in many nations.

In modern international societies, it has become an acceptable fact that the best form of government is founded on principles of democracy. In its international perspective, democracy is defined as government by organized and sustained popular consent characterized by the following essential elements:[30]

(i) Free choice.

(ii) Empowerment and capability.

(iii) Respect for the Rule of Law and equality before the law in theory and practice.

(iv) Promotion and defence of human rights.

(v) Creation of appropriate political and socio-economic machinery.

(vi) Sustained political communication to create trust and confidence among leaders and between them and the general populace.

(vii) Decentralisation of power and authority.

(viii) Periodic and orderly succession to power through popular participation in secret ballot elections.

While emphasizing the Rule of Law as the most inseparable aspect of democracy, the international Commission of Jurists, at its Conference in Athens, 1955 expressed the view that the Rule of Law:

"Springs from the rights of the individual developed through history in the age old struggle of mankind for freedom, which rights include freedom of speech, press, worship, assembly and association and the right to free elections to the end that laws are enacted by the duly elected representatives of the people and afford protection to all ...."

The concept of popular participation in governance has become one of the most internationally accepted attributes of democracy. By the concept, citizens are the most distinctive element in democracies. All regimes have rulers and a public realm, but only to the extent that they are democratic do they have citizens. Historically however, severe restrictions on citizenship were imposed in most emerging or partial democracies based on age, gender, class, race, literacy, property ownership, tax-paying status and the like. Only a dismal part of the population was eligible to vote or run for office. Only certain social categories were allowed to form, join or support political association.

After protracted struggle in some cases involving domestic or international upheaval, most of these restrictions were lifted. Today, the criteria for inclusion are fairly standard. All native-born adults are eligible, although age limits may be imposed on candidate for certain offices. Unlike the American and European democracies of the 19th Century, none of the recent democracies in Southern Europe, Latin America, Asia or Eastern Europe has ever attempted to imposed formal restrictions on the franchise or eligibility for office. But when it comes to informal restrictions on the effective exercise of citizenship rights, the story can be quite different.

In fact, the concept of popular participation in government has been given a legal backing by the African Charter for Popular Participation in development and transformation adopted at the Kenya Conference of 1990[31] to the effect that if African continent is to be truly democratized, the majority of the people must be able to assert and protect their human rights and play a role in decision making. Emphasis should be placed on how to empower the rural population in Africa to ensure their effective participation in democratization. Rural people must be able to articulate their interest in their local government representatives and be heard. The Charter therefore, calls upon African governments to yield space to the people without which participation will be difficult to achieve.[32]

Also, as part of his allocutus upon his conviction on charges of sabotage and of trying to bring down the South African government by force and violence; Nelson Mandel forcefully expressed the view that democracy and stable government cannot be built on the foundation of the permanent superiority of one group and the permanent inferiority of other groups; on the basis of first class citizenship for some and second class citizenship for others. Democracy can only survive and thrive in a free society in which all persons live together in harmony and with equal opportunities to partake in the process of governance.

Over two centuries ago, the Americans had recognized the principle of participatory democracy as a foundation to national stability. This was reflected in the American Declaration of Independence, 1776 to the effect:

> "...that all men are created equal; that they are endowed by their Creator with certain inalienable rights to life, liberty and pursuiti of happiness. To secure these rights governments are instituted among men deriving their just powers from the consent of the governed. That whenever any form of government becomes destructive of these ends, it is the right of the people to alter or abolish it..."

Article 21 of the United Nations Universal Declaration of Human Rights 1948 to which many independent nations are signatories equally confirms the international significance attached to the principle of participatory democracy by stating in part that:

"Everyone has the right to take part in the government of his country, directly or through freely chosen representatives.

The will of the people shall be the basis of the authority of government, this will shall be expressed in periodic and genuine elections which shall be by universal and equal suffrage and shall be held by secret vote or by equivalent free voting procedures."

The principle of popular participation has further been amplified by article 1 of the united Nations International Covenants on Civil and Political Rights and Economic, Social and Political Rights, 1966 which provides that:

"All peoples have the right of self-determination. By virtue of that right, they freely determine their political status and freely pursue their economic, social and cultural development."

The entire idea of the above cited Article of the two United Nations Covenants is now regarded in modern International Law as the principle of self-determination which is the right of all peoples to determine or choose their political future and freely pursue their economic, social and cultural development.

Concept of Development

The concept of development as viewed from the international perspective in this article refers to the evolution of democratic institutions of government that is based on a common political ideology which can bring about peace and overall development in most nations. It is conceived that the existence of solid socio-economic, political, cultural, educational and technological development in every nation is a prerequisite to the attainment of international growth and global development. Since democracy is now a popular concept well favoured by most advanced and civilized nations, a genuine subscription to its basic principles by other nations may enhance mutual understanding between both developed and developing nations thereby; paving way for mutual benefits that are mostly required for comparative development at all levels. Therefore, the idea of development in international perspective is taken to mean the acceptance of the principles of a common political philosophy by most nations subject to their socio-economic and cultural identities. Such political philosophy being capable of fostering their relationships in terms of foreign policies, trade, politics, education, culture and technology. In this piece, we consider an effective democracy as that political philosophy which is capable of achieving that purpose. This contention is based on the reasoning that democracy presupposes the existence of a good government which is founded on freedom, equality and justice. Adherence to such fundamental principles is likely to guarantee peace, respect for human rights and national development.

The World Summit for Social Development (Copenhagen, 1995) adopted the Copenhagen Declaration and Programme of Action which underlined the urgent need to address profound social problems, especially poverty, unemployment and social exclusion which affect every nation. The Declaration stresses further that "people are at the center of our concern for sustainable development and ... they are entitled to a healthy and productive life in harmony with the environment"[33].

A landmark in the enunciation of new human rights occurred when on December 4, 1986, the United Nations General Assembly adopted the Declaration on the Right to Development via its Resolution 41/128. The right to development had been put on hold since 1981, when the United Nations Commission on Human Rights established a working group of 15 governmental experts which had also received very substantial contributions from other non-governmental organizations[34]. However, despite the adoption of the Declaration on the Right to Development, the major task of finding concrete ways and means to develop this right is still on the agenda of States and peoples of the world. The universal notion on this issue at present is that human person is the central subject of development and to make him or her an active participant and beneficiary of the right to development, persistent discussions concerning this right must continue at all levels of policy making and actions.

Relationship between Human Rights, Democracy and Development

A consideration of the relationship between human rights, democracy and development at this juncture is desirable with a view to proffering solutions to some of the problems raised at the onset of this article. First, it will appear that each of the three terms is identifiable with certain fields of study. Human rights is more related to law, democracy is more of a political science while the term development is more technologically oriented. It may be argued that this identification is a matter of academic exercise because the three disciplines to which each of the terms belongs are likely to overlap, not only in their theoretical and practical context, but also, in their daily application. What is important to note is that the terms human rights, democracy and development are popular and of much relevance in the political affairs and process of governance of every nation.

Second, by our philosophical contention, the concept of human rights has been propounded to be tracedental, inalienable, primordial and that it constitutes the ark of the constitution.[34] In fact, a one-time Chief Justice of Japan once said that the fundamental human rights were not created by the state but are external and universal institutions common to all mankind and antedating the State and founded upon natural law.[35] These postulations go to show that in order of priority or importance, the protection and promotion of fundamental rights should come before democracy and development. This contention is based on the fact that since citizens are the most distinctive elements in democracy, their fundamental rights must be guaranteed and protected before they can be in a position to render their human resources for effective democratization and overall development of their nation. In other words, promotion of human rights is primarily fundamental to the emancipation of an enduring democracy and national growth.

Third, a thorough intellectual analysis of this topic would seem to suggest that the three concepts of human rights, democracy and development should exist side by side in every nation for the survival of human race. That is to say, no matter how important one of the three concepts appears to be, a political entity is not likely to survive without the concurrent existence of the three. For instance, the rights of man can better be guaranteed in a stable democratic system. Effective promotion of citizens' fundamental freedoms paves a way for peace that is mostly needed for the survival of a democratic government; while development in terms of economy, education, science and culture remains an essential attribute of a sovereign nation in which citizens are given the opportunity to pursue their safety and happiness. In the context of the Nigerian situation, it has never been possible to realize effective protection of human rights, democracy and development because of the following major problems among others.

Problems Besetting Effective Realisation of Human Rights, Demcoracy and Development in Nigeria

At a period when Nigeria was under a colonial rule, it was not possible to hold that her citizens were under a democratic regime. Shortly after independence and particularly between 1960 and 1966, the parliamentary system of government in practice by then could not be said to have actually consolidated the gains of democracy for the people. For a short period of Presidential System of government between 1979 and 1983, the nature of democracy then, was more in theory than in practice. Painfully too, out of a period of thirty-nine years (till 1999) as an independent nation; Nigeria had experienced agonizing periods of twenty-nine years under various military regimes. The entire political periods of years spent so far by Nigeria as a sovereign independent nation have been characterized by many problems besetting effective realisation of human rights, democracy and development.

Bad Leadership

Within the context of this article, the term 'leadership' means the power vested in political office holders by law to lead the electorate that constitute people who voted them into power. Leadership also entails the qualities possessed by those individuals who are supposed to lead a set of race in a political entity. Democracy depends on the presence of rulers and persons in authority who can give legitimate commands to others. Such persons in authority must be seen by their followers to be realiable, dependable and of impeccable characters who are ready to serve and not to be served. In line with democratic principles, political leaders must be tolerant and always ready to give opportunities to others to make their contributions towards the overall development of the nation. Democratic leaders must encourage opposition. They must not consider opposing views of others as undue confrontations aimed at humiliating them out of power.

An enduring democracy requires just leaders who respect the Rule of Law and Fundamental Rights of Citizens. Leaders of a democratic system must not be greedy and corrupt. It is unfortunate that few of the very serious problems confronting effective realization of human rights, democracy and development arise from the negative attitude of bad leaders in Nigeria who have corruptly enriched themselves, violated fundamental rights of opposing groups, disobeyed court orders, mismanaged national resources and disregarded international human rights norms and democratic principles. AS a result of bad leadership, most of the factors of production have either been ignored, under-utilised, or misused. Fertile agricultural lands lie dormant while unemployment and crime rates soar. The windfall during the oil boom was badly misspent, much of it stolen, thus leaving most of our national oil refineries grounded. The resultant effect has been fuel scarcity in the country with its attendant escalation in transport costs and unbearable increase in prices of commodities in the markets. The exchange rate of Naira has greatly fallen, thereby reducing the purchasing rate of industrial materials which could have been gainfully used to improve the nation's technological development.

Military Intervention in Politics

Nigeria did not start with the military in the process of her political history. When the military boys first struck on January 15, 1966, part of the reasons given for such an abrupt intervention was to wipe out political profiteers in high and low places that sought bribes and kept the country divided permanently so that they could remain in office.[36] In the same vein, the Buhari Military regime which dismissed the Nigerian Second Republic under President Shehu Shagari also gave a catalogue of political errors which characterized that civilian regime. In fact, the spokesman for General Buhari, late Sanni Abacha said:

> ".... We are ready to lay our lives for our dear nation, but not for the present irresponsible leadership.. I am referring to the harsh, intolerable conditions under which we are living.." [37]

Giving the political circumstances which led to military usurpation of political powers in Nigeria as enumerated above, it could be argued that by the philosophical propositions of Hans Kelsen, Hobbes, Rousseau, John Loke and the principles of American declaration of Independence; military leaders were justified for snatching political powers from irresponsible leaders who abandoned their political obligations, thus leaving innocent citizens to suffer. Specifically, the American declaration of Independence, 1776 provides *inter alia* that:

> "...To secure these rights, governments are instituted among men, deriving their just powers form the consent of the governed. Whenever any form of government becomes
>
> destructive of these ends; it is the right of the people to alter or abolish it"

It is however sad to observe that Nigerian experience of military rule has revealed that military leaders have never been able to provide effective and enduring solutions to most of the problems which they often claimed have brought them to power. Thus, it has been stories of coups and counter coups in Nigeria since 1966. While dismissing the military regime of general Buhari who claimed to have seized political power from the 'irresponsible' civilian government of Shehu Shagari; Brigadier Joshua Dongoyaro, the military spokesman of General Ibrahim Babangida said:

> "Fellow countrymen, the intention of the Military at the end of 1983 was welcomed by the nation with unprecedented enthusiasm Almost two years later, it had become clear that the fulfillment of expectations is not forthcoming Any effort made to advise the leadership is met with stubborn resistance and was viewed as a challenge to authority or disloyalty
>
> In such a situation, if action can be taken to arrest further damage, it should and must be taken. This is precisely what we had done.... [38]

A greater percentage of military leaders who have tasted political powers in Nigeria. Haven discovered how sweet it is; are no longer ready to relinquish same. To achieve this goal, political leaders and human rights activists have been held in detention without trials, many have been killed while others have fled to foreign nations for the safety of their lives. Through this process, the country had lost a lot of human resources that would have been employed for her socio-economic, cultural, political, educational and technological development. In every attempt to prevent opposition, military leaders in Nigeria have also formed the habit of promulgating decrees consisting of ouster clauses which prevent courts of law from exercising jurisdiction to entertain matters often regarded by the military as confrontational. By so doing, many citizens have not been able to defend their rights over certain matters that are crucial to the overall development of the nation.[39] In every attempt to make their power supreme, military tribunals have been employed to disregard human rights and principles of natural justice well recognized by civilized nations. A typical example was the case of *Kunule Benson Saro-Wiwa* which led to the suspension of Nigeria from the commonwealth of Nations in 1995. By this suspension, a lot of priviledges and advantages of membership of the commonwealth hitherto enjoyed by Nigerians to promote the nation's development ceased.

Military governments in Nigeria have also not allowed the judiciary to be truly independent. Military leaders were often the sole hirers of judges and so, they could decide at any time to dismiss any judge who was not on their side. By gross disobedience to orders of courts,[40] military leaders have rendered the judiciary seriously incompetent in its onerous function of dispensation of justice. This military posture has not paved way for effective growth and development of the nation's legal system. In a desperate bid to perpetuate their rule, some Nigerian military leaders have scuttled processes of political transitions form military to civil rule. For example, General Ibrahim Badamosi Babangida annulled the Presidential election of June 12, 1993 while General Sanni Abacha also employed a lot of political manouvres which were detrimental to the nation's development with a view to staying longer in power until his sudden death on Monday, June 8, 1998. It may be relevant to point out that the refusal of some military leaders in Nigeria to yield to the advice of the international communities for a quick return to a democratic system of government led to the imposition of economic sanctions which had seriously retarded the development of the nation in all its ramifications.

Illiteracy and Poverty

Many problems which are not legal in nature such as illiteracy and poverty also hinder the effective realization of human rights, democracy and development in Nigeria. Education has been on the decline in Nigeria, both in terms of enrolment as well as physical infrastructure, material and equipment. There has been little advancement in technology. By statistics, it has been confirmed that Nigeria has a male literacy rate of a mere 54 percent while the female literacy rate is 31 percent.[41] Democracy grows from the confidence and faith of a people in their abilities to tap their human and natural resources effectively for national growth and development. It is therefore totally dependent upon an educated and informed electorate who have access to ideas. Illiteracy affects the sustenance of democracy because uneducated people cannot make informed political decisions. Likewise, uneducated people cannot possess the required skills and man-power for industrial growth and technological development of the nation. The impact of poverty on democracy is profound. Lack of education impedes participation in government. In order to participate in government, a person must understand the principles of government and the nature of political operations.

Education is also vital for human resources development and that in turn, builds a foundation for increase productivity, improvement in health and nutrition as well as improved ability to handle innovative scientific tools for technological advancement of the nation.

Poverty also contributes to a litigant's incapacity to meet the cost of litigations in Nigerian courts of law. An action to enforce a person's right includes payment of solicitor's fees, transport cost sand other incidental expenses that normally go with the filing of actions in courts. A person who is unable to secure three square meals a day is not likely to go to court for the enforcement of his fundamental rights because of the cost of litigation. Instead, poor persons often take laws into their hands thereby increasing the rate of violence in Nigeria. This is a threat to democracy.

Illiteracy, ignorance and wrong perception of the government have also been identified as some of the problems militating against human rights litigations in Nigeria. A person who can neither read or write may not even be aware of the existence of his fundamental rights let alone bringing an action to enforce them. Even where some people are aware of their rights, their erroneous impression and perception of the government as an institution too powerful to be sued may prevent them from filing actions to enforce any breach of their fundamental rights against the government. Again, while some believe that Police Officers are noted for their unpredictability since they can turn around to arrest and deal with any person who takes them to court over an alleged infringement on his right; others see the act of going to court as a time wasting exercise which, not only disturb their business endeavours, but also portrays them as irresponsible members of the society.

CONCLUSION

Based on the philosophical approach to the operational definitions and scope of human rights, democracy and development, it is observed that the three concepts are virtually inseparable in the scheme of human affairs for effective governance and national development. Some Nigerians have suggested that sound economy that is necessary for the survival of democracy and development need to be seriously pursued before the intensification of effects for the promotion of citizens' fundamental rights. [42] Our recommendation is that the rights and freedoms of citizens who constitute the work-force and human resources of the nation must be well protected and guaranteed first, before democracy and development can be meaningfully realized and sustained. Once the basic rights and fundamental freedoms of citizens are adequately guaranteed, democracy and development are bound to flourish.

In the course of our analysis, it was also observed that though, the three concepts are basic factors that are *sine qua non* to good governance, the status and position of human rights appear to be most fundamental thus placing it as the Highest of the three common factors. It is therefore suggested that all administrative and legal functionaries, especially members of the armed forces, executive and courts of law must continue to lay more emphasis on the protection and promotion of human rights.

It is equally observed that poverty remains the greatest threat to the survival of human rights, democracy and development in Nigeria. Added to this is the tendency on the part of some leaders to perpetuate their regimes at the expense of democratic ideals and values. If democracy is to take hold in any meaningful way in Nigeria, there must be economic democratization. The economic structure must be altered to allow for a mixed economy that has some built-in mechanisms for equity and open access for all to the system. This can better be achieved if both the leaders and followers are ready to be more patriotic and shun all corrupt and disloyal practices in our private and official capacities.

Finally, it is observed that unpredictable incident of usurpation of political power by military leaders remain the most serious problems besseting effective realization of human rights, democracy and development in Nigeria. Concerted efforts must be made by all Nigerians to continue to tell military leaders that we are tired of their autocratic regimes and so, military leaders must continue with their traditional role of defending the nation from internal and external aggression. This bold step must also include all pragmatic constitutional, legal and diplomatic actions to resist despotic tendencies through free and fair elections in order to sustain democracy for the present and future generations.

REFERENCES

1. See his speech at the English House of Commons, 7th May, 1782 in the *British House of Commons Proceedings.* May, 1782. p. 31.
2. See theories of Natural Law and Social Contract in "Edmund Burke and Natural Law", *Natural Law Forum,* Vol. 6 (1961), OUP, p. 201; Leski, *A Grammar of Politics* (George Allen & Unwin Ltd., London), 4th ed., p. 94; Cicero D'entraves; *Natural Law* (1960), France, pp. 20-25,etc.
3. See Osita C. Eze, (1984) *Human Rights in Africa,* Macmillan (Nig.) Ltd., pp. 5-8, Peter Schneider, Social Rights and the Concept of Human Rights in D.D. Raphael, (ed.) *Political Theory and the Rights of Man* (1967), Bloomington, Indiana University Press, p. 81; Marx/Engels, (1968), Selected Correspondence, Moscoe, p. 500.
4. G. Ezejofor, (1964), *Protection of Human Rights under the Law,* Butterworths, London, p. 3.
5. Lois Henkin, quoted by Umezurike in Constitutional Rights Journal (Nigeria) Vol. 5, 1995 at p.11. See also Oji Umezurike, "The Status of Human Rights" in *Constitutional Rights Journal,* (1995), CRP Publications, Lagos, Nigeria, at p. 11, Vol. 5.
6. Osita, C. Eze; (1984). *Human Rights in Africa, op. cit.*, p. 5.
7. *The Status of Human Rights in Constitutional Rights Journal,* op. cit., p. 5.
8. *From Human Wrongs to Human Rights* (1996), Danie Brand (ed.) Pretoria, p. 44.
9. L. Sohn, "Protection of Individuals" (1982) 32 *American Law Review,* pp. 17-18.
10. See *From Human wrongs to Human Rights;* op. cit., see also, R. Bahlla, "Fundamental Objectives and Directive Principles of state Policy under the Constitution of Nigeria," *Nigerian Bar Journal* (1982), Vol. 18 at p. 9.

11. K. Vasak, *For the Third Generation of Human Rights: The Right to Solidarity.* Denis Broiwn (1996); *op. cit.*, p. 44.
12. P. Alston, A Third Generation of Solidarity Rights; Progressive Development or Obfuscation in International Human Rights Law", in (1982) 29 *Netherland International Review;* p. 307 at 310-311.
13. *Constitutional Problems of Federalism in Nigeria:* Record of Proceedings of a Seminar held at King's College, Lagos, 8-15 August 1960 under the auspices of Ford Foundation of America, edited, by Lionel Brett at p. 43.
14. Chapter III.
15. Sections 30-40 of the Constitution of the federal Republic of Nigeria, 1979 and Sections 33-43 of the 1999 Constitution.
16. (1981) 1 N.C.L.R. 218.
17. Ibidat p. 35. See *also Adewole & Ors. V. Alhaji Jakande & Ors.* (1981) 1 N.C.L.R. 262.
18. Walter Lanqueur; (1973), *A Dictionary of Politics.* Pan Books Ltd., London, 2nd ed. Pp. 139-140.
19. See Webster, *The Lexicon Webster Dictionary* (1980), Encyclopedia edition, Vol. 1, Delair Publishers, U.S.A. at p. 265.
20. Aristotle; *Politics,* ed. B. Jowett (1885), Oxford, V.I.X, (12898, 15-18) 151.
21. See Hon. C. Oputa (1981) *Democracy: What is it all About?* Being the title of a paper presented at the Second Conference of Attorneys-General in the Nigerian Federation at Abuja on 9-12, September, 1991 at p. 2.
22. *Ibid at p.* 3.
23. *Ibid* at p. 5.
24. Quoted by C. Oputa in "Democracy: *What is it all About?* (1991), *op. cit.,* at p. 5.

25. See Webster A.M.; (1986). *Third New International Dictionary of the English Language,* Mariam Webster Inc., Publishers, U.S.A. at p. 618.

26. See Akinola Aguda, (1991), *"Law and Human Rights in Democracy" in Farm House Dialogue* 17, 2nd- 4th August,

27. *Ibid.*

28. *Ibid.* See also Thomas Jefferson's letter to James Madison on December 21, 1891.

29. His paper titled *"In search of a New World Order"* delivered at the Institute of International Affairs, Lagos, 1992 and quoted with approval by Mr. Agbakoba in his paper titled *"Human Rights and the Culture of Silence in Nigeria"* delivered at a Lecture organized by the Juris Chambers of the Obafemi Awolowo University, Ile-Ife, Nigeria, June 1992 at pp. 3-4.

30. See *Farm House Dialogue* 17, *op. cit.,* p. 5.

31. See B.P. Ambrose; (1995), *Democratisation and the Protection of Human Rights in Africa:* Westport, Connecticut, London at p. 174.

32. *Ibid.* at p. 175. See also *African Charter for Popular Participation in Development and Transformation,* Kenya, (1990), p. 21.

33. Janusz Symonides: *Human Rights: New Dimensions and Challenges* (1998), Ashgate Publishers, England, pp. 3-4.

34. Philip Alston, "Making Space for Human Rights: The Case of the Right to Development" *Harvard Human Rights Year Book* (1998) Vol. I, p.1.

35. See Hon. C. Oputa, (1991) *Democracy: What is it all About?* Being the title of a paper delivered at the Conference of Attorneys-General of Nigeria in Abuja, Nigeria, 9-11 September, 1991 at p. 17.

36. By Justice Chundrahund of India quoted with approval by Akinola Aguda in his paper titled *"Law and Human Rights in democracy" in Farm House Dialogue;* op. cit. p. 19.

37. *Ibid.* [38] See Late Major Nzeogwu, P.S. broadcast to the Nigerian people after the *coup d'etat* of January 15, 1966 as quoted by Ademulgeun; (1981), *Why We Struck: The story of the First Nigerian Coup,* Evans Brothers, Ibadan, 87-89.

39. See *Sunday Times* (Nigeria): January 1, 1984, pp. 1 and 32.

40. *Daily Times* (Nigeria); August 28, 1985.

41. See cases like *F.S. Uwaifo v. A.G. Bendel State* (1983) 4 N.C.I.R. 1; *Nwosu v. Imo State Environmental Sanitation Authority* (1990) 2 N.W.L.R. (Pt. 135) 688; *Abavol v. Perm. Sec. Civil Service Commission* (1991) 3 NWLRD (pt. 183) 693; *Ortese v. Gov. of Benue State* (1991) 4NWLR (pt. 184), 157.

42. See *Govt. of Lagos State v. Ojukwu* (1986) 1 NWLR (pt. 18) 621; *Tewogbade v. A.G. Oyo State* (1991) 2 NWLR 32 etc.

43. See *Africa Recovery,* Vol. 5 Nos. 2-3 (September 1991) at p. 29.

44. See the views expressed by General Yakubu Gowon and Earnest Shonekan in the *Punch,* (Nigerian Newspaper) of May 20, 1998 at pp. 1 & 2.

3

Concept of Democracy and Human Rights

Introduction

The principles of democracy and human rights have been persistent, if at times secondary, themes within the rhetoric of American foreign policy toward Africa since the end of World War II. The linking of such Wilsonian precepts with foreign policy practice, however, has been an altogether different story. US policy makers consistently followed the dictates of realpolitik in the era of the Cold War, leaving concerns for democracy and human rights aside. With the collapse of the Soviet Union and the end of the Cold War, conditions are now in place for the tangible and coherent pursuit of an American foreign policy based on democracy and human rights. In the current era, the question emerges as to the resonance of such Wilsonian principles in US foreign policy towards Africa. This essay examines the salience of Wilsonian precepts in United States foreign policy towards Africa in the past and in the current era of Clinton's visit to Africa.

In his foreign policy pronouncements vis-a-vis the European colonial powers President Woodrow Wilson advocated for the pursuit of democracy and human rights conceptualized within the context of self-determination for the colonized peoples. The idea of universal morality was central for Wilson. In his view, the realization of individual freedom, limited government, and legitimacy of power held the key to both international peace and the emancipation of humanity from injustice[1]. It was within this philosophical context that he advocated for the need to make the world safe for democracy. This, he argued, would promote America's long term interests[2].

Wilsonianism emerged as a distinct policy philosophy at the end of the First World War. One of the central concerns at the time was how to avoid war and conflict in general. For Wilson, the crucial priority was the need to establish people-oriented internal and international democratic institutions that would act as the custodians of democracy and human rights as conceptualised within the general rubric of self-determination[3]. This idealism culminated in the formation of the League of Nations in 1919. Thus, Wilsonianism was not only internationalised but also institutionalised. Although the United States did not become a contracting party to the League, Wilsonianism had a global impact.

Such thinking would go on to inform the founding fathers of the United Nations. The UN system tangibly paved the way for the process of decolonization in Africa through the UN General Assembly resolutions, with African countries which were independent at the time as well as India and the socialist countries taking the lead[4]. In this respect, Wilsonianism not only challenged dictatorial and authoritarian systems worldwide but it also helped oppressed people become aware of their rights. For the colonized peoples of Africa, democracy and human rights (or self-determination in general) was equated with the absence of colonialism[5]. Moreover, the momentum on the issues of democracy and human rights was evidenced with the appointment of Eleanor Roosevelt to Chair a Commission on Human Rights. The results of Roosevelt's Commission were the establishment of the Universal Declaration of Human Rights and its corollaries the International Covenant on Civil and Political Rights and the International Covenant on Economic, Social and Cultural Rights.

President Wilson's global campaign as the champion for the silent majority also set the stage for a United States democracy and human rights foreign policy in the twentieth century[6]. Wilsonian precepts resonated clearly in the messsage of the Atlantic Charter which, although promulgated by Franklin D. Roosevelt, Wilson's intellectual heir, manifestly indicated US dissatisfaction with the lack of sovereignty for colonised peoples.

The concern for the promulgation of democracy and human rights is thus part of the legacy of United States foreign policy towards Africa. The salience of these moral principles in foregn policy practice, however, has always stood in the face of a more realist agenda guiding US policy. This was particularly evident during the Cold War. The status of such ideas in the post-Cold War foreign policy of the United States remains an open question.

In the spirit of Wilsonianism, the US welcomed decolonization and independence in Africa in the 1960s. However, with Cold War prism taking a centre stage, emerging American national interests became defined in terms of combatting communism in Africa and other parts of the world. Indeed, such concerns were evident even prior to much of Africa's independence. After his visit to Africa, Vice-President Nixon in his report to Eisenhower explained that "the course of Africa's development...could well prove to be the decisive factor between the forces of freedom and international communism"[7].

To be sure, the concerns with democracy and human rights occasionally surfaced in the discourse of US foreign policy. For instance, the US Congress, particularly since the 1960s has enacted legislation linking economic and military aid to democracy and human rights. Section 116 of the 1961 Foreign Assistance Act prohibited the President from providing development assistance "to the government of any country which engages in a consistent pattern of gross violations of internationally recognized human rights"[8]. Similarly, the 1976 Congressional Foreign Assistance Act stipulates, among other things, that the US is "to promote and encourage increased respect of human rights and fundamental freedoms throughout the world." US security assistance was to be given in a manner which will "provide and advance human rights and avoid identification of the United States, through such programs, with governments which deny their people internationally recognized human rights and fundamental freedoms"[9].

These episodic legislative efforts should not blind us to a more general pattern wherein US foreign policy actually worked against the precepts of Wilsonianism. The overall history of US activity in Africa during the cold war reads like a litany of anti-Wilsonian practices justified in the name of containing communism. This included US support of such brutal dictators as Mobutu, Moi, Barre, Nimieri, and Selassie, whose human rights records were among the worst in Africa. Billions of dollars were spent to roll back communism. Indeed, US weapons played major roles in conflict situations in Angola, Ethiopia, Liberia, Zaire (now the Democratic Republic of Congo-DRC), Namibia, Somalia, Sudan, Uganda, and Sierra Leone.

The more specific chronology of US foreign policy further confirms US reluctance to support Wilsonianism. President Kennedy, guided by US strategic interests, was unable to support anti-colonial forces in Portuguese colonies in Africa due to his concern for the strategic North Atlantic Treaty Organization (NATO) bases in the Azores [10]. Even the 1960 decolonization and self-determination-oriented UN Resolution 1541 (XV), in which Wilsonianism was clearly inscribed, was not supported by the Eisenhower Administration. The US was one of nine countries (Australia, Belgium, Britain, the Dominican Republic, France, Portugal, South Africa, and Spain) to abstain during the voting in the UN General Assembly [11]. The abstention clearly indicated that the US sanctioned oppression, racial discrimination, and the violation of human rights in Africa by the colonial powers, if to do so meant containing communism. US ambivalence on the Rhodesian question was also a clear manifestation of a reluctance to pursue democracy and human rights policies in Africa [12]. Although the administrations of Presidents Kennedy (1961-1963) and Johnson (1963-1969) were generally concerned with the issue of apartheid in South Africa, the Vietnam war occupied most of their time.

Whereas the Johnson Administration upheld the UN economic sanctions against the white regime in Rhodesia because of its human rights violations, President Nixon permitted the US company Union Carbide to import 150,000 tons of chromium ore from that country [13]. Similarly, the Nixon Administration also increased military aid to South Africa, violating the UN embargo. This policy clearly placed the US on the side of the white regimes in southern Africa and in support of the violation of human rights policies that were part of the systems. The Nixon and Ford Administrations's policies of replacing Wilsonianism with national security only enhanced the status quo in the region. These trends in foreign policy behavior underwent a gradual, though inconsistent, shift during the Carter Administration (1977-1981).

Carter defeated the Vietnam War weary and Watergate scandal plagued Republican Administration by building on a domestic constituency rife with Cold War disillusionment[14]. His new vision de-emphasized the view that conceptualized conflicts in Africa within the prism of communist adventurism. For Carter, conflicts arose as a result of domestic disorder or simply socio-economic and political stress [15]. Carter, like Wilson, brought to the White House religious and moral virtues which translated into his foreign policy-making process [16]. One of his concerns was how to bring about democracy in Africa. To help him achieve this objective, he appointed a number of African-Americans, in addition to others, who shared his views to key foreign policy-making positions [17]. It was during the Carter Administration that a real qualitative leap in the prominence of American human rights foreign policy was reactivated [18]. Carter was able, at least initially, to move America away from the realpolitik of the Nixon-Ford-Kissinger years to a vision of Wilsonianism. Specifically, he made the issues of democracy and human rights the subject of international diplomatic discourse. This policy initiative was pursued more vigorously in his first two years in office, raising the hopes of pro-democracy and human rights advocates both in the US and Africa. For example, export and import restrictions were imposed on South Africa, Ethiopia, and Uganda [19]. By linking economic and military aid to human rights violations, the Carter Administration intended to influence the policies of the repressive regimes in Africa.

Carter's idealism was aimed at encouraging countries in Africa considered to be progressive. His Administration dismissed the Kissinger plans in southern Africa as inconsistent with democracy and human rights principles and supported instead the anti-apartheid efforts of the Front-Line States. Carter also increased diplomatic efforts aimed at resolving the Angolan, Mozambican, and Namibian questions. Racism and dictatorship rather than communism were seen as the main threat to American interests in Africa[20]. The Carter Administration also nullified the 1971 Byrd Amendment which allowed American companies to import chrome from Rhodesia and signed U.R. 1746 to law prohibiting US companies from dealing in trade with the white minority regimes in southern Africa and limiting military sales restrictions on countries in Africa that violated human rights in general.

These moves placed the Carter Administration on the side of the pro-democracy and human rights movements in the region and the anti-apartheid advocates in the US[21]. President Carter's shift from Wilsonian idealism to realpolitik became apparent during the 1979 Soviet invasion of Afghanistan and the taking of American hostages in Iran. Carter hurriedly negotiated for military bases in Kenya, Somalia, and Sudan in 1980 at a time when human rights violations were rampant in these countries. Carter needed logistical support for the Rapid Deployment Force (RDF) which was established as a result of the 1979 Soviet invasion of Afghanistan and the US hostage crisis in Iran.[22]. His Administration's inconsistency, however, was displayed on a number of occasions. Whereas he was concerned with the Soviet intention in Africa, his Administration was also insistent on the issue of the observance of human rights [23]. In Fiscal Years 1980 and 1981, for example, Zaire became one of the first victims in Sub-Saharan Africa whose military aid was reduced by Congress during the Carter Administration . Ethiopia and South Africa also were earmarked for sanctions and denial of military aid.

The Reagan and Bush Administrations viewed the issue of democracy and human rights largely within the context of the containment of communism in Africa. This was clearly symbolized in their continued support for what Reagan called freedom fighters such as the National Union for the Total Independence of Angola (UNITA). The Contact Group of Western countries established during the Carter Administration to oversee the Namibian transition to independence was relaxed by the Reagan Administration. Instead, Reagan established the policy of constructive engagement which accommodated the views of the apartheid regime[24]. The US-USSR rapprochement that began in 1984 with the Reagan-Gromyko meeting set the stage for the close of the Cold War. These developments paved the way for the Reagan Administration's accommodative approach to human rights that was expanded under the Bush Administration[25].

A New Trends in US Foreign Policy

The collapse of the Soviet Union ushered in great opportunity for the pursuit of foreign policy based on Wilsonianism. We find such an emphasis emerging in the foreign policy orientation of both the Presidency and Congress. To be sure, it will take some time, perhaps decades, before such a policy becomes meaningfully established. Our aim here is to try to demonstrate that a trend is emerging within the US foreign policy-making establishment in favor of the pursuit of democracy and human rights policy in Africa. The linkage of Wilsonianism to foreign policy and development acquired a central theme under President Bush following the collapse of the Soviet Union. The US advisor to the UN Commission for Human Rights, Marc Northern, clearly articulated President Bush Administration's foreign policy on democracy and human rights. In his address to the Commission, Northern stated that "the US makes no apology for insisting that where human rights are concerned, every nation, including my own must be held to the highest standard... . We stand ready to help those governments committed to human rights move ahead"[26]. He further emphasized that "the division in the world today is not between East and West... . The real division in the world is between those committed to democracy and liberty and those against"[27]. This trend of thinking , did not however, manifest until in the 1990s. In 1989 the Bush Administration opposed aids cuts to some of the leading African old guards-cum-dictators such as Moi (Kenya), Barre and Mobutu. The same dictators were to face political conditionalities in the 1990s imposed by the US and other donor countries.

In Kenya, for example, relations with the US and other donor countries in general began to deteriorate in 1989. The years 1989-1991 witnessed great internal and international pressure on the Kenyan Government to allow multipartism. The US Ambassador to Kenya, Smith Hemstone, brushing diplomatic ethics aside, stated publicly that US assistance would be directed to countries that "nourished democratic institutions, defended human rights and practised multiparty politics"[28]. In conformity with Section 116 of the 1961 Foreign Assistance Act and other democracy and human rights legislation, President Bush acquiesced to the Congressional freezing of $25 million in military aid to Kenya[29]. Kenya's foreign aid was subsequently withheld by the US and other donors in 1991 forcing the Moi regime to allow multipartism. The other African countries which were victims of Congressional legislation in the late 1980s to early 1990s included, Cameroon, Malawi, Sudan, Togo, and Zaire. The Bush Administration was also involved directly or indirectly in peace initiatives in Sudan, Mozambique, Angola, Ethiopia, and Zaire among others. These efforts were augmented by Congressional support.

The effort of Bush Administration on the issue of human rights and democracy were carried on by President Clinton who acknowledged that when he became President, the US had no policy towards Africa. The policies existing at the time, he argued, focused mainly on specific countries. He stated that "for decades we viewed Africa through Cold War prism... We supported leaders on the basis of their anti-Communist or anti-apartheid rhetoric perhaps more than their action ... And... the United States... simply ignored the realities of Africa"[30]. He further emphasized that the United States would like to "see more prosperity and more well-functioning economies and democracy... We'd like to see sustainable development that promotes the long-term interest" defined in terms of global stability[31]. This Wilsonian liberal internationalism constituted part of Clinton's foreign policy orientation.

In one of his public speeches, the American Secretary of State at the time, Warren Christopher, emphasized that "promoting democracy and human rights is a pillar of American foreign policy" conceptualized within what he called the "moral and strategic imperative of the 1990s"[32]. The concern of the Clinton Administration, rhetoric or otherwise, on these issues is centred on the need to establish viable internal and international stability defined in terms of democracy and human rights. These values are increasingly being linked to foreign aid by donors. This foreign policy framework is based on the thesis that liberal democracy and free markets are the best guarantors of world peace, stability and development[33]. Financial institutions such as the International Monetary Fund(IMF) and the World Bank(WB) in particular, have joined the bandwagon in supporting the emerging donors' perspectives on the issues of democracy and human rights. These policies are bound to enhance internal and international pro-democracy efforts.

A further example of Clinton's commitment to human rights is witnessed in the Administration's response to the cancellation of election and killings of innocent people by the Abacha regime in Nigeria. The Clinton Administration cut off $450,000 aid for military training and $11 million in grants. The US, the European Community, the Commonwealth Countries, and some members of the UN also imposed sanctions against the Abacha regime following the hanging of Ken Saro-Wiwa, a human rights advocate, and eight other Ogonis[34]. In her address to the UN General Assembly on November 28,1995, the US Ambassador to the UN at the time now Secretary of State Madeleine Albright singled out Nigeria and Sudan as countries in Africa whose governments are associated with dictatorship, coercion and violation of international recognized human rights principles[35].

However, concerns with democracy and human rights did not supplant more fundamental American interests. The US, however, as one of the major importers of Nigerian crude oil, did not impose stiff economic sanctions against Nigeria. This indicates that realpolitik still guides important aspects of US foreign policy. Indeed, this is a clear indication that regardless of a President's avowed politics, US economic interests always take precedence over other issues.

Moreover, stability in Africa is increasingly understood within the context of Wilsonianism. This is evidenced by the steady decline in military procurement to the continent, particularly in Sub-Saharan Africa. For example, the US arms deliveries to Sub-Saharan Africa started to show a steady decline from 1985 to 1994. Under the Clinton Administration, the term Security Assistance since 1994 has been changed to Assistance for Promoting Peace and Building Democracy. This shows a clear shift in the Administration's policy on security issues in relation to Africa. The focus by his Administration is on the peace-building military training in conjunction with the Organization of African Unity (OAU) and the individual African states. This new concept, under the name African Crisis Response Initiative (ACRI), introduced in 1996 by the Clinton Administration, is designed to prepare African countries' military personnel for future peace-keeping missions in trouble-spots in the continent. While Botswana, Uganda, and Zimbabwe participated in this joint military training program with the US Marines in late 1997, Kenya, Uganda, and Tanzania did so in 1998. What is emerging within the US foreign policy-making establishment is the inclusion of democracy and human rights even on matters pertaining to security.

To augment its peace-building initiatives in Africa the Clinton Administration has also supported the concept of denuclearization of Africa. The US played an active role in drafting the final text of the African Nuclear-Weapons-Free Zone Treaty also known as the Treaty of Pelindaba which was opened for signature in April 1996 in Cairo, Egypt. During the Cold War the US was persistently opposed to this concept, particularly in relation to the Indian Ocean as a zone of peace proposed by the African and Indian Ocean littoral states.

One of the central questions which needs to be asked is the extent to which President Clinton's March 1998 visit to Africa helped solidify the US policy of Wilsonianism? Or was his visit influenced largely by narrow American realpolitik perspectives thus missing the opportunity to lay the foundation for a well established Wilsonian idealism?

While in Uganda President Clinton emphasized that "if we

work together to strengthen democracy and respect for human rights, we can help this continent reach its full potential in the 21st century — its true greatness, which has too long been denied"[36]. This was the message Clinton re-emphasized during his official tour of the continent. President Clinton also stressed a number of things, which according to him, are different from the course US took during the Cold War period. First, he emphasized the importance of good governance, accountability, freely elected governments, and the need for African governments to provide democratic space. Second, he stated that African stability, security, and prosperity are consistent with US interests. Third, he stressed that respect for democracy and human rights constitutes the centre stage of US interest in Africa. Clinton's US-Africa foreign policy pronouncements centred on trade, security, and democracy and human rights [37]. These statements were carefully chosen and linked to Clinton's priorities and strategies at home and in Africa.

Within the domestic context it can be argued that the Clinton Administration's main objective was designed to enlarge its domestic constituency, particularly among African-Americans. His recent recognition of the role played by the American slaves during the Civil War and his apology for the US transAtlantic slave trade can be understood in this context. An expanded domestic constituency would enhance support for the Democratic Party in future elections. Louis Farrakhan's visit to Africa earlier, particularly to Libya and Sudan(dubbed terrorist nations by the US), could not be taken lightly given his increasing influence in the US [38]. Clinton also wanted to enhance his Administration's image in Africa by engaging in a mutually beneficial human relationship with Africans, or simply a comprehensive form of "neo-constructive engagement". This was an important aspect of his visit. It was an attempt to move Africa away from marginalisation and mere US stereotypes to a continent that needs to be engaged in a reciprocal partnership. In other words he brought America to Africa by way of focusing the attention of Americans on the African continent. Clinton may have succeeded in these areas at home-gaining support of the African-Americans and establishing a different image of Africa among the American people-but what are the potential ramifications in the African context?

With the exception of Rwanda, Clinton visited countries (Ghana, Uganda, Rwanda, South Africa, Botswana and Senegal) considered by the Administration to be democratising and promoting market-oriented economies. But what package did he bring? His trip was boosted, at least by the perspectives of his Administration, with the passage of the African Growth and Opportunity Act on March 11,1998 by the US House of Representatives. Yet, to some observers the Act "poses significant threats to Africa's long term interests in sustainable economic development and democracy-building"[39]. The central displeasure with the Act is that it imposes certain conditions- a form of "trickle down theory"- on the African countries. For example, the African countries must comply with IMF rules which require the privatisation of their assets through divestiture; they must acquiesce to World Trade Organization rules such as tariff cuts and the removal of import restrictions and adopt currencies and investment deregulations which allow foreign investors to establish ownership over natural resources in the continent[40]. The initiative is obviously a good one and it indicates a willingness on the part of the Clinton Administration and Congress to engage in meaningful economic relations with Africa. The Act in its present form, however, constitutes a threat to the sovereignty of the African states and renders the idea of mutual respect and reciprocal partnership entailed in some of Clinton's speeches nugatory.

Whereas Clinton emphasized that US-Africa economic policy is to be based on trade as opposed to foreign aid, he failed to offer a historic package to the debt plagued continent. Economic development and more so Wilsonian idealism inscribed in his speeches cannot thrive in a continent trapped in debt. Currently, sub-Saharan Africa alone has foreign debts totaling over $200 billion. Clinton's message could have had great impact for generations to come in the new millennium if it contained a plan for writing-off the 48 sub-Saharan African states' debts, 31 of which are classified as severely indebted and low-income. Something of great foreign policy magnitude like the 1948 Marshall Plan could have made a difference. Even if the plan (or let us call it Clinton-Albright African Plan) were to target only some of the African countries perceived by the US leaders to be in the processes of nourishing democratic ideals, good governance, and respect for human rights, it could have set the stage for a tangible and historic US-Africa policy. The fact that the US and its allies managed to mobilize about $100 billion debt relief under the 1996 Highly Indebted Poor Country Initiative (HIPC) to salvage the East Asian countries trapped in economic crisis, make Clinton's rhetoric in Africa suspect. After all, even under the debt chocking conditions, about eleven sub-Saharan African countries managed to experience 6% growth rates in the period 1996-97, faster than their 3% population growth rates. It is along these lines that Clinton could have made his visit more historic which in turn could have served long term US-Africa interests. Instead, US aid to Africa has undergone a steady decline in recent years. Whereas sub-Saharan Africa received an average of $700 million from the US between 1990-98, down from $ 841 million in 1992, Israel's aid increased from $3 billion to $5.5 billion in the same period[41] What is more revealing is that in Fiscal Year 1999, Sub-Saharan Africa is allocated only $155 million compared to $225 million for Bosnia alone[42].

Clinton's strategic initiative in Africa conceptualised within the context of peacekeeping missions or simply "African solutions to African problems" sounds more like a new form of the Nixon doctrine of the early 1970s, a policy based on the strategy of transferring arms to regional American proxies to enhance their military capabilities to guard US interests. If the Clinton Administration's decision to withdraw American troops from Somalia in 1994 is anything to go by, then the idea of introducing African peacekeeping forces (ACRI) only re-enforces my interpretation. Compare the decision by the US to withdraw from Somalia to its commitment in the former Yugoslavia? The NATO peacekeeping forces are still busy patrolling the area a few years after they were deployed. This is not to argue that the US should become a policeman in Africa. The central point is that even in the post Cold War era the US commitment to Africa is still questionable. It remains at the level of rhetoric defeating the objective of promoting Wilsonian idealism, a policy that would serve US long term interests. The same level of political will established to combat communism in Africa and elsewhere during the Cold War era should be directed toward "rolling back dictatorship and oppression" from the continent and replacing it with Wilsonian idealism. President Clinton had the best opportunity to put such a policy in place while he was in Africa. Although his speeches in Africa were coached in Wilsonian conceptions, they will continue to be interpreted as mere political rhetoric. An inclusive and tangible US-Africa foreign policy orientation can still be put in place by the Administration before the new millennium. After all this was the central thrust of Clinton's keynote address at the White House Conference on Africa in June 1994. In my view, such a policy, would catalyse and solidify the political and institutional reforms that are dubbed "the African Renaissance" sweeping across the continent.

REFERENCES

1. See generally, Stanley Hoffmann, "The Crisis of Liberal Internationalism", Foreign Affairs, 98(Spring 1995):159-177. Wilsonianism is hereinafter used interchangeably with democracy and human rights.

2. Tony Smith, "Making the World Safe for Democracy", The Washington Quarterly (Autumn 1993), pp. 198-199 See also Anthony Whelman, "Wilsonian Self-Determination and the Versailles Settlement", International and Comparative Law Quarterly 431(January 1994): 99-115.
3. See, Bruce M. Russett, Grasping the Democratic Peace (Princeton: Princeton University Press, 1993, James L. Ray, Democracy and International Conflict: An Evolution of the Democratic Peace Proposition (Columbia: University of South Carolina Press, 1995), and Bruce M. Russett, Controlling the Sword (Cambridge: Harvard University Press, 1990).
4. See generally, United Nations, Declaration on the Granting of Independence of Colonial Countries and Peoples (Doc. A/L/325,1960), Report of the Special Committee on the Situation with Regard to the Implementation of the Declaration on the Granting of Independence of Colonial Countries and Peoples (Doc. A/5800/Rev. 1,1964), Robert Me Coroudale, "Self-Determination: A Human Rights Approach", International and Comparative Law Quarterly 43(4) (October 1994): 857-885, and Korwa G. Adar, "The Principles of Self-Determination and Territorial Integrity Make Strange Litigants in International Relations: A Recapitulation", Indian Journal of International Law 26(3/4)(July-December 1986: 425-447.
5. Michla Pomerance, "The United States and Self-Determination: Perspectives on the Wilsonian Conception", American Journal of International Law 70(l)(January 1976), p.19.
6. On the evolution of the US human rights foreign policy see for example, David P. Forsythe, Human Rights and the United States Foreign Policy: Congress Reconsidered (Gainsville: University of Florida Press, 1988, David L. Cingranelli, Ethics, American Foreign Policy, and the Third World (New York:St. Martins, 1993) and Joshua Muravchik, The Uncertain Crusade: Jimmy Carter and the Dilemmas of Human Rights Policy (Lanham:Hamilton Press, 1986.

7. US Government, The Vice-President's Report to the President on His Trip to Africa, February 28-March 21 1957, White House Office Files, Dwight D. Eisenhower Presidential Library, 1957.

8. Stephen B. Cohen, "Conditioning U.S. Security Assistance on Human Rights Practices" American Journal of International Law 76(1982)p.247. See also generally, R. Weissbrodt, "Human Rights Legislation and U.S. Foreign Policy", Georgia Journal of International and Comparative Law 231 (1977):247-268.

9. Quoted in W.F. Buckley, "Human Rights and Foreign Policy: A Proposal "Foreign Affairs (Spring 1980), pp. 785-787.

10. Todd J. Moss, "U.S. Policy and Democratization of Africa: The Limits of Liberal Universalism), Journal of Modern African Studies 33(2) (1995), p.193.

11. Marion Muchkat, "The Process of African Decolonization", Indian Journal of International Law 6(1966) p.495 and D. A. Kay, "The Unites Nations and Decolonization", in James Barros, (ed.), The United Nations: Past, Present and Future (New York: The Free Press, 1972), pp. 152-153.

12. See generally, Anthony Lake, The 'Tar Baby' Option: American Policy Toward Southern Rhodesia (New York: Columbia University Press, 1973), Mohamed A. El- Khawas and Barry Cohen (eds.), The Kissinger Study of Southern Africa: National Security Study Memorandum 39 (Westport, CON.: Lawrence Hill & Co., 1976), Z. Brezinski, Power and Principle:Memoirs of the National Security Advisor, 1977-1981 (New York: Farrar Straws Ginoux, 1983) and Peter J. Schraeder, United States Foreign Policy Toward Africa: Incrementalism, Crisis and Change (Cambridge: Cambridge University Press, 1994).

13. P. M. Kamath, "Human Rights and National Security: US Experience in Africa During the Cold War Era", in M. MuneneJ. D. Olewe-Nyunya, and K. G. Adar (eds.),The United States and Africa: From Independence to the End of the Cold War (Nairobi: East African Educational Publishers, 1995 p.57 and

T. Szulc, The Illusion of Peace: Foreign Policy in the Nixon Years (New YorkThe Viking Press, 1978), especially pp. 176-177.

14. G. Macharia Munene, "Cold War Disillusionment and Africa", in Munene, Nyunya, and Adar, (eds.), The United States and Africa, op. tit, p.30

15. On this view as it relates to Africa in general see, Helen Kitchen, US Interests in Africa (Washington, DC: Praeger, 1983), pp.1-14 and Korwa G. Adar, "Kenya-US Relations: A Recapitulation of the Patterns of Paradigmatic Conceptualization, 1960s- 1990s", in Munene, Nyunya, and Adar, (eds.), The United States and Africa, op. cit, pp. 89-104.

16. David Mervin, Ronald Reagan and the American Presidency (New York: Longman, 1990), pp.63-64.

17. Michael Clough, Free at Last? US Policy Toward Africa and the End of the Cold War (New York: Council on Foreign Relations Press, 1992), p.42.

18. Dilys M. Hill, "Human Rights and Foreign Policy", in Hill, (ed.), Human Rights and Foreign Policy: Principles and Practice (London: Macmillan Press, 1989),p. 22.

19. For the Ugandan and the South African case see, Foreign Relations Authorization Act, Fiscal Year 1979, PL 95-426 and Export-Import Bank Act Amendments of 1978, PL 95-630 respectively. Further restrictions were imposed on Uganda under the International Security and Development Cooperation Act of 1980 PL 96-633.

20. Cyrus Vance, "Human Rights and Foreign Policy", Georgia Journal of International and Comparative Law Quarterly 7[J]97[7], pp. 223-225. See also David Carleton and Michael Stohl, "The Foreign Policy of Human Rights: Rhetoric and Reality: From Jimmy Carter to Ronald Reagan", Human Rights Quarterly 7(May 1985): 54-81. Cyrus Vance,Hard Choices: Critical Years in American Foreign Policy (New York: Praeger, 1983), pp.450-

451.

21. W. F. Buckley, "Rhodesia and the Hypocrites", The Washington Star, March 16,1979 and D. Clark, "Africa's Policy's Big Test", The New York Times, January 30,1979.
22. Korwa G. Adar, Kenyan Foreign Policy Behavior Towards Somalia, 1963-1983 (Lanham:University Press of America, 1994), p.156.
23. R. Cohen, "Human Rights and Decision Making in the Executive Branch: Some Proposals for a Coordinated Strategy", in D. P. Kommers and G. D. Loescher (eds.), Human Rights and American Foreign Policy (Notre Dame:Notre Dame Press, 1979):216- 246 and Morgan, "Panel Rebuffs U.S. Bid to Relax a Rights Sanction", Washington Post (March 23,1979), p.A2, col.3. For the US sanctions against Sudan for what Washington calls state sponsored terrorism see Korwa G. Adar," A State Under Siege: The Internationalization of the Sudanese Civil War", African Security Review, 71(1998) :44-53.
24. US Government, The United States and South Africa: United States Public Statements and Related Documents, 1977-1985 (Washington,DC.:United States Department of State, September, 1985.
25. Tamar Jacoby, "The Reagan Turnaround on Human Rights", Foreign Affairs 64(Summer 1986): 1066-1086.
26. "Fledgling Democracies Can Count on U.S. Help, Maoni Ya America, 53 (April 1992), p.l.
27. Ibid., p.l.
28. "Storm Over USA's Views "The Weekly Review, May 11,1990, p.14. See also, "U.S. Envoy Steps into Political Firestorm in Kenya", New York Times, May 6,1990, p. 13 and generally, Smith Hempstone, Rogue Ambassador: An African Memoir (Sewanee, TN.:University of the South Press, 1997).
29. Barbara Grosh and Stephen Orvis, Political

Conditionality,Democratization and Economic Performance in Africa: Aid in Kenya in the Post Cold War Era, no. Publisher, no date., p.6. See also, Senator T. Kennedy, "Suspend All American Aid to Kenya for Human Rights Violations", Congressional Record 136(93) (July 19,1990), pp. 15-16.

30. Bill Clinton, "Developing a New U.S. Policy Towards Africa", The White House Conference on Africa, June 26-27,1994 (Washington, D.C.: Africa Regional Services, US IS July 1994), p. 14.

31. Ibid.

32. Warren Christopher, "A New Relationship", Africa Report (July-August 1993), p.37. Warren Christopher, "Democracy and Human Rights: Where America Stands" Address at the World Conference on Human Rights, Vienna, June 14,1993.

33. "U.S. Policy for a New Era in Sub-Saharan Africa" (Washington, D.C.: State Department Fact Sheet, January 27,1993) p.6. See also, Marlin Fitzwater, "U.S. Policy for New Era in Sub-Saharan Africa" U.S. Department of State Dispatch 4(3) (January 18,1993), p.35 and George Moose, "Top U.S. Official Defends Africa Programs Before Congress, Maoni Ya America 86 (April 1995), pp.3-9.

34. For Nigeria's human rights record see, U.S. Government, Department of State, Nigeria: Human Rights Report, 1995 (Washington, D.C.: U.S. Government Printing Office, 1996), pp.1-26.

35. Madeleine Albright, "U.S. Challenge Nations on Lack of Respect for Human Rights", Moani Ya Amerika, 95 (January 1996) pp.25-26.

36. See, The White House, Office of the Press Secretary, Kampala, Uganda, "Remarks by the President at Entebbe Summit for Peace and Prosperity", Imperial Botanical Beach Hotel, Entebbe, Uganda, March 25,1998., pp.1-2.

37. See generally, The White House, Office of the Press Secretary,

"Remarks by President to the People of Ghana", Accra, Ghana, March 23,1998, The White House, Office of the Press Secretary, Press Conference by President Clinton and President Mandela", Garden of Tuynhius, Cape Town, South Africa, March 27,1998 and The White House, Office of the Press Secretary, "Remarks by the President at Entebbe Summit for the Peace and Prosperity", Imperial Botanical Beach Hotel, Entebbe, Uganda, March 25,1998.

38. "Clinton in Africa", The Economist, March 21,1998, p. 56.
39. "African Americans Urge Senate to Modify Africa Trade Bill", Letter from Several Prominent African Americans to Members of the US Senate Urging Modification of the US-Africa Trade Bill, Transafrica, March 13,1998, pp. 1-10.
40. Wafula Okumu, "Reflecting on Clinton's Africa Safari", The Perspective, July 14,1998, p. 4.
41. Ibid. See also generally, "Oxfarm Briefing Statement on President Clinton's Africa Trip", Oxfarm International, March 23,1998, pp. 1-4; USIA, "Africa Wants Support Provided by Trade Bill-Summers", (Washington, DC: United States Information Agency, June 22, 1998), pp.1-9.
42. "Clinton Trip Doesn't Mean Change in Policies", The Times of Zambia, March 27,1998, p.l.

4

Democracy and Socioeconomic Rights in India

"Compelling action by authorities of the states through the power of mandamus is an inherent power vested in the judiciary," said India's Prime Minister, but warned that "substituting mandamus with a takeover of the functions of another organ may, at times, become a case of over-reach... these are all delicate issues which need to be addressed cautiously." Manmohan Singh was speaking at a conference of regional chief ministers and high court chief justices. A similar point was made by a former Chief Justice of the Supreme Court who cautioned the courts on legitimate and illegitimate intervention; and also by the Speaker of the legislature who said, "I will be failing in my duty if I do not point out that there has been an encroachment in the legislative arena." These cautionary words from the heads of the legislature, executive, and the judiciary imply that the Indian courts have not just been activist, but over-activist. Is that true?

In the last two decades, the higher judiciary in India transformed non-justiciable economic and social rights such as basic education, health, food, shelter, speedy trial, privacy, anti-child labor, and equal wages for equal work into legally enforceable rights. In a famous judgement on the right to education, the judges even said that a right could be treated as fundamental even if it was not present in the fundamental rights section of the constitution. Subsequent judgements established the rights to a healthy environment, nutrition, food, shelter for the poor, and the primacy of the right to health and privacy for an HIV-positive employee who was fired after taking the company physical.

These judgements have triggered a view that the interpreters of the law became lawmakers in India. Some scholars and parliamentarians agree, but others argue that the judiciary did not encroach into legislative or executive space. Drawing on evidence from litigation on the rights to health and education, we argue that Indian judges have not become lawmakers or have even been activist in these two spheres if activism is defined quantitatively in terms of the number of decisions that find government actions unconstitutional. In fact, the judges were reluctant to strongly penalize the government even when the state failed to fulfill its statutory obligations. Instead, courts adopted what Tushnet calls weak remedies such as setting up committees and negotiation channels. We discuss the probable reasons for such behavior within theories of institutionalism and civil society activism. Our evidence questions whether the judicial arena provides the right avenue for improving the realisation of social rights to health and education.

The first section addresses the constitutional framework of social and economic rights and the power of the courts. The second and third sections focus on the nature and extent of legalisation of health and education rights, highlighting the argument that courts have, at best, played an indirect role in influencing policy. The fourth section assesses the impact of the courts for the effective delivery of these rights. In the conclusion, we return to the implications for the debates on the court's role in delivering social goods.

The Constitution and Economic Rights

Rights, which are guaranteed by the state and enumerated in

the constitution, are enforceable claims on the delivery of goods, services or protections by specific others.[8] Social rights are at systemic risk in legislative democracies because those who would benefit from them lack political power. As Tushnet points out, there are three ways in which a constitution can recognize social and economic rights: (a) by enumerating them but making them non-justiciable; (b) by making them justiciable but allowing courts to find a violation only when the legislature dramatically departs from the constitutional requirements; or (c) by making them enforceable to the same extent as civil and political rights. Tushnet argues that in the long run it would be better to opt for non-justiciable social rights because enforceable rights would force courts to adopt strong remedies that could spark political opposition and even noncompliance.

Constitutional provisions dealing with rights - of whatever generation involve trade-offs between norm articulation, the availability of individual remedies, and the strength and credibility of the institutions created to enforce those rights....Coupling strong rights with weak remedies, particularly when those remedies are rarely deployed because of resource constraints on plaintiffs, maybe a formula for producing cynicism about the constitution.

Drawing on the Irish experience, the Indian constitution distinguished between enforceable fundamental rights, which were to be protected from incursions by the state, and non-enforceable directive principles, which were goals and duties of the state and included social and cultural rights highlighted in the Universal Declaration of Human Rights; the International Covenant on Civil and Political Rights; and the International Covenant on Social, Economic and Cultural Rights. It was "the intention of the Assembly that in future both the legislature and the executive should not merely pay lip-service to these principles enacted in this part but that they should be made the basis of all executive and legislative action that may be taken thereafter in the matter of governance of the country," said B.R. Ambedkar, the chairman of the constitution drafting committee. The framers made the fulfillment of the rights to food, health, and basic education contingent on the state's economic capacity.

The people, rather than the courts, were supposed to prod the state to provide these goods.

India is a federal republic with a Westminster-style parliamentary system, a strong central government and a unified judiciary under an apex court. The Supreme Court, assisted by twenty-one high courts and numerous lower courts, is often described as the most powerful court in the world. The Supreme Court has original, appellate, and advisory jurisdiction on any dispute between the central and state governments, and between state governments. Apart from a brief hiatus during an emergency regime (1975-77), the Supreme Court has rebuffed every legislative amendment aimed at curtailing judicial review and even increased its power to interpret the constitution through a basic structure doctrine. Judicial independence increased in the early 1990s when the apex court appropriated the power to appoint itself and lower court judges.

But this power is offset by the high case load because the apex court, unlike its American counterpart, has no control over its docket. As one serving judge pointed out, the government (a litigant in more than 70 per cent of the cases) is responsible for the high case load because it appeals automatically when it loses in a lower court. Epp highlights the incoherence in the Supreme Court's agenda caused by overload in cases, fragmentation of the twenty-six supreme court justices into small panels that allows inconsistency to creep into decision-making, and the short terms served by the justices (1-6 years). Of approximately 100,000 cases (admitted and pending) in 2006, the court disposed of 56,540 cases, which means that each judge dealt with 3,846 cases that year. A high court judge deals with seventy to one hundred cases a day. These institutional obstacles raise questions about whether judges even have the time to be activist on non-enforceable social and economic rights.

In the initial decades after independence in 1947, the Supreme Court endorsed the distinction between fundamental rights and directive principles citing the economic incapacity of the state. By the 1970s, the court (nudged by the executive) shifted toward the view that one of the basic features of the constitution was harmony and balance between the directive principles and fundamental rights. The judges began incorporating rights to health, food, education, shelter, and so forth into the fundamental rights to equality (Article 14) and life and liberty (Article 21).

Why the shift? Scholars attribute the transformation to the post-emergency attempt by judges to recoup legitimacy after their capitulation to an authoritarian executive from 1975 to 1977. According to legal scholar Upendra Baxi, "Judicial populism was partly an aspect of post-emergency catharsis....Partly, it was an attempt to refurbish the image of the court tarnished by a few emergency decisions and also an attempt to seek new, historical bases of legitimation of judicial power." Judicial activism of the post-emergency period, according to Sathe, involved a liberal interpretation of constitutional provisions like Articles 21 and 14 and the reconceptualisation of the judicial process by making it more accessible and participatory. There is some basis to this claim because the judges who were tarred by their acquiescence to the executive during the emergency era were also among those who championed the court's orientation toward social rights. Supreme Court judges like Krishna Iyer and P. N. Bhagwati liberalised rules of locus standi (the right to bring an action) and simplified the appeals process through the introduction of public interest litigation (PIL). Common law systems permit only those persons whose rights are directly affected to approach the court. The PIL system allows any member of the public (individuals or

NGOs) to espouse public interest causes by sending a letter or petition to the Supreme Court (and now also to the high courts). Since the mid-1980s, the court has heard PILs on environment, women's rights, poverty issues, among others, brought by public-spirited individuals and organisations. The Right to Information Act, 2005 provided a new tool for NGOs to litigate on some socioeconomic rights. For instance, NGOs spearheading the right-to-food campaign decided to approach the Supreme Court after the Right to Information Act allowed them to see letters between the central and state government on food stocks.

Some analysts charge that the courts used PILs as a tool to creatively read rights into the constitution, later becoming law makers, and even super-executives.[21] Is the observation valid? Let us examine the behavior of the higher courts in health and education.

Defining a Right to Health and Education

In 1992, a minority opinion of Justice K. Ramaswamy in a three judge panel (which included the Chief Justice) argued:

> The term health implies more than an absence of sickness. Medical care and health facilities not only protect against sickness but also ensure stable manpower for economic development. Facilities of health and medical care generate devotion and dedication to give the workers' best, physically as well as mentally, in productivity. .. In the light of Articles 22 to 25 of the Universal Declaration of Human Rights, International Convention on Economic, Social and Cultural Rights, and in the light of socio- economic justice assured in our constitution, right to health is a fundamental human right to workmen.

Although commending Ramaswamy for his concern, the majority opinion, however, held that in the absence of legislation, one could not talk of a right to health. Health and education rights of citizens including securing the health and strength of workers (Article 39e), effective provision within the limits of the state's economic capacity for rights to work, education and public assistance in event of unemployment, old age, and sickness (Article 41), and raising the level of nutrition and standard of living and public health (Article 47) belonged to non-enforceable directive principles.

By 1997, the minority ruling had become settled law that right to health is integral to right to life" and the government had a "constitutional obligation to provide the health facilities" for its employees, which later expanded to cover all citizens by the turn of the century.

In 1992, the court declared that all citizens had a right to education.

Every child's of this country has the right to free education until he completes the age of 14 years. Thereafter his right to education is subject to the limits of economic capacity... the effect of holding that the right to education is implicit in the right to life is that the state cannot deprive the citizen of his right to education except in accordance with the procedure prescribed by law.

Did judges address the main problems in the sectors? Did these judgements have any impact on the government's health or education policies? A big problem with linking judgements to policies is the following: how does one determine whether the court was responsible for a policy? For instance, ten years after *Unnikrishnan,* the Parliament passed the 86th constitutional amendment providing for free and compulsory education for all the children between six to fourteen years as a fundamental right under Article 21 A. But interviews with government officials and other experts suggest that the amendment was induced by political motives (it was piloted as part of an election promise by a political party) rather than the court's ruling. The fate of the Right to Education Bill in 2005, slated for debate in parliament in 2006, and then shelved indefinitely by the government on grounds of a budgetary crunch, confirms their contention. In this study, the court would have an impact on policy if the government or the relevant institution cites the judgement as the reason for formulating it. To assess the impact on policy, we must examine the extent and impact of legalisation of health and education rights.

The extent of legalisation depends on three factors: demands made for these rights in court, ease of litigation, and the enforcement of a decision. We collected cases in the higher courts where the judges or litigants explicitly used the right to health or education to justify their arguments. Our analysis captures only a fraction of the total litigation on health and education, but we deliberately limited our scope to assess the impact of courts on policy because a court's use of a right to health or education would have greater legal and policy influence. We focused on the higher judiciary because they establish the final interpretations of the law and were most likely to influence policy.

From 1950 to 2006, the Supreme Court alone disposed of 1,158,303 cases, and the twenty-one high courts disposed of hundreds of thousands of cases each, of which cases dealing with a right to health or education (HE) composed only 382 cases. Using the classification of socioeconomic rights that Gauri and Brinks develop in the introduction to this volume, almost half the caseload on HE rights dealt with enforcing the obligations of providers and clients, whereas a third focused on regulation. Only 15 per cent involved provision and financing of health care or education. The impact of the decision in more than 80 per cent of the cases favored a citizen's right to health and education.

The impact of the judgements overwhelmingly favored the citizen rather than the violator, who could be the plaintiff or defendant; poor (BIMARU) states had significantly lower rates of litigation on HE, and PILs were used in only a third of the cases. Only eight PILs were registered from poor states and were

Table 4.1. Health and education cases profile

Category of states	*Total cases*	*Impact favors citizen*	*Impact does not favor citizen*	*Private obligation*	*Government obligation*	*PIL*	*Writ petition*	*Other*
BIMARU	64	49	15	25	35	8	15	41
Non-BIMARU	318	248	70	118	180	39	110	169

successful in 75 per cent of the cases. The state/government was the defendant in 77 per cent of the cases, whereas individuals (43 per cent),

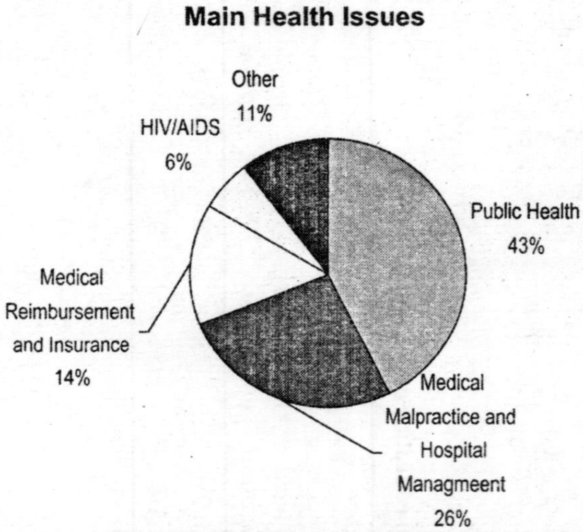

Fig.1 : Main issues in right-to-health litigation.

NGOs/public-spirited citizens (19 per cent) private institutions (16 per cent) and unions (12 per cent) were the main plaintiffs.

Of the 209 right-to-health cases, only a quarter were decided in the Supreme Court. The rest were in the high courts, with 70 per cent of the cases litigated in Delhi, Bombay, Allahabad, and the southern states. Regulation accounted for the bulk (44%) of the cases, provider/client obligations (35%) and provision/financing (18%). The state was the defendant in 86 per cent of the cases, but was likely to win only around 30 per cent of the time.

Despite the high (80 per cent) success rate of PILs, only a fifth of the health cases were PILs. These cases focused on the absence rather than the quality of facilities promised by the government. These low rates of litigation by NGOs confirm the contention that the rights-based approach to social needs in India was judge-led rather than NGO-led. It corroborates other research

Table 2 : Winners in right to health litigation

Issues	*Individual v. state*	*Individual v. private institutions*	*NGO v. state*	*Private institutions v. State*	*Unions v. State*	*Total*
Public Health	7 (14)	1 (1)	34 (40)	4 (16)	2 (8)	48 (79)
Med Negligence	12 (18)	5 (6)	5 (7)	0	1 (2)	23 (33)
Med Reimbursement	23 (25)	0	0	0	1 (2)	24 (27)
HIV	4 (6)	1 (2)	3 (3)	1 (1)	0	9 (12)
Other	5 (6)	1 (1)	4 (5)	0 (1)	0	10 (13)
total	51 (69)	8 (10)	46 (55)	5 (18)	4 (12)	114 (164)

Note: Numbers denote winning cases; total cases are in parentheses.

on the negligible emphasis by NGOs on litigation as a public action strategy owing to the time-consuming and costly nature of approaching courts and the poor enforcement of decisions. Although more than half the cases were filed after 1997 and 70 per cent of the cases were decided within two years of being registered in the relevant court, a case could take more than five years if it was appealed in the Supreme Court.

The higher levels of litigation in urban areas and richer states reflect the importance of income and access to courts in facilitating litigation. Poor people rarely approached courts, and when they did, it was through NGOs. For instance, several cases dealt with the reimbursement of hospital expenses incurred by middle class government employees. Public health concerns were reflected predominantly by NGOs or public-spirited persons who were plaintiffs in more than 50 per cent of these cases and won more than 80 per cent of the time.

Using the notion of a right to life with dignity, judges expanded the ambit of health to include physical, social, and mental well-being and aimed at the policy goals of a healthy environment, nutrition and socioeconomic justice. NGOs won 80 per cent of their cases against the state, whereas private institutions and unions were less likely to win against the state.

The procitizen trend of judgements was uniform across health issues. But what do the judgements imply for the effective enjoyment of these rights by the citizens? Did judges address the main issues plaguing the health sector and deliver effective rights to citizens? Effective rights means that individuals are likely to get the social good they ought to receive. The next section examines that issue.

The impact of legalisation depends on the enforcement of the decision in conjunction with the relevance to the broader needs of the health sector. India accounts for a third of global tuberculosis (TB) incidence and the largest number of active TB patients, 20 to 30 million episodes of malaria per year, and the largest number of HIV-positive persons in the world, though proportionately prevalence is low compared to many developing countries. The health-care system in India favors those who can pay. In India, the richest fifth receives three times the curative healthcare subsidy of the poorest fifth. A World Health Organisation (WHO) report revealed that public health subsidies disproportionately benefit higher quintiles, though such imbalance was lower in southern states. Southern and western states performed well on health indicators, but BIMARU states did poorly. In India's federal set up, health is a shared subject between the center and states. Despite the availability of free medical treatment in government hospitals, poor people prefer private providers because of the inefficiency of the state run services. Medical care is now the second most common cause of rural family debt. The number of people not taking any treatment in the mid-1990s because they could not afford it was double what it was a decade earlier, composing nearly one in every four rural Indians and one in five urban Indians. This stemmed from a mismatch between stated goals and low levels of public expenditure, 0.9 per cent of the Gross Domestic Product (GDP) on medical services (versus 2.2 per cent by lower-middle income countries).

The urgent requirements were the reform of the public delivery of curative services (more doctors, equipment, and medicines), the provision of municipal services for a disease-free existence, and the regulation of private health care, particularly the complaints mechanism. How does the litigation address these issues? The attitude of courts varied depending on whether the issue was a tussle between an employer and employee, state and citizen, provider and client, or regulation of providers.

Courts had a direct influence on making doctors legally accountable for negligence, and an indirect influence on facilitating a complaints redressal mechanism. Medical malpractice suits favored the patient's rights a majority of the time even though the burden of proof to demonstrate negligence rested on the patient. More than half of the thirty-three cases were brought by individuals (patients) against state-run hospitals and doctors, and 66 per cent of the rulings favored patients, and the enforcement mechanism was clearly specified with damages and time limits. Doctors were defendants in a third of the cases, and only one case was registered in a poor state. In *Jacob Mathew,* the apex court framed guidelines under which a doctor could be tried in criminal courts for negligence. "Negligence is the breach of a duty caused by omission to do something which a reasonable man guided by those considerations which ordinarily regulate the conduct of human affairs would do, or doing something which a prudent and reasonable man would not do."[43] *Intention* and *lack of proper care and caution* were key in determining negligence. A doctor would have "no absolute or total immunity... from liability for his negligence." In *Cosmopolitan Hospitals,* the court allowed patients to get remedies through the consumer redressal forum. Consequently, except primary health centers and hospitals that offered free treatment to all patients, all doctors and hospitals are now liable under the Consumer Protection Act.

The court favored the patient when a delay in operating and providing oxygen led to brain damage, an abdominal pack was left in the body, death was caused by failure to perform an appendicitis surgery, and the state's failure to maintain electric lines led to amputation and death. The court said,

If people go to such Government Hospitals and Public Health Centres for improvement of their health but instead return with further damage to their health on account of infection at such Government Hospital or Public Health Centre, their fundamental right to life under Article 21 of the Constitution would stand infringed.

But judges were aware of the limits of their expertise. In

complex operations or where the technical equipment did not reveal complications, the court gave the benefit of doubt to the doctor/ institution.

Medical reimbursement cases constituting 16 per cent of the health cases were primarily about the obligations of the state to its primarily middle class employees. In nearly 90 per cent of the cases, the court favored full reimbursement of medical expenses of the employee-patient, arguing that a welfare state had a constitutional obligation under Article 21 and Article 47 to provide health facilities to its employees. The remedies were straightforward -judges fixed the amount of damages to be paid within a time limit, with monetary penalties for noncompliance. The court's intervention had a larger policy impact, albeit for a small and already favored fraction of the population (about 10 per cent of the population consists of formal sector workers and their families) - eligibility requirements were relaxed to include new entitlements and new classes of persons, and even overturned existing policies. At the high court level, the judges extended the coverage to new groups such as wives, pensioners, and municipal pensioners. The judgements also expanded the entitlement package to cover emergency treatment in private hospitals, specialised equipment, and expensive treatment.

State-Private Provider Regulation

Judges backed the state's regulation of the private sector, which had only a 28 per cent chance of victory when bringing cases against the state. Manufacturers challenged government orders regulating the manufacture and sale of alcoholic and addictive substances. The court ruled that because the state was bound to uphold the right to life and health (Articles 21 and 45), it could limit the sale of gutka and pan masala, ban the supply of country liquor in polyethylene sachets and abolish country liquor shops. The right to work (Article 19) was not absolute and would be subservient to public health. "Adulterated foodstuff have a direct bearing on public health... well settled principles relating to the matters pertaining to public health should be kept in mind by the Court while approaching such matters. Attending to public health is of the highest priority perhaps the one at the top," said the court.

In cases where the government had failed to comply with existing rules on medicines, the judges asked the government to follow its guidelines on the manufacture and procurement of oral polio vaccine, the associations of drugs and pharmaceuticals to follow new rules issued by the government in line with WHO guidelines, and asked the government to pass legislation mandating severe punishment to those involved in the manufacture of spurious drugs. The court was more effective with specific types of noncompliance; it imposed fines on a chemist for selling spurious drugs and reprimanded the government for not prosecuting the accused, found a hospital guilty of purchasing contaminated IV fluids at exorbitant prices. Few cases dealt with poor access to medicines by the vulnerable groups. Only three high court cases dealt with drug policies, of which only one dealt with the culpability of the chemist in selling spurious drugs. One reason for the low case load on access to medicines could be that generic medicines in India are relatively inexpensive. However, with the Trade Related Aspects of Intellectual Property Rights (TRIPS) compliance by India in 2005, we may see an increase in litigation on access to medicines in the next decade.

Some judgements were more contentious, drawing criticism that the legal rulings could be hijacked by vested interests. For instance, the judges did not recognize practitioners of alternative medicine as doctors because they had not been certified by the Indian Medical Council. This and other rulings on environmental cases raise questions about the capacity of judges to grapple with complicated public policy issues, which willbe addressed in the final section. The high caseload coupled with the short stints of judges at the apex court did not allow sustained scrutiny of compliance. High court judges have a longer tenure (twelve to eighteen years) but their high caseload (eighty to one hundred cases a day) does not give them time to monitor compliance. Evidence from the judgements indicates that once the court's scrutiny lapsed, the situation reverted to status quo ante - and judges were aware of it.

State-Citizen Obligations: Public Health and Medical Services

Public health and medical services posed the most complex and urgent problems in the health sector. The court had a direct policy impact on legally increasing the access of citizens to medical services and free antiretrovirals for HIV patients. One judgement said:

> This is a welfare State, and the people have a right to get proper medical treatment. In this connection, it may be mentioned that in U.S.A. and Canada there is a law that no hospital can refuse medical treatment of a person on the ground of his poverty or inability to pay. In our opinion, Article 21 of the Constitution, as interpreted in a series of judgements of the Supreme Court, has the same legal effect.

However, as we shall see shortly, when it came to enforcement, it was a different story. The judges, who turned a deaf ear to the government's pleas about a resource crunch, said that the state was constitutionally responsible for providing citizens with potable water, clean environment, and sanitation as part of the right to life. "By affirmative action, the court could compel a statutory body to carry out its duties to the community including creation of sanitary conditions," said the court in a *suo moto* (on its own motion) case on the degradation of Jaipur city. Similarly, in environmental disasters such as the leakage of poisonous gas in Bhopal from a Union Carbide plant, which caused the deaths of more than 2,500 persons and damaged the health of thousands, the higher judiciary gave compensation to the victims and directed and monitored compliance by the state in establishing a specialised hospital. The court favored the maintenance of ecology and pollution-free air in urban and residential areas and asked industries like stone crushing units, rice mills, and brick kilns to shift. But in activities beneficial to the public such as hospitals in residential areas, the courts dismissed petitions from the residents.

Several judgements increased the access and availability of medical treatment to citizens. The court issued guidelines to hospitals on providing medical facilities to accident victims, banned strikes by doctors in tertiary referral hospitals because it would infringe the right to medical treatment, quashed a notification appointing doctors on contract saying that the right to life demanded proper treatment, which could be ensured only through fair selection and regularised appointments.

However, the court was more circumspect on the issue of quality of services provided by the state. Relatively few cases dealt with the quality and provision of medical services in rural areas, including the pitiable conditions of government hospitals, health centers, and doctors. The court opted to apply indirect pressure on the government through weak remedies such as committees to improve and fill vacancies in primary health care centers and address the concerns of doctors.

Prevention and Treatment of Key Public Health Concerns

As noted earlier, India is poised to become the world capital of HIV-infected persons by 2015. The major problems in HIV are the regulation and removal of unsafe practices (e.g., blood screening practices), enforcing provider-client treatment and employment obligations, and allocation of adequate funds for public education and treatment. A handful of cases dealt with provision and financing of medicines for HIV/AIDS, and 75 per cent of

HIV rulings favored "public health." The low use of litigation (only twelve cases) by patients, NGOs and the court itself is striking, and reflects the importance of prior legislation and civil society litigation for the court's intervention.

The high courts expanded the access to free medical treatment to AIDS patients including armed personnel and prostitutes, asked the state to start public education on safe sex practices for prostitutes, provided maintenance for a wife suffering from HIV, contracted through blood transfusion during pregnancy, said that the right of a fiancee to a healthy existence (Article 21) overrode the HIV-positive man's right to privacy, gave back wages to a casual laborer who had been deleted from the selection panel because of his HIV-positive state, lowered the cost of diagnostic kits, instituted free medical treatment to HIV-positive prisoners, and deleted a clause from an insurance policy because it excluded poor people.

High court judgements had a direct legal effect in two key areas: they reduced the cost of antiretroviral (ARV) kits and facilitated a government policy to provide free ARVs. The Human Rights Law Network along with the Punjab Voluntary Health Association (VHA) filed a petition in the Supreme Court in 2003, asking for free and equitable access to ARV treatment. The court issued notices to the government National AIDS Control Organisation (NACO) and the state governments. The Delhi Network of Positive People, an NGO formed by persons living with AIDS, dashed off a similar petition to the Delhi High Court asking for free access to medicines, treatment, and care. Earlier petitions by the VHA dealt with equitable treatment of AIDS patients by health-care workers and the right to a safe working environment for health-care workers and doctors. In response to the Punjab petition and pressure from domestic and international actors, the Indian government announced a new policy in 2003 of providing free ARVs to 100,000 patients in six high incidence states by 2005. From March 2006, three ARV drugs were available free of cost to patients below the poverty line at all Delhi hospitals. However, none of the twenty-six hospitals had kits to detect the extent of HIV infection and calculate the dosage of ARVs. But the legal effect did not translate into effective rights for 770,000 (WHO estimate) AIDS patients who are too poor to afford even the reduced cost ARV kits, while their access to free ARVs was stymied by poor compliance by the government.

The evidence shows that the judiciary directly facilitated policies that increased legal access to medical services, environmentally friendly areas, and regulatory mechanisms. First, the court's rulings expanded access of some services (like medical reimbursement, access to ARVs, food, use of consumer courts to complain about doctors) to new classes of beneficiaries. The judges were instrumental in expanding the ambit of the right to food to all states even though the initial case was registered in Rajasthan. The court's receptiveness to the petition prompted the original plaintiff (an NGO) to file PILs on the right to food in a number of regional high courts. Although the introduction of cooked midday meals in primary schools "would not have happened without the Supreme Court cracking the whip," the court's effectiveness in mandating enforcement of its directives has been low. In an attempt to cope with the ramifications of the court's rulings on the right to food, the government introduced an education levy to finance a midday meal scheme in schools.

Second, the court also influenced new policies on health related issues such as a ban on smoking in public places in Kerala, a switch to clean fuels in Delhi and Mumbai, oversight of the pesticide content in soft drinks such as Pepsi and Coke Citing the obligation of the government to improve public nutrition (Article 47), the court struck down a new method of distributing sugar, which allotted more quantity to persons with higher income, saying it would result in inequitable distribution and nutrition.

A 1996 apex court judgement, which came in response to a PIL on the malpractices and malfunctioning of blood banks, directed the government to set up a national council and state councils of blood transfusion and consider legislation on regulating blood banks. An analysis of the court's role in the eventual regulation of blood banks illustrates the promise and the inadequacy of court interventions. The councils were established in most states by 2004 with budgets allotted by the NACO, and a national blood policy was evolved in 2000 to finance, regulate, and provide safe and adequate quantity of blood, blood components, and blood products. Government officials claimed that "the blood transfusion service has sufficiently been cleaned up based upon the Supreme Court order... the per centage of HIV infection occurring through blood has come down from 8 per cent to 3.4 per cent in the last four years" However, experts point out that the transfusion of infected blood continues to be responsible for around 6 per cent of AIDS and hepatitis cases in the country. Drug controllers were ill-equipped to handle the task of monitoring blood banks because of the multiplicity of agencies involved; whereas advisory councils lacked the authority to punish erring blood banks. These inefficiencies generated a gap between growing demand and reduced supply of clean blood, leading to noncompliance by commercial blood banks who do not always conduct the prescribed tests and the illegal re-entry of professional blood donors, who had been banned in 1998.

The judiciary had an indirect impact on facilitating regulatory mechanisms of nongovernment agencies. The Supreme Court prodded the Medical Council of India to institute a formalised mechanism for hearing complaints on medical negligence. "The decision to formulate guidelines has been taken in view of the Supreme Court directive in the Malay Ganguly Case, which was a PIL filed in the year 2000 alleging lack of transparency and lack of proper mechanism on the part of MCI in dealing with cases of medical negligence."

Thus, despite the expansive nature of the judgements, selective impact on some policies, and the expansion of selected social goods to new classes of beneficiaries, the courts had a limited and indirect impact on increasing the efficacy and access of citizens to better health. The courts avoided grappling with core issues of poor management of the public health and medical services by the government. And NGOs and others did not challenge these gaps in court. Only one PIL dealt with the poor functioning of a state AIDS Control Program and the judgement said that "the funds released by the Government of India shall not be diverted to any other Heads of Account except for the purpose of implementation of the programme as per guidelines and strategies formulated by the NACO and the funds withheld so far shall be released for the Programme." The poor enforcement of these directives, addressed in the final section, highlights the question of the court's effectiveness in generating policy and delivering health rights to citizens. But first, let us examine the situation of education rights.

The Extent of Legalisation in Education

Forty-five years after independence, the court transformed education into a fundamental right for children ages six to fourteen years. We looked at all cases where either the litigant or the court expressly relied on the right to education to argue their position. The constitution promises the right only to children in primary and elementary education, but in our cases we included secondary school cases within "schools" and university level cases in "university." Let us examine the patterns in court.

Only 47 per cent of cases focused on primary (the focus of the right) and secondary education, whereas the rest (including most Supreme Court rulings) related to university-level concerns. At the high court level, of the 149 cases, Allahabad, Bombay, and

Table 3 : Winners in Right to Education Litigation

Issues	*Individuals v. state*	*Individuals v. private*	*NGOs v. state*	*Private v. State*	*Unions v. State*	*Total*
Students	34 (51)	2 (5)	4 (5)	0 (2)	4 (5)	44 (68)
Teachers	4 (8)	2 (2)	2 (3)	1 (1)	10 (15)	19 (29)
Private Sector/ Minority Institution	2 (3)	1 (3)	1 (2)	15 (33)	0 (1)	19 (42)
Government	0 (1)			1 (1)	1 (2)	
Other	1 (1)		1 (1)		0 (1)	2 (3)
total	41 (64)	5 (10)	8 (11)	16 (36)	15 (23)	85 (144)

Note: Numbers denote winning cases; total cases are in parentheses.

the four southern states accounted for half the litigation. Despite experiencing much greater need in this area, the poorer BIMARU states accounted for only 28 per cent of primary and secondary school level cases and 18 per cent of university-level cases. The distribution of education cases across courts of different jurisdictions. As ondividuals, private institutions, and unions (mainly student and teacher) - the more literate, urban and well-off sections - were most likely to come to court. The negligible use of courts by NGOs (7 per cent of plaintiffs) is evident from the fact that PILs accounted for only 4 per cent of the cases. The Supreme Court dealt mainly with university-level issues relating to the autonomy of private and minority institutions to admit students, charge capitation fees, charge differential fees, and general administration. These cases mainly focused on the access of well-off students to higher education rather than the access and quality of education for the poorer sections. A handful of cases dealt with the poor quality of rural schools and teacher absence. Admissions, exams and activities of students accounted for 45 per cent of the case load, whereas 32 per cent of cases were brought by private institutions on issues relating to autonomy, permission to start new schools/universities, and affirmative action. Obligations (62 per cent) between the providers and citizens were more frequently litigated than were regulation (25 per cent) and provision/financing (13 per cent).

Judgement

An overwhelming majority of judgements favored a citizen's right to education. About 77 per cent of the cases were decided within two years in the high court, and if appealed, within four years from start to finish; so judges seemed to be aware of the time constraints imposed by the academic system.

The state, which was the defendant in 80 per cent of the cases, lost more often than it won. NGOs had a high success rate, followed by individuals and unions who won 65 per cent of the time, whereas the private sector had a 44 per cent chance of victory against the state. Individual plaintiffs arguing for student related issues had a 67 per cent chance of winning in court against the state, while teacher salary and tenure issues had a 66 per cent chance of success. Individuals had only a 50 per cent chance of winning against private and minority institutions. If one were to loosely group NGOs and Unions into collective cases and compare them to noncollective cases, both had approximately similar chances of victory (65 per cent). The courts commonly used the fundamental right to education and public safety arguments to favor education rights. A second rung rationale involved the "duty of the state" argument. So, for instance, the courts said student safety included physical and mental safety, which meant that they deserved access to better quality education. Does this mean that judges had a great impact on policies and an effective right to education?

The Impct of Legalisation in Education Schools

The litigation patterns did not reflect the main sectoral concerns: high dropout rates, poor teaching record evident from the low functional literacy and numeracy of students, rampant teacher absence, and poor quality of school infrastructure. Most cases dealt with access rather than quality. The case load in court reflects the malaise affecting the education sector in India, where the emphasis is on access, often at the expense of quality and learning outcomes. India has one of the largest education systems in the world. At the elementary level, of the 931,471 schools in twenty-five states, 80 per cent were located in rural areas. The government ran 65 per cent of the schools and the rest were managed by private (government aided and unaided) organisations.[86] The government launched the Sarva Shikha Abhiyan (SSA) program to achieve universal primary education by 2007, but the results were mixed. School infrastructure was poor: only 42 per cent of schools had common toilets, and not all schools had drinking water facilities. Boys outnumbered girls in enrollment, with the poorer BIMARU states showing the lowest enrollment for girls; there were low Scheduled Caste (20.84 per cent) and Scheduled Tribe (9.71 per cent) enrollments in government-run schools. Surveys by the National Institute for Education Planning and Administration (NIEPA) show that about 42 per cent of children drop out of school before reaching Grade V. The average pupil-teacher ratio was 39 to 1. Almost 44,000 schools were getting by with para-teachers rather than regular appointees.

The primary school level -a key area of concern for the state - took a back seat to litigation on teacher-related issues of salary and tenure. The judgements overwhelmingly favored teachers when they challenged the state on appointments, parity of pay, and other issues discussed in the next section, but there were almost no cases on teacher absence and quality of teaching. Private institutions managed by religious minorities and others often came to court and won their cases against the state's intervention in their institutions. Very few cases focused on the functioning of government schools. In a case in Meghalaya, the courts said that public schools established and maintained by the government and providing quality education with better facilities than those of government primary and upper primary schools could not be made beyond the reach of weaker sections of the society by fixing higher fees for the students. At the university level, admissions- and fee-related issues followed by new institute approvals and facilities and conduct of exams were the main areas of litigation. Let us examine the main issues fought out in court.

Students (Access and Quality of Education)

Admissions (access to education) were among the most frequently litigated issues in primary education. The judges supported students when the authorities acted in an arbitrary fashion in admission, expulsion, and exam policies; banned corporal punishment on grounds that it affected attendance and increased the dropout rate; and included the right to study in a language medium of one's choice in the right to education. Very few cases focused on the quality of education. The courts increased the facilities for children by mandating that the government provide free textbooks until Grade IV.

In view of the fact that a large amount of rupees 827.39 crores is available for primary education, it cannot be said that the financial position of the state is such that it is not possible for the state government to provide for free textbooks to students below the age of 14 and studying standards I to IV. The financial requirements as envisaged in article 41 of the constitution is thus met with.

Courts held the government in contempt for not complying with the court's directions in granting courses; allowed the state to make policy decisions to improve the quality of education by mandating that school children pass a middle standard exam within fourteen years, and study English/Hindi before taking the matriculation exam, and fulfill attendance requirements; and allowed students who were unable to take exams because of riots to retake them; provided state financial aid to a school for students with handicaps, dismissing the government's excuses of a budgetary crunch and their contention that the deaf and hard of hearing were more capable than the blind.[93] The judges also tried to curtail misuse of the right by noting that no student could insist that a school of his choice should provide him with education in the manner he wanted or could get his exam papers reevaluated.

Teachers (Selection, Salaries and Quality)

Teacher absence and appointments are major concerns in education policy. Teacher absence ranged from 17 per cent in Maharashta to 30 per cent in Bihar. In 2001 to 2004, of the 535,203 approved teacher positions at the All-India elementary level, only 310,506 positions had been filled. The court cases did not reflect teacher absence, but did focus on the selection, salaries, and to a lesser extent on the quality of teachers. On selection criteria, the court upheld the parity of Bachelor of Education degrees with teacher training certificates and asked the state to appoint these teachers to the 21,000 posts vacant in the primary school program. The court rejected the government's decision to reserve seats for women and for science subjects in teacher appointments and prevented the state from unlawfully terminating a teacher appointed under a welfare scheme.

A handful of cases touched on the quality of teachers. The court agreed with a PIL that only qualified teachers should be appointed to provide quality education to children; that criminals could not be presidents of educational institutions; and dismissed petitions from teachers who were unqualified or who challenged universally applicable policy decisions of the state. The judgements obliquely addressed teacher quality by instituting regular payment of salaries and parity of pay for teachers and nonteaching staff of private (government-aided) and public institutions. The judges said that irregular payments and inequality would result in disgruntled teachers and would negatively affect the quality of education. The standard of teaching should not suffer because of nonpayment of salaries resulting from a budgetary crunch, said the court, pointing out that by denying primary school teachers proper salaries and allowances the state violated Articles 21, 14, and 19 (1) (a) of the constitution. The claim of the teachers of the primary classes to get proper salaries and the fundamental right of children to get education were two sides to the same coin, said the court. However, the court held, teachers had no right to strike despite nonpayment of their salaries.

Since right to education is a fundamental right, and right to uninterrupted education in School or College is also a fundamental right, and that Articles 39,41,45 and 46 have also highlighted the importance attached to children, this judgement [denying the teachers the right to strike] is made applicable not only to

Government schools, Government aided schools, but - also to similar other schools and other institutions which impart education.

Private Institutions: Regulation and Provider-Client Obligations

Private institutions frequently challenged access-related regulations of the government such as the refusal of permission to establish new schools. In response, the court said that the right to establish and administer an educational institution was a fundamental right available to all, as was the right to impart education. However, none had a right to get state recognition without satisfying the validly imposed requirements of infrastructure, teacher recruitment, and so forth. Poor quality, particularly of private schools, was immediately penalised by the court. Unrecognised schools "with little or no infrastructure and with a lack of qualified teaching staff cannot be permitted and the State would be justified in dealing with such institutions with strictness." Where government aided schools lacked teachers and other facilities because of a budgetary crunch, the court directed the state to rectify the situation by supplying teachers. The private sector also challenged the government's incursions into their autonomy, to which the court replied that there was no right to impart education and no right to government grants,[108] that government-funded private schools could not refuse to implement the government's reservation policies, and the state could regulate admissions and make reservation policies applicable to private unaided schools.

Judges accepted budget shortfalls as a sufficient reason to close private schools because the private companies were not obliged to open schools when they could not afford it. Neither was the government duty bound to pay salaries of teachers in aided higher secondary schools if it could not afford to do so.

The court's impact on policy was primarily indirect—it upheld state policies on educational standards rather than forcing the government to formulate new policies. The court's rulings upheld quotas for "backward classes" in private schools, and policies on curriculum. In a few cases like *Ravindra Kumar, Advocate v. State of UP,* the court directed the state to increase budgetary allocation for education. It also expanded salary benefits to new classes of teachers and access to better quality schools for poor people. However, the court's response fell short of addressing the key concerns in the sector - remedies focused on improving access rather than quality, and they penalised private rather than government providers for failing in their obligations.

If we assessed the court's impact vis-a-vis constitutional rights, then we would have to give judges a poor grade because a majority of the right-to-education cases were at the university level. In the next section, we ignore the constitutional extent of the right and focus more broadly on the court's impact on higher education.

University

The constitutional right to education was not meant for higher education, which suffered from lack of quality rather than access. However, litigants who came to court from educated, middle class and urban areas used the right to argue for a host of issues ranging from a right to strike to a right to get government aid.

University-level students used a right to education to argue for admissions to professional courses, political activities on campus, and fees. The Supreme Court disagreed with a Delhi court decision and agreed with a Kerala court ruling that the right to participate in elections was a statutory right, not a fundamental one. The high courts upheld the right of students to higher education and professional courses; rejected quotas for nonresident Indians (NRIs) but upheld reservations for Delhi city students in professional colleges; rejected an upper-age limit, a merit limit, and a time limit for applying to a course; and chastised the Calcutta government for "criminal" delay in publishing examination results. The court was more lenient when students and women were involved. It asked the college to admit a woman who had not received the relevant information by mail saying that the right to education of weaker sections especially women was important. But powerful groups also benefited from the court's leniency; candidates admitted because of political influence were allowed to continue the course because it would affect their future. Some high courts had a more expansive interpretation of the state's obligations on education - a college had to resume teaching a course despite lack of funds.

Teachers got a favorable response from the court because of need for "good quality teachers." On the issue of parity of pay for teachers of recognised, aided private schools with their counterparts in government schools and the subsequent obligation of the state to bear the expenditure, the judges argued that the state was obliged to treat both sets of teachers equally and should "endeavour to review and increase the budget allocation" for education. The judges chastised the state government for ad hocism in regularising teacher appointments; instructed the state to reappoint a librarian who had been fired because of withdrawal of government funding; and upheld a district-based selection of teachers in Himachal Pradesh on grounds that locals would know the culture better.

Private institutions used the right to education to challenge nonrecognition by the government, but the court rejected these petitions on grounds of quality. The court held that the right to education did not include the right to conduct courses without government approval. "We cannot convert the University into an orphanage for these students," said the court in a judgement denying permission to an unrecognised college for veterinarians on grounds that these courses were specialised subjects needing course work and training. The court objected to the policy of giving guest lecturers in Chennai preference during hiring, saying that their quality was questionable. Thus, courts acted as quality controllers, vetting the entry and operation of new institutions.

Government regulation was challenged on the issue of the extent of affirmative action in minority institutions and quotas in government and private colleges. In *Inamdar* the court clarified that private, minority, and nonminority self-financed institutions had the autonomy to fix fee structure and admissions policy, subject to reasonable restrictions of public interest. Aided minority institutions would have to submit to some amount of regulation as a condition of receiving aid or recognition. The courts struck down 100 per cent reservations for in-state students saying that it contravened the right to education; allowed quotas for candidates from hill areas because the beneficiaries were socially and educationally "backward" classes but deemed reservations for rural areas as unconstitutional because the classification was based on residence. The courts said that the state had "the legal duty, subject to availability of the seats in the institutions, to make the right to medical education available to every eligible person"; but then chastised a southern state government for permitting medical colleges to overfill their seats. One case even held that the state had a constitutional mandate (Articles 39 and 21) to grant legal aid to society and ought to permit a private entity to open a law college. In one case, the apex court said that the government could be forced to provide grant in aid to government-recognised private law colleges, despite the government's argument that the judiciary was interfering in a policy decision. "It is open to the Court to direct the executive to carry out the directive principles of the Constitution, when there is inaction or slow action by the state."

Overall, it appears that the courts have done little to secure the right of students to a decent primary and secondary education. The higher level of activity on private school and university education might be the result of more legal resources available to private providers, who can contest the state's accreditation decisions. Courts had a direct impact on quality by enforcing mechanisms to ensure that only good quality private institutes were given approvals to run schools and universities. However, they could do little about the 65 per cent of schools that were government run, and which educated 73 per cent of all enrolled students. Overall, the judiciary focused more on client-provider obligations and less on regulation and financing. The reason for this may well be that Indian courts, as courts elsewhere, see issues related to state provision and financing as a legislative or executive prerogative.

Let us now turn to the compliance with court orders. Our argument was that the judiciary was aware of its inability to elicit executive branch compliance because of its overloaded dockets, panel-style treatment of cases, rules regarding judicial tenure, and its other institutional constraints. Therefore, it adopted weak remedies.

Compliance

More than half the cases in education and more than 60 per cent in health dealt with the obligations of government providers. According to Mark Tushnet Constitutional provisions allowing governments to adopt reasonable programs to achieve social welfare rights, a willingness to find some programs unreasonable and a remedial system that does not guarantee that any particular plaintiff will receive individualised relief: these are the characteristics of weak substantive social rights.

Tushnet outlines several types of weak remedies: declarations that identify the strength of the right rather than the remedies; or a requirement that the government develop plans (through committees or other means) within a reasonably short but unspecified time to eliminate constitutional violations. Indian judges used both types of weak remedies to deal with cases of government failures to meet statutory obligations. The court typically used two types of supervision for weakremedies: (a) A supervising ministry or authority had to report to the court from time to time, following which the court would issue new directions; and (b) in some cases, the court itself monitored implementation, leaving open the window for petitioners to come back to court if the directives were not implemented.

The type of enforcement preferred by judges in cases involving the government shows that judges were more likely to favor a committee-style approach for public health issues where complexity was high and the judge's own grasp of the myriad interlocking policies was low. In medical reimbursement, a relatively less complex issue, we see more emphasis on time-bound actions with penalties for delays imposed on the states. In education, on the other hand, judges favored strong enforcement of government and private provider obligations. Of the seventy-eight cases where the government was a defendant, the court favored strong enforcement and the status quo a third of the time, and weak and no enforcement 10 per cent of the time.

Judicial directions were usually couched in the language of suggestions and recommendations generated through committees. For instance, although agreeing with a PIL petitioner that authorities should not provide ground water with a high fluoride content, the court *asked* the state to consider evacuating the effected villagers. The Calcutta high court judges *asked* the government to investigate charges that ground water was contaminated because of overuse by soft drink companies, and *recommended* that the state make rainwater harvesting mandatory for these companies. It directed a committee to *examine* ways to improve services in government hospitals, and *asked* the government to pass legislation banning the use of carcinogenic insecticides and color additives. The judges rarely issued strong remedies for government providers. In a Jharkhand case, the judge issued detailed instructions to local officials to certify within two months that the meals (served in a mandatory midday meal scheme) were fit for human consumption after an NGO filed a PIL alleging adulteration of the food.

Compare this to the compliance mechanism favored in education cases. Judges opted for strong enforcement (with time limits and penalties) in 27 per cent of the school and university cases, and weak enforcement in only 11 per cent of the cases. Evidence from the follow up on enforcement of Delhi High Court education decisions suggests that the authorities complied with court directives. This could be because of the nature of these cases - follow up by the affected individuals and the relative noncomplexity of the solutions as compared to public health or medical negligence. Even here, the unwillingness of the court to penalize the government is evident in their satisfactory rating of the government's efforts to strengthen the standard of education despite criticism in a PIL on the government's inept implementation of compulsory elementary education.

It is doubtful whether the reliance on intermediate mechanisms has helped in the effective delivery of social and economic rights. Judges were aware of the disconnect between their directives and the government's propensity for non-compliance but could do little about it. The problem with weak remedies is the higher possibility that the rights remain unenforced - in several cases the government shelved committee reports citing budgetary shortfalls. Even when the court instituted time limits, enforcement depended more on monitoring by the litigant. The right-to-food and right-to-education campaigns demonstrate the importance of NGOs in monitoring progress. Even when NGOs supervised progress, the results did not match the promise contained in the judgement. For instance, despite a Supreme Court judgement in 2001 giving each enrolled child up to Grade V, at least 300 kcal of a cooked meal, several glitches, including slow implementation in Bihar, Jharkhand, and Uttar Pradesh; poor quality of meals; and cost cutting by panchayats because of lack of separate earmarked funds for midday meals, undercut effectiveness. Despite judicial support, even the Right-to-Food campaign is looking beyond legal tools to carry out and sustain its work. Some of the problems of litigation included the access, time, funding, and efficacy of court judgements.[133] A survey of the court's orders shows that the state governments have been quite reluctant to enforce the directives. As Jean Dreze points out, the basic food policy remained unchanged even while committed civil servants did commendable work in specific areas, such as Baran district in Rajasthan.

CONCLUSION

Critics and our opening quotes point to the recent spate of judgements on school admissions, affirmative action in elite institutions, and environmental policies as an instance of larger involvement by the judiciary in policy making. They would be correct in the environmental arena, perhaps because of the higher NGO activity and interest of judges in the issues.[134] But in health and education, the patterns show low impact of courts on policies, the reluctance of judges to penalize government providers as compared to private providers, and the corresponding lack of emphasis by NGOs and others on litigation as a strategy to obtain social goods.

Judges could get involved if one of three conditions exists: (a) no law on the issue (judgements in the 1980s and 1990s transforming social rights into justiciable rights); (b) the legal framework exists but is not implemented (judgements on municipal failures to provide potable water); or (c) the legal framework is inadequate to meet new challenges (judgements on intellectual property rights and drug policies). Our evidence shows that the court's role in health and education policies was indirect and minimal at best, focusing more on (b) and less so on (a) and (c). Even here, the courts can only intervene if cases are brought before it. The low rates of litigation by NGOs and the minimal use ofPILs confirm Epp's (1998) argument that social rights litigation (except environmental) lacks the support structures for a full-fledged rights revolution. Interviews with the right-to-food campaigners suggest that litigation has been time consuming, costly, and relatively ineffective as compared to traditional mobilisation strategies. Social Jurist, a civil rights group consisting of lawyers and activists, filed several petitions in the Delhi High Court on health and education issues, but progress is slow.

This can be explained by the fact that judges are members of an institution whose rules emphasize restraint rather than activism. The allocation of cases by the Chief Justice, lack of enforcement capacity, and the emphasis on collaboration rather than dissent in the two- or three-judge panels encourage conformity and status quo behavior. Judges realize that their decisions may not be enforced, and they will not be there long enough to ensure compliance. Hence, they only pick battles that they can win - less complex issues that pit the court against private providers rather than the government.

The behavior of the Indian courts belies theories about the conditions for activism. There are two sets of theories about the conditions for activism. Juris-tocracy theories focus on the motives underlying the creation or empowerment of the judiciary by legislators or other elites. The argument is that political elites transfer power to judges in hopes that they will be conservative and/or protective of rights.[137] In India, the Supreme Court seised some elements of independence (the power to appoint itself) through its own judgements; political elites did not transfer power to judges. The second set of theories attributes such empowerment to legal choices of judges rather than to the short-term self-interest of elected power holders. In fact, Gillman points out that these scholars saw activism as being inconsistent with the preferences of legislators. Within this tradition, one sees theories about fractured governments generating more room for expansion of judicial power or post-crisis judges engaging in activism . The transformation of unjusticiable social rights into legal ones in the post-emergency era confirms a post-crisis behavior, but the results from our analysis show that the position of judges on social rights was consistent with and not opposed to the promises of successive governments. Take the example of a right to education. The constitutional amendment was piloted in 1996 by a minister from a political party who had made it an election promise, and it finally passed during a different party's rule in 2002.

But it is not a completely pessimistic story. Court interventions did extend benefits to larger groups of beneficiaries and included poorer and backward classes. In health, the judgements expanded the concept of access, but not actual access to ARVs for the large number of AIDS patients. But the same example shows that the effective delivery of these rights depends on the government. Some findings from the Delhi High Court suggest that the court's scrutiny, in conjunction with NGO and media attention, may force the government to implement directives.

The evidence raises concerns about whether the court is the right arena to ensure the provision of social goods like education and health. Are judges qualified to assess the implications of their judgements? For instance, a recent interim ruling by the Supreme Court permitting the implementation of a 2002 pharmaceutical policy that sought to put in place a mechanism that would allow the government to intervene when prices of essential drugs behaved abnormally was interpreted by the government as allowing a drug price control policy. In education, it is debatable whether the court's ruling in *Unnikrishnan* has been beneficial or detrimental to the quality of learning. Preliminary evaluations of the government's SSA shows that the emphasis is on putting children in schools (i.e., the targets are met) rather than on ensuring learning outcomes. Even PILs have come under a huge strain. The Prime Minister warned that PILs have great utility in initiating corrective action, [but] PILs cannot become vehicles for settling political or other scores. We need standards and benchmarks for screening PILs so that only genuine PILs with a justiciable cause of action based on judicially manageable standards are taken up. This will also ensure consistency in judicial pronouncements... the Supreme Court could take the lead in framing rules in this regard.

Courts have at best provided temporary solutions to complex problems of public health and primary education, but they were more effective in addressing simpler issues dealing with government regulation of private providers and obligations of private providers to citizens. The declaratory language of the judgements focused on the strength of the right rather than the remedies. Perhaps that is all overburdened and understaffed courts in countries like India can do.

BIBLIOGRAPHY

Andhyrarujina, T. R. 1992. Judicial Activism and Constitutional Democracy in India. New Delhi: M. N. Tripathi Private Ltd.

Austin, G. 2000. The supreme court and custody of the constitution. In B. N. Kirpal et al (eds.). *Supreme but not infallible: Essays in honour of the Supreme Court of India* (pp.1–15). New Delhi: Oxford University Press. G. Austin 1996. *The Indian constitution: Cornerstone of a nation*. Oxford: Clarendon Press.

Barak, A. 2002. A judge on judging - The role of a supreme court in a democracy. *Harvard Law Review* 116: 16–162.

Baruka, G. C. 2007. Contemporary views on access to justice in India. In A. K. Hazra and B. Debroy (eds.), *Judicial reforms in India - Issues and aspects* (pp. 101–18). New Delhi: Academic Foundation.

Baxi, U. 1980. *Indian supreme court and politics*. Delhi: Eastern Book Company.

Baxi, U. 1985. Taking suffering seriously: Social action litigation in the supreme court of India. In R. S. R. Dhavan and S. Khurshid (eds.), *Judges and the judicial power* (pp. 289– 315). Bombay: Tripathi.

Baxi, U. 2002. The (im)possibility of constitutional justice: Seismographic notes on Indian constitutionalism. In E. S. Z. Hasan and R. Sudarshan (eds.), *India's living constitution – Ideas, practices, and controversies* (pp. 31–63). New Delhi: Permanent Black.

Baxi, U. 2007. The rule of law in India. *SUR* 6: 7–27.

Bhandari, L. 2006. Class monitor needed. *Indian Express*, October 20, http://www. indianexpress.com/story/14984-2.html

Cameron, C. M. 2002. Judicial independence:How can you tell it when you see it? And, who cares? In S. B. Burbank and B. Friedman (eds.), *Judicial independence at the crossroads: An interdisciplinary approach* (pp. 134–147). Thousand Oaks, CA: Sage.

Choudhry, S., and C. E. Hunter. 2003.Measuring judicial activism on the supreme court of

Canada: A comment on *Newfoundland (Treasury Board) v. Nape.McGill Law Journal* 48: 525–562.

Clayton, C. W., and H. Gillman, eds. 1999. *The supreme court in American politics: New institutionalist interpretations*. Chicago: University of Chicago Press.

Cover, R. 1983. Nomos and narrative. *Harvard Law Review* 97: 4–68.

Dahl, R. 1957. Decision-making in a democracy: The supreme court as a national policymaker. *Journal of Public Law* VI,(2): 279–95.

Dam, S. 2005. Lawmaking beyond lawmakers: Understanding the little right and the great wrong. *Tulane Journal of International and Comparative Law 13*: 109.

Das, G. 1987. *Supreme court in quest of identity*. Lucknow, India: Eastern Book Company.

Davis, D. (1992). The case against inclusion of socio-economic rights in a bill of rights except as directive principles. *South African Journal on Human Rights* 8: 475.

Desai, A. and S. Muralidhar. 2000. Public Interest Litigation: Potential and Problems. In B. N. Kirpal et al (eds.). *Supreme but not infallible: Essays in honour of the Supreme Court of India*. New Delhi: Oxford University Press.

Dhavan, R. 1977. *The supreme court of India: A socio-legal analysis of its juristic techniques*. Bombay: N. M. Tripathi.

Dhavan, R. 1980. *Justice on trial: The supreme court today*. Allahabad, India: A.H. Wheeler & Co.

Dreze, J. 2003. Hunger admidst plenty. India Together December 2003: http://www.indiatogether.org/2003/dec/pov-foodsec.htm

Dua, B. D. 1983. A study in executive-judicial conflict: The Indian case. *Asian Survey* 23(4): 463–483.

Dworkin, R. 1986. *Law's empire*. Cambridge: The Belknap Press of Harvard U. Press.

Dworkin, R. 1999. *Taking rights seriously*. Delhi: Universal Law.

Epp, C. 1998. *The rights revolution*. Chicago: University of Chicago Press.

Epstein, L., ed. 1995. *Contemplating courts*.Washington DC: CQ Press.

Epstein, L., and J. Knight. 1998. *The choices justices make*. Washington, DC: Congressional

Quarterly Press.

Feeley, M., and E. Rubin. 1998. *Judicial policy making and the modern state: How the courts reformed America's prisons*. Cambridge: Cambridge University Press.

Ferejohn, J. 1999. Independent judges, dependent judiciary: Explaining judicial independence. *Southern California Law Review* 72(2–3): 353–84.

Forbath, W. E. 1994. Why is this rights talk different from all other rights talk? Demoting the court and reimagining the constitution. *Stanford Law Review 46*: 1771.

Gadbois, G. H. 1968. Indian supreme court judges – A portrait. *Law & Society Review 3*: 317–36.

Gadbois, G. H. 1977. Indian judicial behaviour. *Economic and Political Weekly*, 149–66.

Gadbois, G. H. "The Supreme Court of India as a Political Institution." In *Judges and the Judicial Power*, edited by R. Sudarshan Rajeev Dhavan, and Salman Khurshid. Bombay: Sweet and Maxwell, 1985.

Gajendragadkar, P. B. 1965. *Law, liberty and social justice*. Bombay: New Age Printing Press.

Galanter, M., and J. K. Krishnan. 2004. Bread for the poor: Access to justice and the rights of the needy in India. *Hastings Law Journal 55*: 789–834.

Galanter, M. 1997. *Law and society in modern India*. Delhi: Oxford University Press.

Gillman, H. 2002. How Political Parties Can Use the Courts to Advance Their Agendas: Federal Courts in the United States, 1875–1891," American Political Science Review *96*: 511–524.

Goldstein, L. F. 2004. From democracy to juristocracy. *Law and Society Review 38*: 611.

Hazra, A. and B. Debroy, editors. 2006. *Judicial Reforms in India: Issues and Aspects*. New Delhi: Academic Foundation.

Helmke, G. 2002. The logic of strategic defection: Court-executive relations in Argentina under dictatorship and democracy. *American Political Science Review 96*(2): 291–303.

Hirschl, R. 2000. The political origins of judicial empowerment through constitutionalisation: Lessons fromfour constitutional revolutions. *Law and Social Inquiry 25*(1): 91–149.

Hirschl, R. 2004. *Towards juristocracy – The origins and*

consequences of the new constitutionalism. Cambridge, MA: Harvard University Press.

Hirschl, R.,N.Tate, andT.Ginsburg. 2003. *Judicial reviewin newdemocracies –Constitutional courts in Asian cases*. Cambridge: Cambridge University Press.

Iyer, K. 1992. *Justice at crossroads*. New Delhi: Deep and Deep.

Iyer, K. 1987. *Our courts on trial*. New Delhi: B. R. Publishing.

Kashyap, S. 1994. *Our constitution*. Delh: National Book Trust.

Krishnan, J. 2006. Lawyering for a cause and experiences from abroad. *California Law Review*, March: 574–615.

Levi, E. H. 1949. *An introduction to legal reasoning*. Chicago: The University of Chicago Press.

Llewellyn, K. 1931. Some realism about realism – Responding to Dean Pound. *Harvard Law Review 44*: 122–1264.

Mehta, P. B. 2005. India's judiciary: The promise of uncertainty. InD. Kapur and P. B.Mehta (eds.), *Public institutions in India*. New Delhi: Oxford University Press.

McCann, M.W. and G. L. Houseman, eds. 1989. *Judging the constitution – Critical essays on judicial lawmaking*. London: Scott, Foreman/Little, Brown Series in Political Science.

Misra, R.,R.Chatterjee, and S.Rao. 2003. *IndiaHealth Report*.New Delhi:OxfordUniversity Press.

Muralidhar, S. 2002. Implementation of court orders in the area of economic, social and cultural rights: An overview of the experience of the Indian judiciary. Paper presented at the First South Asian Regional Judicial Colloquium on Access to Justice, New Delhi, November 1–3.

Rao, K. S. 1974. *Social justice and law. First Shyama Prasad Mookerjee memorial lectures*. New Delhi: National Publishing House.

Rau, B. N. 1960. *India's constitution in the making*. Edited by B. Shiva Rao. Bombay: Orient Longmans.

Rosenberg, G. N. 1991. *The hollow hope: Can courts bring about social change?* Chicago: University of Chicago Press.

Rosenberg, G. N. 1992. Judicial independence and the reality of political power. *Review of Politics* 54: 369–398.

Rosenberg, G. N. 1998. Knowledge and desire: Thinking about courts and social change. In Schultz, *Leveraging the law – Using the courts to achieve social change*. New York: Peter Lang

Rosencranz, A., and M. Jackson. 2003. The Delhi pollution case: The Supreme Court of India and the limits of judicial power. *Columbia Journal of Environmental Law 28*: 223.

Sainath, P. 2006. The health of nations. *India Together*, Feb 18, http://www.indiatogether. org/2006/jan/psa-health.htm

Sathe, S. P. 2002. *Judicial activism in India*. Delhi: Oxford University Press.

Sathe, S. P. 2002. Judicial enforcement of socio-economic and cultural rights. Paper presented at the First South Asian Regional Judicial Colloquium on Access to Justice, New Delhi, November 1–3.

Scheingold, S. 1989. Constitutional rights and social change: Civil rights in perspective. In M. W. McCann, and G. L. Houseman (eds.), *Judging the constitution – Critical essays on judicial lawmaking*. London: Scott, Foreman/Little, Brown Series in Political Science.

Seervai, H. M. 1983. *Constitutional law of India* (3rd ed.). New Delhi: N.M. Tripathy.

Segal, J., and H. Spaeth. 2002. *The supreme court and the attitudinal model revisited*. Cambridge: Cambridge University Press.

Sen, A., and J. Dreze. 1995. *India: Development and participation*. New Delhi: Oxford University Press.

Setalvad, A. M. 2000. The supreme court on human rights and social justice: Changing perspectives. In B. N. Kirpal et al (eds.). *Supreme but not infallible: Essays in honour of the Supreme Court of India* (pp. 232–255). New Delhi: Oxford University Press.

Shapiro, M., and A. S. Sweet. 2002. *On law, politics and judicialisation*. Oxford: Oxford University Press.

Shue,H. 1980. *Basic rights: Subsistence, affluence, andU.S. foreign policy* (2nd ed.). Princeton, NJ: Princeton University Press.

Sousa, M. 2006. Judicial roles in the policy making process and public policy in Latin America. Paper presented at the American Political Science Association, Philadelphia, August 31.

Sunstein, C. R. 1995. Propter honoris respectum: Rights and their critics.*Notre Dame Law Review 70*: 727.

Tate,C.N. 1993.Courts and crisis regimes – A theory sketchwith Asian case studies. *Political Research Quarterly 46*(2): 311–38.

Tate,C.N., andT.Vallinder. 1995. The global expansion of judicialpower:The judicialisation of politics. In C. N. Tate and T. Vallinder (eds.), *The Global expansion of judicial power* (pp. 1–24). New York: New York University Press.

Tushnet, M. 2004. Symposium: Constitutional courts in the field of power politics: Social welfare rights and the forms of judicial review. *Texas Law Review 82*: 1895.

UNAIDS. 2003. *AIDS Epidemic Update*. Available from: data.unaids.org/Publications/IRCpub06/ JC943-EpiUpdate2003 en.pdf

Verma, J. S. 2007. The Indian polity: Separation of powers. Pandit Kunji Lal Dubey Memorial Lecture. April 26, 2007. Available here: http://speakerloksabha.nic.in/speech/ Speech Details.asp? SpeechId=212

Vandenhole, W. 2002. Human rights law, development and social action litigation in India. *Asia Pacific Journal on Human Rights and the Law 2*:136–210.

Voigt, S. & Salzberger, E.M.,2002. Choosing Not to Choose: When Politicians Choose to Delegate Powers, *Kyklos* 55(2): 289–310.

5

Economic Reforms and Social Democracy

Introduction

In the second half of the 1990s, parties of the center-left briefly dominated West European politics, with Socialist, Labour or Social Democratic parties in power in almost all the EU member states. But this electoral dominance was shortlived, and two of these left governments suffered resounding defeats after just one term in office. Of those that won reelection, some, such as the UK Labour party and the German Social Democrats, have been subject to fierce criticism from within their own ranks for their perceived compromises with the neo-liberal, pro-market orthodoxy.

Much criticism has focused on the apparent reluctance of the European centre-left to challenge the mainstream view that globalisation has made distinctive social democratic strategies impossible. Indeed, the most visible result of this period of Social Democratic dominance was the 2000 Lisbon summit, which exhorted EU governments to embrace neoliberal structural reform rather than continue with traditional Social Democratic goals such as income redistribution, public provision of important services or employment rights. The Lisbon summit appeared to confirm the most pessimistic arguments about how globalisation has made Social Democratic policies unworkable.

This article seeks to assess the prospects for West European Social Democratic parties following distinctive, progressive programmes in the current, apparently inhospitable, political climate. It moves beyond the kinds of crude accounts of globalisation and social democracy which have driven much of the public debate, drawing on the insights of two distinct fields of research: comparative party politics and comparative institutionalist political economy. These two fields provide accounts of both the electoral opportunity structures facing Social Democratic parties, and the institutional legacies and global economic constraints facing these parties when they govern. However, the close connections between the two have not been fully drawn out by the existing scholarship on social democracy. As Peter Hall has argued, political economists tend to interpret policy change in terms of broad dynamics of social coalition-building, without looking too hard at how electoral coalitions are filtered through the institutions of representative democracy. Research into party politics, on the other hand, studies coalition-building and the electoral process in all its complexity, but pays little attention to the policy process. This article seeks to exploit the potential of bringing these two literatures together.

I will therefore make two inter-related arguments. First, I argue that the debate between proponents of neo-liberal 'structural reform' and an essentially conservative defence of existing West European models of welfare capitalism is misleading and unhelpful to Social Democratic parties. In fact, structural reforms can be combined with social democratic welfare institutions, as the example of the Scandinavian countries demonstrates. Second, I show that the difficulties Social Democratic parties face in achieving a virtuous combination of structural reform and welfare provision lie not only in the institutional legacies of their welfare states, but also in long-standing patterns of party competition that provide incentives for Social Democratic parties to adopt particular political discourses.

This article examines the electoral strategies of Social Democratic parties in the five largest West European democracies, and finds that discursive traditions and electoral incentives deriving from historical cleavage structures can explain differing responses to the economic and social challenges of globalisation and technological change. The Social Democratic parties of the largest West European states face a double dilemma, since their electoral incentives often do not square with the opportunities for progressive policy change in their political economies.

Globalisation and Policy Change

Recent work in comparative political economy has brought a much needed correction to some of the more sweeping claims about globalisation that characterised the debate in the early to mid-1990s. Many early contributions to this debate predicted dire consequences for the autonomy of the nation-state as the internationalisation of capital flows and the dismantling of trade barriers unleashed a 'race to the bottom' among Europe's complacent and inflexible welfare states. Social democratic policies such as welfare entitlements, publically funded services, and employment protection legislation would have to be rolled back if Western Europe was to 'compete' in the new global economy. Such claims have been revealed to be overblown however, and careful analyses of the realities of policy change under globalisation depict a variety of responses dictated, in large part, by the different institutional arrangements governing politics and the economy in the advanced democracies.

Contrary to the convergence hypothesis, the institutional constraints on welfare retrenchment appear decisive in determining the extent to which governments respond to globalisation by cutting back social protection. Countries with majoritarian electoral systems, decentralised wage bargaining, federal arrangements and limited welfare states have tended to reduce social provision, while those with inclusive electoral institutions, centralised wage bargaining, unitary structures and more encompassing welfare institutions have tended not to. In other words, the countries that have cut back social protection in recent years have for the most part been those that had less generous welfare arrangements in the first place.

Similarly, extensive research on wage bargaining has demonstrated that both decentralised and centralised labour market institutions can contribute to economic efficiency, although 'intermediate' models are likely to be penalised by globalisation. Other research stresses the complex interactions between institutions, interests and exogenous constraints, concluding that institutional divergence has actually increased in recent decades, in spite of, and in some ways because of, globalising pressures. Finally, it has also been persuasively argued that many of the imperatives attributed to globalisation are actually the result of other pressures, such as demographic and technological changes, and the shift in advanced democracies from a manufacturing-oriented economy to a services-oriented economy.

Varieties of (Non-Convergent) Capitalism?

Much of this work implicitly or explicitly draws on longstanding models or types of advanced welfare capitalism in order to make sense of the variety of responses to globalisation. Most prominently, Hall and Soskice and their collaborators see these responses reflecting two broad types of institutional arrangements in advanced industrialised capitalism: liberal market economies (LMEs) and coordinated market economies (CMEs). In LMEs markets and the price mechanism regulate most economic activity, whereas in CMEs markets coexist with various kinds of coordination and cooperation between economic actors. The crux of the 'varieties of capitalism' argument is that neither model is inherently more economically efficient, and both can harness their respective institutional comparative advantages to good effect in the unforgiving global economy. However, Hall and Soskice note that the coordinated market economy, with strong labour market institutions and generally more generous social provision, is clearly less socially divisive than the liberal market model.

This school of thought therefore has emerged as a powerful counter to the convergence theorists' insistence that only 'structural reform' - liberalisation and welfare retrenchment - will allow advanced industrial democracies to adapt successfully to globalisation. These critiques of the 'globalisation as convergence' thesis seem to offer some reassurance and encouragement for the disoriented left parties of Western Europe. However, Social Democratic parties remain on the defensive, advocating liberalising measures at the European level, whilst struggling to protect existing welfare arrangements in the domestic arena. Why then has the evidence against the neo-liberal interpretation of globalisation failed to provide left parties with the confidence to defend social democratic values?

Part of the reason is the poor economic performance of the largest CMEs -Germany, France and Italy - over the past decade. These countries' slow growth contrasts with the relatively stronger growth of Western Europe's LMEs. Given this, international economic institutions and the financial press frequently draw on comparisons of ideal-typical LMEs (the US and UK) and CMEs (usually Germany) to argue the case for the increased marketisation of economic and social life. This places their left parties in a particularly difficult position, as structural reform runs contrary to their ideological traditions, and threatens the interests of part of the left electorate.

This structural reform discourse, however, rests on a potentially misleading dichotomisation of economic models. Although there is relatively little controversy over membership of the market-friendly group of English-speaking democracies, the 'social Europe' alternative is more diverse. In much of the policy debate, the non-English speaking advanced industrial countries tend to be lumped together as market-averse welfare states, with sluggish growth and high unemployment brought about by well-meaning but wrongheaded systems of social protection. Sweden's generous social benefits, Italy's state pension liabilities, Germany's restricted shopping hours, and France's insistence on 'national champions' are mixed together in the same Eurosclerotic bag. This 'continental corporatist' model is then contrasted with the 'Anglo-American' market-based model: a 'capitalist culture-clash' in which the latter is usually tipped as the winner.

Much of the debate surrounding globalisation and social democracy has revolved around this choice, with proponents of structural reform arguing that the European social model is unsustainable, and those on the left often denying the need for any fundamental reform. Given continental Europe's recent poor economic record, framing the debate in such terms places the left in an unpromising position. However, the following section demonstrates that the choice is far less stark and the political dilemma of the left therefore less intractable than the rhetoric might suggest.

Variation Within the Varieties of Capitalism: LMEs, CMEs and Structural Reform

The distinction made by the 'varieties of capitalism' school between liberal market capitalism and coordinated market capitalism lumps together political economies that other typologies have perhaps more usefully separated out. For instance the CME group contains countries that Esping-Andersen divided into social democratic and conservative/Christian democratic welfare state types, whilst more recently Schmidt has revived a further distinction, between 'statist' and 'managed' CMEs. Of course, any comparative effort will tend to elide some differences whilst emphasising others, and the LME/CME dichotomy does indeed capture important features of the economic dilemmas facing advanced industrial democracies. However there are patterns of differentiation within the CME group which have important implications for the strategic opportunities facing the West European left and the policy choices that they can make.

The importance of disaggregating CMEs can be illustrated by drawing on Geoffrey Garrett's analysis of globalisation and European political economies. For Garrett, globalisation reinforces divergence since it benefits both economies with decentralised wage bargaining and those with highly centralised wage bargaining. Under globalisation, states with 'intermediate' labour market institutions will face most pressure to converge around one of these two types. Thus, according to Garrett, CMEs face two diametrically opposed fates: the Scandinavian social democracies are well equipped to prosper in the global economy without having to sacrifice their generous welfare arrangements, while the continental 'Christian democratic' welfare states (such as France, Germany and Italy) face a more unpalatable set of choices. By distinguishing between 'social democratic' and 'Christian democratic' CMEs, Garrett is able to present a powerful argument for the sustainability of welfare capitalism.

This line of argument can be taken further. In fact, in some of the policy areas where the pressure for structural reform is greatest, the CME-LME distinction all but disappears. Analysis of financial markets, business conditions and labour markets shows just about as much variation within the CME group as within the full range of Western European states. For example, as Figure One below shows, standard measures of financial market liberalisation group some of the highest spending welfare states (the Northern European social democracies) close to the finance-friendly UK, whilst the conservative/Christian democratic welfare states tend to cluster towards the bottom of the scale.

A similar picture emerges regarding product market regulation and business conditions. In Figure Two, the UK - the poster child of economic reform in Western Europe - fails to outperform the Northern European social democracies in providing a lightly regulated environment for business, with Finland and the Netherlands scoring higher for a broad measure of business conditions, and Denmark and Norway enjoying lower start-up barriers.

Finally, even in the controversial area of labour market flexibility (Figure Three), there is a striking degree of variation amongst CMEs. Although the UK stands out here for its combination of low employment protection and decentralised wage bargaining, there are again some surprises. Denmark and Switzerland have even more liberal hire and fire rules than the UK, and Finland is not significantly more restrictive.

Two important points emerge from this analysis. First, the LME-CME dichotomy fails to capture the variation of economic institutions amongst Western European states. Instead, in many policy areas the differences between Western European economies are best analysed through continuous variables, which reveal graduations of 'market-friendliness' rather than clear demarcation lines between liberal and coordinated economies. To the extent that typologies remain useful, the picture is still better captured by Esping-Andersen's 'three worlds of welfare capitalism', in which LMEs (liberal welfare states) are contrasted with two kinds of CME: the Scandinavian social democratic welfare state, and the continental European Christian democratic welfare state. Second, there is surprisingly little correspondence between the degree of market-friendliness of economic institutions and government size. Northern European social democracies such as Sweden and Denmark, which have enthusiastically embraced structural reform, also have larger governments than than both the LMEs (the UK and Ireland) and the other CMEs.

This suggests a way out of the left's strategic paralysis. Economic reform, often portrayed as a one-way street towards free market capitalism, is actually far more compatible with the institutions of the social democratic welfare state than is generally acknowledged. The Northern European social democracies have managed to combine market-friendly regulation of key areas of the economy with high levels of state spending, which permit generous welfare provision and public services. The relatively good economic performance of this group of economies through the difficult period of the 1990s has not been achieved at the expense of social solidarity. This of course has important lessons for Social Democratic parties in the rest of Western Europe. Social Democratic parties in Christian democratic welfare states can, in principle, liberalize their economies and maintain high standards of welfare provision. Similarly, Social Democratic parties in liberal welfare states such as the UK can aim to expand social provision without necessarily undermining the functioning of markets. European social democrats can both defend left values and respond to the challenges of a changed economic situation. *So what is stopping them doing exactly this?*

Institutional Constraints, Party Strategies and Policy Change

One possible answer to this question is that Social Democratic parties are locked into particular policy choices by the institutional constraints they face when in power. Long-standing formal and informal institutions not only refract the pressures of economic internationalisation in particular ways; they also constrain and condition policy change. Comparative political economists have stressed the ways in which the broad institutional features of advanced industrial states provide strong disincentives for certain types of policy changes, constraining political parties of both the left and right in the development and implemention of their preferred policies. Political systems with large numbers of veto players create an inbuilt bias towards policy continuity. Different constellations of economic and political institutions have varying degrees of openness to policy change, particularly in the crucial areas of labour markets and the welfare state. Hence, it is held that extensive welfare states are difficult to reform since they create a wide range of beneficiaries intent on protecting their positions. Faced with a broad range of vocal opponents, governments desist from fundamental policy changes with redistributive consequences, and choose instead to 'go with the flow', adopting policies which are consistent with existing institutional arrangements.

This line of argument is persuasive, but cannot alone explain the programmatic positions and electoral strategies of Social Democratic parties in Western Europe. Although globalisation pressures are refracted through extant economic and political institutions, change in these institutions, and hence change in the available range of policy choices, is frequent and significant. For example, decentralisation has been cited as a factor facilitating cuts in welfare provision, and yet Social Democratic parties have often been the promotors of decentralising reform and such reforms have often occurred at the same time as *expansions* in welfare provision. Similarly, inclusive electoral institutions have been cited as a barrier to welfare retrenchment and economic reform since they increase the number of veto players in the system. However, these institutions have been changed by Social Democratic parties in both directions, again without the predicted consequences for economic and social policy. Finally, the 1990s have witnessed a powerful shift towards centralised corporatist bargaining in some of the Christian democratic welfare states.

Certainly, welfare arrangements are very sticky, with most reforms having some redistributive effects that can provoke fierce political resistance. However, policy change can overturn apparently 'immovable' policy institutions. The UK was perhaps closer to the Scandinavian social democratic model of welfare state than to American liberalism in the 1970s, and yet the Thatcher governments overcame strong resistance to impose structural change by making use of a highly centralised state apparatus. The Netherlands successfully reformed its welfare and labour market in the 1980s and 1990s, moving from a Christian democratic model to a more social democratic one. Even in frequently cited cases of policy stagnation - such as France and Italy Social Democratic parties have been able to adopt economic and social reforms which challenged to some degree the existing institutional structure.

So without wishing to underestimate the obstacles in the way of progressive reform in Western European political economies, there is evidence to suggest that the range of policy choices is wider than some observers, and some left party leaders, appear to believe. Indeed Social Democratic parties' reluctance to embark on radical progressive agendas may well be explained as much by their willingness to subscribe to a particular view of the way the world economy works as by the real concrete opportunities and constraints they face.

While not disagreeing with such perspectives, an alternative understanding of this phenomenon based around social cleavages is developed here. Specifically, in the rest of this article I focus upon the electoral opportunity structure facing Social Democratic parties *and examine how this provides incentives for parties to adopt particular views of the world and policy prescriptions that derive from them.* In this regard I suggest how national patterns of party competition and the organisational dynamics of Social Democratic parties themselves can affect economic policymaking under globalisation. I show how the institutions of party politics provide Social Democratic party leaders with incentives to adopt particular theories of the political economy which fit in with the most advantageous strategies of electoral coalition-building and party management. This approach can make sense of the variations in Social Democratic parties' responses to economic change, and explain the obstacles in the way of a realistic but progressive strategy of reform.

Governing With or Against Globalisation? The Importance of Party Competition

The nineties appeared to present the Western European centre-left with two broad options, each of which was identified with a prominent Social Democratic party. The UK Labour party under Blair espoused the 'third way', a centre-oriented strategy which accepted globalisation as unavoidable and adapted traditional social democratic policies to this new reality. Schroeder aligned the German SPD with Blair by signing a common document in 1998, although his closeness to Blair has oscillated since then[36]. In contrast, the French Socialist Party under Jospin was markedly less enthusiastic about globalisation and reluctant to countenance an abrupt 'updating' of his party's traditional ideological identity. The Spanish Socialist Party and Italian Left Democrats have also, although less explicitly, taken some distance from the Blair-Schroeder position. Although the differences between Western European Social Democratic parties are less stark on closer examination of their policy choices in government, the Blair-Jospin debate reflected a real tension within Western European social democracy over how to deal with the changing political economy of advanced industrial states under globalisation.

These contrasting positions cannot easily be explained in terms of the broad structural and institutional features of their respective political systems and political economies. Although the UK economy is more open to global trade than Germany, and France is less open than either, the differences are not particularly striking. Germany has higher industrial employment than France and the UK, but there is little difference between the latter two. The UK certainly stands out for the size and importance of its financial services sector, but in this respect there is little difference between France and Germany. France and the UK, although in different ways, have strongly majoritarian political institutions and relatively centralised states, whilst Germany is a federal state with more inclusive political institutions. In short, macro-structural variables and political system characteristics, although they should be integrated into any account of responses to globalisation, do not seem to correlate in any consistent way with the discourses and policy preferences of Social Democratic parties.

A more fruitful approach is to examine the opportunity structures the parties face in their attempts to win votes and obtain political power. Formal political institutions such as the territorial distribution of power, the level of inclusiveness of electoral institutions, and the balance of power between executives and legislatures, are an important feature of these opportunity structures. But just as important is the nature of the party system. By providing incentives for adopting particular electoral strategies and discourses, the structure of party competition gives Social Democratic leaders strong reasons for favouring one theory of the world economy over another. Responses to globalisation may in fact be responses to the exigencies of party competition.

Class, Religion, and Left-Wing Rivals

Two features of party systems appear particularly important for understanding Social Democratic parties' strategic imperatives, and the ways in which a discourse on globalisation and the national economy develops. First, the presence of rivals within the left bloc that set constraints on how the Social Democratic party can make strategic shifts without losing support. Social Democratic parties tend to face two types of left rivals: communist parties, and left-libertarian or Green parties. Second, Social Democratic parties' strategic choices are also affected by the nature of the cleavage structure, and in particular the role of class and religious cleavages in channeling votes towards the political parties. Although the class cleavage has been important in structuring party competition in all of Western Europe in some countries the religious cleavage has had a major impact on the strategic incentives facing Social Democratic parties.

Although the processes of deindustrialisation and secularisation have changed the ways in which the class and religious cleavages filter through into electoral and party behaviour, these cleavages remain relevant for two reasons. First, social class identity and religious practices remain important predictors of the vote, although weaker than in the past. Second, the organisational and ideological legacies of party experiences in the period when social identities were stronger than today continue to permeate party behaviour and choices. On this basis I propose an alternative account of why Western European parties choose to 'embrace' or 'resist' globalisation.

Industrialisation, Incorporation and Cleavage Structure

Social Democratic parties in Western Europe emerged as the parties of the industrial working class and the landless peasantry, mobilising society's 'have-nots' around a programme of political emancipation and social transformation. European societies in the first part of the 20th century were deeply polarised, and the majority of citizens had a desperately poor material standard of living. This class of politically excluded poor people constituted a formidable support base for early Social Democratic parties. In early industrialising countries, left parties could mobilize the excluded on the basis of class identity - the communality of interests amongst workers in the manufacturing sector facilitated the emergence of cohesive trade unions which underpinned the growth of Social Democratic parties. In contrast, in many of the European countries where industrialisation was late or patchy, class identity was slower to develop, as industrial manual workers and landless peasants had less obvious shared interests. Communist parties tended to be stronger in these countries, so that Social Democratic parties were unlikely to enjoy a monopoly of representation of the industrial working class. To compound this dilemma, in Catholic Europe the religious cleavage tended to cross-cut the class cleavage, so that left identity became as much a question of a shared hostility to the temporal power and social influence of the Catholic church as one of shared economic interests. For Social Democratic parties seeking to protect their working class vote from Communist pressure whilst attracting sections of the middle classes, the optimal strategy was to mobilize around the religious as well as the class cleavage.

The development of political cleavages and the resulting patterns of party competition have therefore affected the ways in which West European Social Democratic parties mobilize around materialistic issues. In Northern European countries, earlier industrialisation and the limited role of religious conflict allowed Social Democratic parties to institutionalize as parties of the industrial working class, and mobilize around issues of economic policy, income redistribution and material security. The Social Democratic parties of Catholic Europe, on the other hand, had heterogeneous social bases permeated by deep economic contradictions, even in the 'golden age' of post-war Keynesian welfare states. These Social Democratic parties (with the help of long period of opposition) therefore maintained their economic discourse at a high level of abstraction, shunning detailed economic policy prescriptions. Especially since the post-materialist 'silent revolution' of the 1960s and 1970s, the 'Latin' Social Democratic parties have emphasised non-economic issues of socio-cultural norms, lifestyle choices and intellectual freedom. An essentially anti-clerical and anti-authoritarian discourse has proved an effective way of maintaining an electorate with no real class identity. Appeals to the memory of past conflicts against authoritarian regimes and fascism play a key role in articulating this discourse.

Cleavage Structures, Globalisation and Varieties of Policy

These differing paths of Social Democratic party development imply that the challenges of deindustrialisation and globalisation look very different to different Social Democratic parties. For the 'Northern' group of Social Democratic parties which developed as the representatives of a sizeable industrial working class, deindustrialisation in particular has been a major threat to their existence, forcing them to look for ways of extending their reach beyond the *classe gardée* to attract new electoral clienteles. In part, as Herbert Kitschelt argued in his influential book on social democracy, they have done this by integrating post-materialistic concerns such as the environment and personal freedoms, especially when pressed by left-libertarian rivals. But this strategy requires the parties' economic discourse to be adapted so that an increasingly heterogeneous social base can be held together.

Globalisation is an extraordinarily useful concept for these purposes. The external constraints imposed by global markets push Social Democratic parties to embrace public sector reform, restrictive fiscal and monetary policy and labour market liberalisation, as necessary tools for survival in a competitive global economy. Structural reform is therefore *presented as an imperative rather than a choice,* and the discourse of external constraints helps hold together a heterogeneous and potentially contradictory social coalition of the 'winners' and 'losers' in economic change. On the one hand, the policies deriving from the globalisation discourse tend to be the same policies that benefit the middle classes; on the other, the view that such policies are imposed by outside forces provides a defence against working class accusations of 'betrayal', and the suggestion that new jobs will be created by labour market and welfare reforms offer some hope to the economically excluded. The material conflict of interests within this coalition the issue of progressive taxation and transfer payments - is therefore attenuated by appeals to the external constraint of footloose international capital.

For the 'Latin' group of Social Democratic parties, which have traditionally elided many of the economic conflicts within a necessarily heterogeneous social base, globalisation is a threat rather than an opportunity. For these parties, the conflict of interests between 'winners' and 'losers' of the market economy within the Social Democratic electoral base is not a novelty, and has been dealt with by stressing non-economic issues such as the liberalisation of social policy, the modernisation and democratisation of the state, and the defence of lay values in the public sphere. Therefore globalisation, if anything, makes maintaining the cohesion of the Social Democratic electorate more difficult, for two reasons.

First, the prominence of globalisation in the public debate highlights economic issues about redistribution and the institutions of welfare capitalism which these Social Democratic parties prefer not to address in any detail. Second, countries where the religious cleavage has traditionally been strong also tend to have welfare state and labour market institutions which appear particularly ill-suited for dealing with the socio-economic pressures resulting from globalisation. In the 'Latin' Europe, welfare states tend to rest on cumbersome social insurance arrangements and protective labour market regulation, both of which appear unsuitable for job creation in increasingly competitive markets, but which are difficult to reform. Globalisation is therefore an opportunity for Social Democratic parties in countries where the class cleavage is dominant, and a threat for Social Democratic parties in countries where the class cleavage cross-cuts the religious cleavage. The following section will present some qualitative empirical support for this explanation of the strategic choices of West European Social Democratic parties.

Global Opportunities and Threats in Europe's Divergent Capitalisms

The British Labour Party under Tony Blair, and more haltingly the German Social Democrats under Schroeder, are the most visible representatives of the 'third way' in Western Europe. These two parties share a similar dilemma. For much of the twentieth century they were able to draw on a traditional industrial working class constituency for social democracy, but as industrial employment began to decline, a class-based appeal was an increasingly inappropriate electoral strategy. Both suffered defeats around the beginning of the eighties, and after long periods of opposition were ultimately able to win power in the late nineties, building a cross-class coalition by overtly appealing to centrist voters.

The British Labour party is a paradigmatic case of a left party whose electorate was predominantly composed of the manual working classes and which managed to win political power on that basis until the 1970s. The party's decline between the 1970s and the 1980s is emblematic of the fate of class-oriented Social Democratic parties in advanced societies: as the size of the traditional working class shrank the Labour vote declined accordingly. Electoral analysts in Britain disagreed over whether social democracy could survive such a change in the social structure: some suggested that Labour's fortunes were dependent on the size of the working class and that little could be done[47]; others contested that class voting had declined in Britain and that Labour had simply adopted unpopular policy positions and could recover by moving to the right. Labour's recent electoral trajectory provides strong support for the latter thesis, with historically low levels of support in 1974-1983 with more radical manifestoes, and a recovery to a more respectable level in 1997 with a clearly centrist programme. In particular, it is worth noting the party's historically high levels of middle class support in 1997 and 2001, with the party's least left-wing manifestoes in its history.

In the German case the religious cleavage cross-cut the class cleavage to an extent. However the similarities with the UK case outweigh the differences. The SPD shared with Labour (from the early 1950s on) the lack of a Communist rival, which allowed it to monopolize the left political space until the arrival of the Greens in the mid-1980s (with the help of Germany's relatively high electoral threshold). Although religion did push some German workers into the Christian Democratic camp, the relative weakness of the Catholic Church and strength of lay values denied the SPD an obvious alternative to a class-based, materialist appeal. Of course, as in Britain, an appeal was made to a broader electorate; the SPD's abandonment of Marxism at Bad Godesburg, like Labour's retreat to 'Butskellism' in the early 1960s, showed an awareness of the need to win middle class votes. But the core of SPD and Labour support remained the industrial working class, and the extent of 'class voting', as measured by the Alford index, was very similar in Germany and the UK in the 1950s and 1960s. The SPD therefore faced a similar dilemma to Labour in the 1980s and 1990s, as its natural social base declined as a proportion of the electorate, and the need to attract new supporters amongst the middle classes became more pressing.

Crucially, Labour and SPD responded in similar ways to this dilemma in the 1990s. The 'Third Way' in Britain and the 'Neue Mitte' in Germany were clear attempts by formerly workerist parties in post-industrial states to overcome their electoral dependency on traditional manual labour and construct a new coalition of workers and sectors of the middle class. Appeals to globalisation play an important role in this strategy. As the intellectual inspiration of Blair's 'third way' discourse, Anthony Giddens, argues, 'third way politics should take a positive attitude towards globalisation', and adapt to it whilst rejecting the path of 'market fundamentalism'. This adaptation involves reforming economic and welfare institutions to maximize both personal freedom and market efficiency on the one hand, and social cohesion and security, on the other.

Similarly, Gerhard Schroeder cites as a principle of the *Neue Mitte* 'to evolve new policies to exploit the opportunities offered by globalisation', policies which include reducing unit labour costs, increasing flexibility in the labour market and fiscal reforms to improve economic incentives. Globalisation is clearly identified as an external constraint which forces the abandonment of traditional protective social policies. In this way (albeit with varying degrees of conviction) both Labour and the SPD have been able to reconcile the conflicting interests of their working class and middle class electorates.

Global Threats: France, Italy, and Spain

The picture in the large states of Latin Europe France, Italy and Spain is very different. Here the industrial working class was, for most of the democratic period, a smaller proportion of the electorate than in Northern Europe, and socialism was originally as much a movement of radicalised landless rural labour as of the industrial working class. Further (in part because of more inclusive electoral institutions), Social Democratic parties in these countries faced the complication of powerful Communist parties. In the postwar period Social Democratic parties therefore had to expend as much effort on competing for left-wing voters with the Communists as on competing for middle class voters with conservative or Christian parties. The persistence of strong communist or radical left movements in these countries, and in France and Italy the added complication of Green parties capable of winning parliamentary representation, has made 'third way' strategies extremely risky for Social Democratic parties.

The role of the religious cleavage, which has played an important role in structuring voter alignments in these countries, created a natural barrier to left support and entrenched conservative or Christian parties in power (and in the Spanish case, an authoritarian regime) for a good part of the post-war period. Long periods in opposition therefore allowed Social Democratic parties to maintain a tough (although often abstract) left-wing discourse without having to damage middle class voters with concrete policy choices. Moreover, the 'Latin' Social Democratic parties were helped rather than threatened by the social changes of the 1960s and 1970s, as the process of secularisation weakened the religious cleavage, making part of the middle class vote available for the left for the first time. The decline of Catholic values and the demands for greater personal freedom of the '1968' generation provided Social Democratic parties with an opportunity to build a cross-class coalition by emphasising their anti-clerical and anti-authoritarian identity, and downplaying the conflicts of material interests amongst the left electorate.

In France, Mitterand's clever strategy of the Left Union *(Union de la Gauche)* allowed the Parti Socialiste to first coopt and weaken the communists (PCF), and then capture the votes of the more progressive middle classes. The themes of modernisation and democratisation served to mobilize both workers and progressive emerging sectors of the middle class around projects to reform archaic and hierarchical state structures and consolidate new social freedoms. In the 1980s, the decentralisation of the 'oppressive' central state and the vague notion of *autogestion* applied to the sphere of production were sufficiently broad themes to unite industrial workers and the growing middle class. In a short time, the strategy *of front de classe* with which the PS was elected in 1981 was replaced by imprecise talk of *Modernisation et Progrès Social*. The PS's control of the institution of the presidency allowed it to present itself as a representative of a higher, national interest, mobilising support beyond narrow sectoral interests. This strategy has allowed the PS to build an extremely heterogeneous electorate. In the 1997 elections, the party won almost identical shares of the vote amongst the upper-middle class, clerks and workers, with only the self-employed (a traditional bastion of conservatism anywhere) deviating from the pattern.

This successful track record of building cross-class electoral coalitions has obviated the need for the PS to address the difficult question of how to reconcile the conflicting economic interests of this social base. As a result, the 'third way' has few attractions for the Socialist leadership. On the one hand, the imperative of structural reform does not serve any useful purpose in the party's electoral strategy. On the other, structural reform threatens the institutions of *dirigiste* French welfare capitalism more fundamentally than the more liberal and universalistic welfare arrangements of Northern Europe. Not surprisingly, therefore, the PS under Lionel Jospin took a much more defensive view of globalisation than Blair and Schroeder. Jospin recognised that globalisation cannot be ignored, but pays much greater attention to its dangers. Whereas Blair and Schroeder have both advocated, and to some degree implemented, labour market liberalisation, the banner policy of Jospin's *gauche plurielle* government was a statutory limitation of the working week to 35 hours, a policy which is difficult to reconcile with the 'third way' declaration.

Similar arguments can be made of SOCIAL DEMOCRATIC parties in Spain and Italy, both of which have sought to distance themselves from the 'third way', particularly after 2000. The Spanish PSOE followed a strikingly similar strategy to that of the PS, although more successfully given the weakness of the PCE. Here too, a rapid process of secularisation from the 1960s on made the Catholic vote available for the left once democratisation took place. The broad notion of modernisation served as a unifying discourse, uniting both workers and the emerging middle classes around the aim of bringing Spain economically, socially and culturally into line with the rest of Western Europe. Economic reforms were explicitly defended in terms of integration into Europe, so the middle classes could be courted whilst the left was reassured that Spain was being modernised and democratised. At the same time, a series of liberalising social and political reforms (legalisation of abortion, support for lay education, administrative decentralisation) served to satisfy the demand for progressive change amongst left voters. Appeals to the imagery of the Spanish Civil War - which became increasingly frequent as the party lost ground in the 1990s - served to identify the Socialist Party with democracy, and implicitly, the conservative opposition with dictatorship. Until the corrupt misuse of state resources provoked outrage in the 1990s, this discourse of modernisation, lay values and anti-authoritarianism was successful in constructing a broad electoral coalition including both workers and the progressive middle classes.

In Italy the picture is complicated by the disappearance of the Socialists (PSI) in the early 1990s and their replacement in the Social Democratic space by the former communists. However, similar dynamics are present. The dominance of the religious cleavage has attenuated real class divisions, making it possible to construct electoral coalitions on the basis of broad notions of political, social and cultural modernisation. The PSI emphasised its lay identity in opposition to its governing partner the Christian Democrats, and supported modernising institutional reforms. At the same time it mobilised poorer voters in the impoverished South through a clientelistic use of state resources, creating an 'alliance of merit with need'. The Left Democrats, after adopting limited structural reforms while in government, have reverted to a defensive view of globalisation once in opposition, setting their stall against the Berlusconi government's proposed labour market and pension reforms. The rhetoric of modernisation and democratisation, bolstered by a strong identification of the left parties with the anti-Fascist partisan movement in the Second World War, serves to win support beyond narrow class lines. Both the PSI and have faced radical left and left-libertarian competition, making a reliance on the votes of the industrial working class impossible.

The divisions between a broadly Catholic subculture and a more progressive anticlerical subculture cut across class lines, and therefore Social Democratic parties in the 'Latin' countries can mobilize middle and working class support with the same broad 'modernising' message. Social Democratic parties have continued to mobilize along the traditional Catholic/authoritarian-secular/progressive faultline, precluding the need to dilute their ideology in order to maximize support in a homogeneous, 'consumerist' electorate. Voting for the left, rather than an expression of economic interests, becomes an expression of socio-cultural belonging, almost of lifestyle. Social class, therefore, has not been a useful predictor of the vote. Social Democratic parties in Latin Europe have been largely successful in averting situations in which the contrasting economic interests of working and middle class sectors of their electorates have become politically salient. This explains the reluctance of the French, Italian and Spanish parties to sign up to the 'Third Way', and suggests that the dilemmas facing Social Democracy may be quite different in countries with different traditions of political conflict.

CONCLUSION

This article has set out to bring party politics back into the debate on social democracy and globalisation. The literature on political parties and electoral politics can make an important contribution to our understanding of globalisation and the constraints it imposes on national governments and their choices of economic policies and institutions. After all, political parties still do the job of governing Western democracies, and although their freedom of action may be more limited than in the past, the ways in which party leaders interpret opportunities and constraints, and the institutionalised patterns of electoral competition they face, refract the pressures of globalisation in different ways. Many political economists have assumed Social Democratic parties' electoral coalitions to be essentially a function of economic interests, yet decades of research into party politics have provided us with a more complete picture of the electoral process. This article has drawn on this research tradition to offer a different interpretation of how West European Social Democratic parties respond to the pressures of globalisation.

It is often argued that Social Democratic parties in Western Europe must choose between two unpalatable options. On the one hand, they can accept the dominant view of a competitive global economy in which market forces economic outcomes, and reduce the expectations of their electorate, insisting on the need for liberalising 'structural reforms', and limiting themselves to smoothing the rougher edges of the market system. On the other, they can take a skeptical view of globalisation, resist structural reform and commit themselves to protecting society from market forces. But this stark choice between neoliberal conformity and an essentially conservative defence of existing arrangements is both unrealistic and unhelpful. Structural reforms can be made compatible with Social Democratic goals, as Social Democratic parties in Scandinavia and the Netherlands have demonstrated. The Social Democratic parties of the largest West European states are finding it difficult to find this virtuous mix of economic efficiency and social solidarity. Although much of the 'new politics of welfare' literature has emphasised the inertial properties of welfare state institutions themselves, rather less attention has been paid to the complexities of the electoral process and the incentives it presents to social democratic party leaders.

This article has shown that the dynamics of electoral politics are an important variable in understanding the way Social Democratic parties approach structural reform. Parties face historical legacies - in the form of ideological traditions and institutionalised patterns of electoral mobilisation - which can push them to adopt discourses which are inappropriate for reforming economic and welfare institutions effectively. In consequence, Social Democratic parties in continental Christian democratic welfare states are often the least inclined to embrace liberalising reforms since they able instead to construct cross-class electoral coalitions on the basis of essentially non-economic policy issues. In contrast, in the UK, probably Europe's most marketised political economy, the Labour party has quite different incentives. Appeals to globalisation and liberalising proposals are essential for the purposes of building a cross-class electoral coalition, even though Britain has already pushed structural reform much further than its neighbours, and would likely benefit much more from greater state intervention and welfare expansion. Political parties often face conflicting incentives in the electoral and policy spheres. In Western Europe's largest states these conflicting incentives stand in the way of a balanced response to economic change.

REFERENCES

Alford, Roger (1963). *Party and Society: The Anglo-American Democracies.* Chicago:Rand McNally.

Bartolini, Stefano (2000). *The Political Mobilisation of the European Left, 1860-1980.* Cambridge: Cambridge University Press.

Bartolini, Stefano and Peter Mair (1990). *Identity, Competition and Electoral Availability: The Stabilisation of European Electorates 1885-1985.* Cambridge: Cambridge University Press.

Blair, Tony and Gerhard Schroeder (2000). 'Europe: The Third Way/Die Neue Mitte', in Bodo Hombach, *The Politics of the New Centre.* Cambridge: Polity, pp. 159-77.

Blyth, Mark (2002). *Great Transformations.* Cambridge: Cambridge University Press.

Boix, Carles (1998). *Political Parties, Growth and Equality. Conservative and Social Democratic Economic Strategies in the World Economy.* Cambridge: Cambridge University Press.

Boy, Daniel and Nona Mayer (2000). 'Cleavage Voting and Issue

Voting in France', in Michael Lewis-Beck (ed.), *How France Votes.* New York: Chatham House, pp. 153-75.

Budge, Ian (1999). 'Party Policy and Ideology: Reversing the 1950s?', in Pippa Norris and Geoffrey Evans (eds.), *Critical Elections. British Parties and Voters in Long-Term Perspective.* London: Sage, pp. 1-21.

Butler, David and David Stokes (1974). *Political Change in Britain.* London: Macmillan, 2nd edition.

Clift, Ben (2002). 'Social Democracy and Globalisation: The Cases of France and the UK', *Government and Opposition* 37: 466-500.

Crewe, Ivor (1986). 'On the Death and Resurrection of Class Voting: Some Comments on *How Britain Votes*', *Political Studies* 35: 620-38.

Curtice, John, Anthony Heath and Roger Jowell (2002). *The Rise of New Labour.* Oxford: Oxford University Press.

Djankov, Simeon, Rafael La Porta, Florencio López-de-Silanes and Andrei Shleifer (2002). 'The Regulation of Entry', *Quarterly Journal of Economics* 117: 1-38.

Esping-Andersen, Gøsta (1990). *Three Worlds of Welfare Capitalism.* Princeton: Princeton University Press.

Esping-Andersen, Gøsta (1996). 'Welfare States Without Work: The Impasse of Labour Shedding and Familialism in Continental European Social Policy', in Gøsta

Esping-Andersen, *Welfare States in Transition. National Adaptations in Global Economies.* London: Sage, pp.66-87.

Esping-Andersen, Gøsta (1999). *Social Foundations of Postindustrial Economies.* Oxford: Oxford University Press.

Evans, Geoffrey (ed.) (1999). *The End of Class Politics.* Oxford: Oxford University Press.

Evans, Geoffrey, Anthony Heath and Clive Payne (1999). 'Class: Labour as a Catch-All Party', in Pippa Norris and Geoffrey

Evans (eds.), *Critical Elections. British Parties and Voters in Long-Term Perspective*. London: Sage, pp.87-101.

Franzese, Robert (2002). *Macroeconomic Policies of Developed Democracies*. Cambridge: Cambridge University Press.

Gamble, Andrew (1988). *The Free Economy and the Strong State*. London: Macmillan.

Garrett, Geoffrey (1998). *Partisan Politics in the Global Economy*. Cambridge: Cambridge University Press.

Giddens, Anthony (1998). *The Third Way. The Renewal of Social Democracy*. Cambridge: Polity.

Glyn, Andrew (1998). 'Internal and External Constraints on Egalitarian Policies', in D. Baker, G. Epstein and R. Pollin (eds.), *Globalisation and Progressive Economic Policy*. Cambridge: Cambridge University Press.

Golden, Miriam, Michael Wallerstein and Peter Lange (1999). 'Postwar Trade Union Organisation and Industrial Relations in Twelve Countries', in in Herbert Kitschelt *et al* (eds.), *Continuity and Change in Contemporary Capitalism*. Cambridge: Cambridge University Press, pp.194-230.

Gwartney, James and Robert Lawson (2001). *Economic Freedom of the World: 2001 Annual Report*. Vancouver: Fraser Insitute.

Hall, Peter and David Soskice (eds.) (2001). *Varieties of Capitalism. The Institutional Foundations of Comparative Advantage*. Oxford: Oxford University Press.

Hay, Colin, Matthew Watson and Daniel Wincott (1999). 'Globalisation, European Integration and the Persistence of European Social Models'. Working Paper 3/99, ESRC 'One Europe or Several?' Programme.

Heath, Anthony, Roger Jowell and John Curtice (1985). *How Britain Votes*. Oxford: Pergamon.

Heath, Anthony, Roger Jowell, John Curtice, Geoffrey Evans, Julia

Field, and Sharon Witherspoon (1991). *Understanding Political Change: The British Voter 1964-87.* Oxford: Pergamon.

Hemerijck, Anton and Jelle Visser (2000). 'Change and Immobility: Three Decades of Policy Adjustment in the Netherlands and Belgium', in Maurizio Ferrera and Martin Rhodes (eds.), *Recasting European Welfare States.* London: Frank Cass, pp.229-56.

Hicks, Alexander and Lane Kenworthy (2003). 'Varieties of Welfare Capitalism', *Socio-Economic Review* 1.

Hincker, François (1997). 'The French Socialists: Towards Post-Republican Values?' in Donald Sassoon (ed.), *Looking Left. European Socialism After the Cold War.* London: I.B.Tauris, pp. 109-23.

Iversen, Torben (2001). 'The Dynamics of Welfare State Expansion: Trade Openness, Deindustrialisation and Partisan Politics', in Paul Pierson (ed.). *The NewPolitics of the Welfare State.* Oxford: Oxford University Press, pp.45-79.

Jospin, Lionel (2002). *My Vision of Europe and Globalisation.* Cambridge: Polity/The Policy Network.

Kaase, Max and Kenneth Newton (1995). *Beliefs in Government.* Oxford: Oxford University Press.

Kirchheimer, Otto (1966). 'The Transformation of West European Party Systems', in Joseph LaPalombara and Myron Weiner (eds.), *Political Parties and Political Development.* Princeton, N.J.: Princeton University Press, pp. 177-200.

Kitschelt, Herbert (1994). *The Transformation of European Social Democracy.* Cambridge: Cambridge University Press.

Kitschelt, Herbert (1999). 'European Social Democracy Between Political Economy and Electoral Competition', in Herbert Kitschelt *et al* (eds.), *Continuity and Change in Contemporary Capitalism.* Cambridge: Cambridge University Press, pp.317-45.

Kitschelt, Herbert, Peter Lange, Gary Marks, John Stephens (eds.) (1999). *Continuity and Change in Contemporary Capitalism.* Cambridge: Cambridge University Press.

Krugman, Paul (1996). *Pop Internationalism.* Cambridge, MA: MIT Press. Lafontaine, Oskar (2000). *The Heart Beats on the Left.* Cambridge: Polity.

Lane, Jan-Erik and Svante Ersson (1999). *Politics and Society in Western Europe.* London: Sage.

Levy, Jonah (1999). 'Vice into Virtue: Progressive Politics and Welfare Reform in Continental Europe', *Politics and Society* 27(2): 259-73.

Lipset, Seymour M. and Stein Rokkan (eds.) (1967). *Party Systems and Voter Alignments.* New York: Free Press.

Llewellyn, John and the Global Economics Team of Lehman Brothers (2003). 'Reinvigorating Structural Reform', in Peter Cornelius (ed.), *The Global Competitiveness Report 2002-3.* Oxford: Oxford University Press/World Economic Forum, pp.69-100.

Mair, Peter (1987). *The Changing Irish Party System.* New York: St. Martin's Press.

Mair, Peter (1997). *Party System Change.* Oxford: Oxford University Press.

Merkel, Wolfgang (1987). *Prima e dopo Craxi.* Padua: Liviana Editrice. Ohmae, Kenichi (1995). *The End of the Nation State: The Rise of Regional Economies.* London: HarperCollins.

Pasquino, Gianfranco (1986). 'The PSI Between Gamblers and Entrepreneurs', *West European Politics* 9: 120-41.

Pierson, Paul (1994). *Dismantling the Welfare State?: Reagan, Thatcher and the Politics of Retrenchment.* Cambridge: Cambridge University Press.

Pierson, Paul (1998). 'Irresistible Forces, Immovable Objects: Post-Industrial Welfare States Confront Permanent Austerity', *Journal of European Public Policy* 5: 539-60.

Pierson, Paul (ed.) (2001). *The New Politics of the Welfare State.* Oxford: Oxford University Press.

Social Democratic Przeworski, Adam (2001). 'How Many Ways Can Be Third?', in Andrew Glyn (ed.),

Social Democracy in Neoliberal Times. The Left and Economic Policy Since 1980. Oxford: Oxford University Press, pp.312-33. Przeworski, Adam and John Sprague (1986). *Paper Stones.* Chicago: University of Chicago Press.

Rhodes, Martin (1998). 'Globalisation, Labour Markets and Welfare States: A Future of "Competitive Corporatism"?', in Martin Rhodes and Yves Mény (eds.), *The Future of European Welfare. A New Social Contract?* Basingstoke: Macmillan, pp. 178-203.

Rhodes, Martin (2001). 'The Political Economy of Social Pacts: "Competitive Corporatism" and European Welfare Reform', in Paul Pierson (ed.), *The New Politics of the Welfare State.* Oxford: Oxford University Press, pp. 165-94.

Rokkan, Stein (1970). *Citizens, Elections, Parties.* Oslo: Universitetsforlaget.

Ross, Fiona (2000). 'Interests and Choice in the "Not Quite So New" Politics of Welfare', in Maurizio Ferrera and Martin Rhodes (eds.), *Recasting European Welfare States.* London: Frank Cass, pp. 11-34.

Royo, Sebastián (2000). *From Social Democracy to Neoliberalism. The Consequences of Party Hegemony in Spain 1982-96.* Basingstoke: Macmillan.

Sarlvik, Bo and Ivor Crewe (1983). *Decade of Dealignment.* Cambridge: Cambridge University Press.

Scharpf, Fritz (1991). *Crisis and Choice in European Social Democracy.* Ithaca: Cornell University Press.

Scharpf, Fritz (1997). *Games Real Actors Play.* Boulder: Westview.

Schmidt, Vivien (2002). *The Futures of European Capitalism.* Oxford: Oxford University Press.

Schroeder, Gerhard (2000). 'Postscript', in Bodo Hombach, *The Politics of the New Centre.* Cambridge: Polity, pp. 153-6.

Stephens, John, Evelyn Huber and Leonard Ray (1999). 'The Welfare State in Hard Times', in Herbert Kitschelt *et al* (eds.), *Continuity and Change in Contemporary Capitalism.* Cambridge: Cambridge University Press, pp. 164-93.

Swank, Duane (2002). *Global Capital, Political Institutions and Policy Change in Developed Welfare States.* Cambridge: Cambridge University Press.

Tsebelis, George (2002). *Veto Players. How Political Institutions Work.* Princeton: Princeton University Press.

6

Fundamental of Human Rights

This chapter explores some of the key issues that arise in the context of efforts to bring the discourses of human rights and development closer together. It does so, by focusing on the right to education, and in particular on an unusually interesting and instructive case study of India. The Indian experience with the right to education illustrates both the central issues that arise in relation to resource constraints and the role played by key actors in relation to economic and social human rights, including civil society, the judiciary and the legislature. In some respects it is a cautionary tale, while in others it provides an invaluable insight into some of the steps that need to be taken if a right to education is to gain community acceptance, take constitutional form, and have a significant impact on both policy and practical outcomes in the field of education.

Legal versus Developmentalist Perspectives on Education

It is relatively uncontentious to say that human rights and development objectives are for the most part complementary. We can even go further and suggest, as does the title of this volume of essays, that they are capable of mutually reinforcing one another. But the sticking point comes when it is suggested that it follows that a human rights lens is not only a desirable way of viewing some of the fundamental challenges facing development, but is actually a superior and perhaps even a mandatory one. Such a formulation immediately raises three questions:

(a) is a human rights approach meaningful and thus useful in the context of complex issues of resource allocation affecting sectors such as education, food, and housing?

(b) are there ways in which such an approach can be shown to be better than non-rights based ways of approaching those issues; and

(c) is a human rights approach mandatory, or obligatory, and if so what does that mean?

The backdrop against which such questions often arise is the disconnect that generally seems to characterize the approaches taken by human rights lawyers on the one hand and development economists on the other. One way of contrasting these two approaches is by thinking of them in terms of over-drawn depictions, almost caricatures, of the positions adopted on each side. Although caricatures are, by definition, distorted or extreme in some respects, they can nonetheless assist us to get a sense of the strengths and weaknesses of the approaches. A caricature of the international law approach (the equivalent of a drawing by Honoré Daumier of a lawyer in nineteenth century France) posits the absoluteness and immediacy of human rights and a refusal to take account of financial constraints in relation to a fundamental value which must take priority over all else. In at least some cases, this would apply equally to a right like the right to education.

A comparable caricature of the development economist's approach posits an open-ended set of policy options, an emphasis on individual and ideally rational decision-making, and a pre-occupation with the financial dimensions of any social options that might be considered. As one World Bank economist has observed, many economists think that 'human rights principles, as commonly defined today, tend to violate the basic principles of traditional' welfare economics,[1] presumably because the rights approach seeks to pre-empt at least some choices and to tie the hands of decision-makers in certain respects.

In reality, economists, whatever their starting point, are rarely likely to adopt the position that human rights considerations have no legitimate place in the overall equation. Similarly, international lawyers rarely entertain an absolutist approach to the right to education, even when they adopt a more dogmatic approach to civil and political rights, such as the right to free speech or the right to freedom from torture. And even in relation to those rights, there is room for a degree of relativism in any sophisticated and frank analysis.

The bigger problem for international human rights lawyers is that they are unaccustomed to having to provide justificatory analyses. For most of them, the issue of justification has long since been settled, whether through the adoption of the Universal Declaration of Human Rights of 1948, the widespread ratification of key treaties (such as the two International Human Rights Covenants) adopted in the 1960s and 1970s, the virtually universal acceptance of the Convention on the Rights of the Child of 1989, or simply the evolution of the customary international law of human rights.

While leaving aside the broader philosophical challenge of defending either the concept of human rights or the catalogue of rights adopted by governments within the United Nations framework, the issue of justification is especially relevant in relation to the cost dimensions of rights and particularly those commonly conceived of as positive rights. In this respect, economists would point, and not without cause, to the reluctance of many human rights proponents to engage in debates over the resource implications of taking seriously a range of economic and social rights such as the right to education. They might cite, by way of example, the very lengthy General Comment on that right adopted by the UN Committee on Economic, Social and Cultural Rights[2] which addresses the resources issue only in order to emphasize that States must use their available resources to the maximum, and that in some respects, a lack of resources can be no defence to a failure to take appropriate measures.

In recent years, however, economists have been increasingly prepared to factor into the overall equation a relatively new set of considerations under the rubric of good governance. The result is that development policy literature and relevant programs are now replete with references to the importance of governance, defined to include not only free elections, the absence of corruption, and the presence of various market freedoms, but also accountability, transparency and participation. These elements are not, however, generally viewed in the way that human rights proponents might present them - as matters of justice, fairness, and right which must simply be included whatever their cost. Instead they are seen in instrumental terms as factors which are empirically justified in economic terms. Similarly, education has long been considered as an important element in the economic balance sheet but the perceived returns on investments in education had not led to the conclusion that it should be supplied to every child regardless of his or her productive potential. But while this approach has now been replaced by the language of universal access, it continues to be a program which is put forward and justified, at least in the discourse of international development organizations, essentially in terms of its economic benefits. Thus, for example, an important study on child labor by the International Labor Organization, sub-titled 'An Economic Study of the Costs and Benefits of Eliminating Child Labor', was entitled 'Investing in Every Child'.[3] While the study does not ignore the issue of values, the language of rights is comprehensively avoided. In order to assert that its inspiration is not solely instrumentalist the report notes that the ILO's perspective is that 'child labour is not only, nor perhaps even primarily, an economic problem. The justifications for [its Conventions on child labour are largely ethical and social in nature, although the economic consequences of child labour are taken into account.'[4]

But rather than highlighting the rights or values dimension, the report's emphasis is very clearly on economic justifications. Thus while it acknowledges the 'personal development and social inclusion' benefits of eliminating child labour it clearly states that the 'two principal benefits' are 'the added productive capacity a future generation of workers would enjoy due to their increased education' and the 'economic gains' which would flow from healthier workers if the worst forms of child labour, such as those that are hazardous, are eliminated.[5] This then leads inexorably into what might be termed a supply-, rather than a demand-, style approach. The challenge is to 'supply' education through 'an expansion of school capacity and an upgrading of school quality'.

The International Monetary Fund takes an even more determinedly 'neutral' or economistic approach to the issue. While the Fund now acknowledges, which was not the case only a few years ago, that user fees for primary education, 'whether taking the form of compulsory benefit taxation or voluntary user fees, are ... second-best compared with free access'.[7] But rather than invoking ethical, let alone human rights, based arguments, the Fund simply observes that requiring payment 'is generally considered undesirable'.[8] The reason, it transpires, has nothing to do with the rights of children, but rather 'because of the burden placed on parents, particularly in low-income households'.[9] The thrust of the report, which includes an analysis of three countries in which user fees had recently been eliminated in relation to primary education (Uganda, Malawi and Tanzania) is that economically rational considerations should determine how a given education budget should optimally be allocated. The report thus sums up the classic dilemma in the following terms:

Voluntary user fees introduce a dilemma in the choice between efficiency and equality. A decision regarding user payments may, for example, require a judgment about whether 45 children attending school and 5 children excluded is preferable to 50 children not attending school.[10]

But this analysis takes for granted the refusal of the government involved to prioritize comprehensive access to free primary education, and assumes that an agency such as the IMF has no role whatsoever in factoring into the equation either the individual government's human rights obligations (an almost universal obligation in relation to the Convention on the Rights of the Child) or the rights of the child in the country concerned to enjoy access to primary education as of right. It is hardly surprising then that the report cautions that 'a strong preference for equality could ... lead to a judgment rejecting financing, through user payments, even when public expenditure cannot provide reasonable schooling, so as to avoid the unequal exclusion of some children. Equality may then mean that all children are functionally illiterate.'[11]

Even studies produced by international organizations which focus specifically on the situation of primary education in India have tended to pay little or no attention to the human rights dimension of the equation. This is well illustrated by a comprehensive 300 page analysis undertaken by the World Bank which opens with the observation that 'the vision of education for India is contained in article 45 of its Constitution',[12] but fails to make any significant reference to this dimension of the issue in the remainder of the report. Even when responding to the question of why children are out of school, in the context of an analysis of potential demand-side interventions, the report mentions a range of factors but does not consider the possibility that characterizing education as a right rather than a possible opportunity might contribute to changing community expectations and stimulating demand for education.[13]

While it is obvious that the instrumentalist and rights approaches are not necessarily incompatible, and that one can advocate universal access to education both on the grounds that it is a right and that it is a sound investment, the point is that most of those who take one approach are at best reluctant to embrace also the other. Thus the language of investment can be an attractive formulation for those who wish to play down, or even deny, the human rights dimension of a right to education. Thus for example the Country Reports on Human Rights Practices, issued by the United States Government in February 2004, contrasts its discussion of the need to protect civil liberties and political rights (or at least to make sure that other countries do) with its references to the desirability of 'investing' in education and health.[14] This enables the State Department to both insist on the importance of education while maintaining its position that economic and social rights should be seen not as entitlements but rather in terms of opportunities.

The language of public goods provides a helpful bridge towards bringing the two approaches together. Few people would disagree that the provision of and access to education is a social good, and an indispensable component of human development, sustainable economic growth and poverty reduction. A number of economists have argued that the provision of education is a public good which produces a variety of beneficial externalities, including health improvements, slowed population growth, the strengthening of democracy and good governance[15] all dimensions of any reasonable definition of'human development' and 'human security.'[16] Drèze and Sen, adopting Sen's notion of development as the enhancement of capabilities and freedoms, enumerate five ways in which a successful program of universal education contributes to development: education is intrinsically important in as much as it directly improves a person's effective freedom in basic social interactions; education facilitates the attainment of employment and other sources of income, and helps persons negotiate and cope with circumstances that may threaten their livelihood (education as self-defense); education facilitates public discussion of social needs and encourages informed collective demands, which can produce better governance and greater effectiveness in the use of public resources; education can help eradicate specific social problems, such as child labour, and; educational achievement among disadvantaged groups increases their ability to resist oppression, organize politically and alter distributive outcomes.[17] Invoking the example of Kerala, Drèze and Sen observe that basic education is a catalyst of social change:

> The historical analysis of Kerala's experience ... brings out the dialectical relationship between education progress and social change: the spread of education helps to overcome the traditional inequalities of caste, class, and gender, just as the removal of these inequalities contributes to the spread of education.[18]

Drèze and Sen's final example points us towards the close conceptual kinship between the idea of education as a 'public good' conducive to development, and the idea of education as a human right. At the very least, the notion of human rights connotes the equal dignity and autonomy of human beings in their pursuit of their conception of a good life, a life worth living. At a foundational level, to speak of something as a human right is to not just make a legal claim to resources or for protection against an abuse of power, but it is also to insist that without those resources or that protection, one's equal dignity, autonomy and participatory parity are fundamentally impaired. The externalities that make the public provision of education welfare-enhancing as a public good (health, greater reproductive choices, employment opportunity, slowing of diminishing marginal returns) are also effects that broadly correspond with the achievement of equal dignity and autonomy. At a certain level of abstraction, then, we might readily conclude that education qua public good and education qua human right share an essential affinity.

It is against this background that we turn in this chapter to explore the practical consequences of entrenching education as a legally enforceable right. What does the idea of education as a human right add to the way in which governments and civil society develop strategies to ensure access to education? This chapter seeks to address these questions through a case study of India, which in 2002 amended its Constitution to make education a 'fundamental right' for children between the ages of 6 and 14. Before addressing those issues it is appropriate to note briefly the status of the right to education in international law.

The International Legal Setting for the Right to Education

While the right to education has been recognized in a great many international human rights treaties, the formulations used and the nature and the scope of the resulting obligations undertaken by states tend to vary significantly.[19] In view of the fact that these different provisions have been analyzed in considerable detail elsewhere,[20] it will suffice for the purposes of the present chapter to note that the relevant provision in the UN Convention on the Rights of the Child is binding on 192 states which have opted to become parties to it and that the only states in the world which are not covered by its provisions are Somalia and the United States. The Convention thus provides a virtually universal basis for examining the right to education.

The key provision of the Convention is article 28 (1) which provides that:

> States Parties recognize the right of the child to education, and with a view to achieving this right progressively and on the basis of equal opportunity, they shall, in particular:
>
> (a) Make primary education compulsory and available free to all; ...

It is also pertinent to note that many state constitutions within the United States recognize a right to education and that they are by no means alone in recognizing education in the context of formulations dealing with rights.[21] The UN Special Rapporteur on the Right to Education indicated that in 2001 there were explicit guarantees of the right to education in the constitutions of 142 countries, and that only 44 countries did not include such provisions within their national constitutions.[22] While the relevant provisions have been significant in the context of a state such as India, they have also had an impact within some developed country. This is true, for example, of the United States where education is characterized in rights terms, albeit in widely varying formulations, in the constitutions of some 40 or more States of the United States. While many of these provisions seem to have lain almost dormant for a good period of time, there have been notable exceptions. Suffice it to note for present purposes that the Constitution of New York State guarantees every child the opportunity for a 'sound basic education'.[23] In 2005 this provision was relied upon by the NY State Supreme Court in Manhattan to order that an $5.6 billion per year be spent on the City's schools over and above current levels. An additional $9.2 billion was ordered to be spent over the following five years to shrink class sizes, relieve overcrowding, and provide the city's 1.1 million students with adequate laboratories, libraries and other learning places. The case had been initiated twelve years earlier by the Campaign for Fiscal Equity and had been fought strongly by the State Government. The New York Times commented that:

> The decision is a major landmark in one of the nation's biggest school- finance cases, and may have ripple effects across all school districts in the state. Though virtually every state in the nation has been embroiled in lawsuits over school spending, the New York suit has been more closely watched, in part because of the number of students and the dollar figures at stake.[24]

The extent to which a right to education has thus found recognition within a wide variety of constitutional instruments and traditions serves to highlight the potential importance of the experience of any country in which the right has been taken seriously in terms of public advocacy, national constitutional arrangements, and international supervision of treaty undertakings. We turn therefore to examine the situation in India, which constitutes a prime example in this regard.

The State of Education in India

India is an interesting and tractable case study for the actual and potential impact of constitutionalizing the right to education, for two reasons. On the one hand, India is a developing country facing considerable resource challenges, particularly in light of its rapidly growing population and the fiscal constraints of the state and federal governments. On the other hand, India has a well-developed judicial system and a recent history of constitutional rights litigation that, in the breadth of issues that it has touched upon and the scope of remedial judgments delivered, is almost unparalleled in either the developing or the developed world.[25]

In a nutshell, almost 50 percent of the population remains illiterate, and an estimated 58 million out of 185 million children aged between 5 and 14 years are not in school.[26] The Indian Government reported in 2003 that the enrolment rate in rural areas nationwide was only 71%, with a gender disparity of 0.84, meaning a 16% lower rate for girls. In some states the levels are considerably lower. In Bihar only 59% are enrolled and in Rajasthan the rate is 61% with a gender disparity of 46% for girls.[27] This result is hardly surprising given that the provision of education (particularly elementary education) appears to have been a relatively low priority for Central and State Indian governments from 1947 to 1980, with less than 2 percent of GDP being expended annually on education until 1979.[28] Expenditures on education grew substantially after the Central government was granted concurrent responsibility for education through a 1976 constitutional amendment,[29] but remained lower (as a share of total government expenditure) than most low-income countries.[30] Significantly, the share of expenditure allocated to elementary education through the 1980s remained below 50 percent, which is low relative to other countries that sought to universalize elementary education at a comparable stage of economic development. Shariff and Ghosh note that:

> Japan invested 84 percent of its educational budget in six years of elementary education in 1885 and a meager 8 percent on higher education. By 1960, the share of higher education had increased to 13 percent and the share of higher education had increased to 13 percent. ... In Sri Lanka too, the case is similar. Sri Lanka allocated 70 percent of its educational budget to the first level of education and 6 percent to higher education in 1970. By 1978, when primary education had become universal, the share of higher education had increased (marginally) to 8.7 percent.[31]

The nature of the resulting challenge is made all the greater by the fact that the overall social picture in the country has been far from rosy. Thus, over the past ten years, India's ranking in the United Nations' Human Development Index has fallen dramatically.[32] A former Supreme Court Justice and former Chairman on the National Commission on Human Rights, M N Venkatachaliah, put the situation of education in its broader context by observing in 2000 that:

> Today we have the dismal situation of a social infrastructure where 670 million people in this country don't have basic sanitary facilities, and 260 million don't have potable water. Forty percent of the world's tuberculosis patients are in India, 25 percent of the world's blind are in India ... Then there is the issue of the enormous corruption in public life, electoral malpractices, the tyranny of wealth, and the insolence of authority.[33]

The poor state of primary education is thus but one of several urgent developmental priorities that the Government of India must balance, and this balancing may well mitigate the value of constitutionally entrenching education as a right.

The Response of the Supreme Court

Beginning in the early 1980s, the Supreme Court of India waived traditional doctrines of standing and pleadings to permit concerned citizens, public interest advocates and non-government organizations to petition it on behalf of individuals or communities suffering violations of constitutionally protected rights. As a consequence, the Court entertained applications for constitutional protection on behalf of a wide range of traditionally powerless persons, including bonded labourers, rickshaw drivers, pavement dwellers, inmates of mental infirmaries and workhouses and victims of environmental damage. In conducting these cases, the Court created its own fact-finding commissions to investigate alleged violations, and dramatically expanded its remedial powers to include detailed supervision of government institutions and the ordering of programs to mitigate the effects of systematic injustice. Through the development of its 'Public Interest Litigation' (PIL) jurisdiction, the Supreme Court of India came to act as a 'combination of constitutional ombudsman and inquisitorial examining magistrate, vested with responsibility to do justice to the poor litigant before it by aggressively searching out the facts and the law, and by taking responsibility for fully implement its decisions ... PIL provides a model for courts struggling to balance the transformative aspect of law against the law's natural tendency to favour those rich enough to invoke it.'[34]

It was in fact a Supreme Court public interest case that set in train the movement to create an enforceable constitutional right to education in India. The unamended text of the Constitution of India had included a right to education under the title of a 'Directive Principle of State Policy.'[35] In the Constitution of India, a Directive

Principle was distinguishable from a Fundamental Right in so far as a Directive Principle 'shall not be enforced in any court.'[36] A Directive Principle is phrased in terms of an important duty incumbent upon the State, but one that is to be implemented by the executive and legislative arms of government without intervention or oversight by the judiciary. Thus, the 'right to education' as contained in the original text of the Constitution of India was cast in imperative terms:

> The State shall endeavour to provide, within a period of ten years from the commencement of this Constitution, for free and compulsory education for all children until they complete the age of fourteen years.

The ten-year deadline for the provision of free, universal elementary education was not met, and remains unmet to this day.

In 1992 and 1993, the Supreme Court of India decided two PIL cases in which the plaintiffs claimed a judicially enforceable right to education.[37] Although both cases concerned the impact of certain state laws on private educational institutions of higher learning, the Court took the opportunity to develop a precedent that also governed the public provision of elementary education. Expressing concern at the obvious failure of the Government of India to uphold its duty under article 45 to ensure free and compulsory elementary education, the Court in Unni Krishnan stated:

> It is noteworthy among the several articles in Part IV, only article 45 speaks of a time-limit ... Does not the passage of 44 years - more than four times the period stipulated in Article 45 - convert the obligation created by the article into an enforceable right? In this context, we feel constrained to say that the allocation of available funds to different sectors of education in India discloses an inversion of priorities indicated by the Constitution.[38]

Based, it appears, on the view that the Central and state governments of India had consistently and systematically failed to apply the Constitution in their decision-making in relation to funding allocations for elementary education in India, the Court held that the right to education up to fourteen years of age contained in article 45 amounted to a 'fundamental right' that was enforceable by the courts. It also relied upon a link between the right to life recognized in Article 21 of the Constitution as a fundamental right, and the right to education as a directive principle. Sripati and Thiruvengadam observe that the immediate effect of the Unni Krishnan decision was that any child below the age of fourteen who was denied facilities for primary education could approach a court for an order directing the authorities to initiate appropriate measures.[39]

While human rights proponents have consistently welcomed the Court's activist approach in this area, and its effective re-characterization of the right to education as a fundamental right, despite the arguably clear contrary intent of the drafters of the Constitution, it must be asked whether such a powerful judicial reinterpretation of the relevant principles could be achieved in any other constitutional system and whether it is desirable. But whatever the outcome of such an inquiry in relation to other countries, it is essential to note that within India the Court's initiative had a huge impact in terms of mobilizing civil society, legitimating demands for a right to education, and unleashing extensive pressures on the government to formally amend the Constitution so as to bring it into line with the Court's approach.

Responding to the Court's Agenda-setting Role

Community activists and non-government organizations began utilizing the decision as a means of pushing the executive and legislature toward action on primary education. At the same time, the decisions became a catalyst for political advocacy and public sphere debate over the state of primary education in India, galvanizing a number of different children's rights groups into a coalition demanding government implementation of the 'fundamental right to education.' The Central government responded by establishing two committees to investigate both the desirability and financial implications of amending the Constitution to establish primary education as a fundamental right. A joint committee of state government Ministers of Education (the Saikia Committee) concluded in 1997 that the Constitution should be amended to create as a 'fundamental right' the right to free and compulsory education from six to fourteen years of age, and to impose a 'fundamental duty' on parents to provide opportunities for education to their children in this age group. A second expert committee (the Majumdar Committee) concluded in 1999 that the universalisation of elementary education for children aged six to fourteen years would require an additional expenditure of Rs 140,000,000,000 per year for ten years; on the assumption of annual GDP growth of 5 percent, this amounts to an additional 0.7 percent of GDP dedicated to education per year, raising education expenditure to approximately 5 percent of GDP.

The Saikia Committee report resulted in a bill to amend the Constitution to introduce a new article 21A, which provided: '[t]he State shall provide free and compulsory education to all citizens of age six to fourteen years in such manner as the State may, by law, determine.' It also introduced a new article 51A which imposed a duty on parents and guardians to provide their children with educational opportunities, in the terms recommended by the Saikia Committee. The bill was tabled in 1997, but would not pass into law until December 2002. In the meantime, a number of important criticisms were made of the proposed new right during the hearings Parliamentary Standing Committee on Human Resource Development.[40] The Standing Committee noted that the 'general feeling' of submissions was that the age restriction was arbitrary and neglected the rights of children below six and above fourteen years of age. The exclusion of the application of the right to children under six years of age was noted to be contrary to the Supreme Court's ruling in Unni Krishna. It was also submitted to the Standing Committee that, at the time of the drafting of the original article 45 (which encoded the fourteen year age limit), a child received a formal certification of education at 7th grade; in modern India, no formal certification was awarded until 10th grade, or when a child would be aged about sixteen years. The constitutional amendment as proposed would thus not ensure that impoverished children could continue until their formal certification had been obtained. Submissions to the Standing Committee also argued that there was a need (potentially in subsequent legislation pursuant to the amendment) to define the meaning of'free' as referred to in article 21 A, and to include some definition of the quality of education that was to be provided.

Two factors which warrant emphasis in the present context are the role played by civil society in mobilizing to demand the formal constitutional recognition of a right to education and the role played by commentators and scholars, both domestic and foreign, in highlighting the claim that resources were not in fact the sole or even the main barrier to a major improvement in India's educational performance. The latter case was pressed with particular force and perseverance by Myron Weiner who rejected outright the claim that the low educational rates in India were due to the lack of financial resources needed to fund universal compulsory primary school education. Focusing on the question of why widespread child labour persisted despite avowed government opposition, he suggested three alternative explanations: (a) child labour was sustained by weak and unenforced government policies on primary education; (b) the middle classes were more concerned to expand government funding for higher education than for primary education; and (c) even more controversially, that child labour was in fact 'part of the government's industrial strategy to promote the small scale sector and to expand exports.'

Weiner depicted compulsory education as a *sine qua non* for the reduction and abolition of child labour. He concluded that: '[t]he sooner India acts, the quicker will be the fall in the illiteracy rate, the more likely it is that child labour will be reduced, and the greater are the prospects for a reduction in fertility rates as children are no longer seen as financial assets to the family. He was particularly critical of what he saw as ameliorative half-measures which involved programs such as the promotion of adult literacy campaigns, the provision of non-formal education to working children, and the provision of free school lunches. In his view, nothing short of a compulsory and constitutionally recognized right to primary education would suffice.[41]

Civil society groups also took up the struggle to give constitutional status to the right to education. As one observer put it, the proposed amendment 'is an initiative which could have far-reaching consequences ... It has the potential to be a major catalyst in achieving the elusive goal of universal elementary education.'[42] Much of the groundwork for this support had also been laid by a major public initiative which produced the path-breaking Public Report on Basic Education in India (PROBE Report).[43] The Report was important not only because of its sophisticated advocacy approach but because it was based upon a detailed empirical study of the situation in five states of northern India, accounting for 40% of the total population but well over half of its children not attending school.[44] In contrast to the economic instrumentalist approach favoured by so many developmental economists, the Report identifies eight arguments which can be invoked to justify the case for universal elementary education. They are:

(1) elementary education is a fundamental right, as stated in the Constitution and determined by the Supreme Court;

(2) there is massive popular demand for universal schooling;

(3) it represents an important investment in human capital;

(4) it should contribute to the joy of learning;

(5) education helps individual well-being in diverse ways;

(6) education assists the social progress of the whole community;

(7) education facilitates effective political participation; and

(8) universal elementary education is a requirement of social justice.[45]

The Report concluded that 'the notion of a fundamental right has great value in overcoming the objections and excuses that are consistently invoked to continue postponing the goal of universal elementary education.'[46] To some degree, the very process of drafting and debating the amendment generated popular mobilization around the need to improve basic education in India, with 40,000 citizens from distant villages and towns around India rallying in New Delhi on the day that the amendment was passed.[47] The protest was organized by a coalition of several thousand grassroots organizations from all over India, the National Alliance for the Fundamental Right to Education (NAFRE), and demanded a common school system providing free education of equitable quality.

The role played by civil society in bringing about the constitutional amendment is instructive. Human rights demands are all too often promoted in a top-down fashion, whether pushed by the international community, or by domestic elites. Although this process is not necessarily doomed to failure, it is less likely to succeed and, more importantly, it is less likely to generate the level of societal support which will, over time, ensure that the relevant value is internalized within the community so that, at least at the level of ideas, it is no longer a matter of contention. While India's vibrant civil society, its relatively longstanding democratic traditions, and its legal heritage might all have combined to provide particularly fertile ground for such an initiative, this does not necessarily mean that a campaign based on the assertion of education as a matter of human rights will not work in other countries.

The Constitutional Amendment

Despite the minimum age restriction also being criticized by the government-sponsored National Commission to Review the Working of the Constitution,[48] the amendment establishing the fundamental right to education passed in the form originally proposed.[49] While controversial in its terms, the constitutional amendment was nevertheless hailed by activists and education-focused non-government organizations as an important step towards improving the condition of basic education in India.

To understand how the constitutional amendment might (or might not) assist in realizing this demand, we need briefly to consider the state of basic education in India and some of the reasons why the goal of universal elementary education remains elusive after 58 years of independence. India's achievements in elementary education have been far less impressive than other developing countries that were similarly situated 40 years ago.[50] As already noted, close to half of the Indian population is still illiterate and almost one-third of the children to whom the Constitutional amendment will apply are not in school. Enrolment rates are suspected of being inflated, and say nothing of whether children actually attend school or learn anything. The PROBE Report and other studies have documented very low levels of learning among enrolled students in those states and regions with high numbers of out of school children.[53] Studies and analyses investigating the reasons behind this poor performance indicate a combination of causes: inadequate financing of education, entrenched social division and discrimination on the basis of caste, class and gender, political apathy and an institutional and management incentive structure that inhibits accountability, responsiveness and quality teaching.[54]

As noted above,[55] elementary education in India has suffered from 'five decades of underinvestment,'[56] a problem compounded by the fact that state governments are responsible for more than 80 percent of education expenditure. This entails very considerable inter-state disparities in education expenditure, but has also meant that national expenditure on education has suffered as a consequence of the fiscal crisis of state governments throughout India, over the 1990s. Shariff and Ghosh observe that, during the 1990s, the share of state budgets devoted to elementary education has declined in all but three states in India to levels below that achieved in the 1980s.[57] The growth in per pupil expenditure on elementary education also declined over this period in all but three states. While the 1980s saw a steady growth of central and state government expenditure on education generally and on elementary education in particular, the share of GDP devoted to education expenditure fell from 4.1 percent in 1990-91 to 3.8 percent in 1995-6.[58] Drèze and Sen observe that the increased education expenditure of the 1980s went almost entirely toward teachers' salaries, even as there was an absolute decline in the number of primary and upper primary teachers between 1991 and 1993.[59]

Adequate expenditure on education is by no means a sufficient condition for universal elementary education of an equitable standard, but it is undoubtedly a necessary condition. Access to lower and upper primary schools within safe walking distance of a settlement remains a problem in the states most afflicted by illiteracy and poor educational attainment, and as the PROBE Report has documented, the mere presence of a school building does not mean that the school is adequately equipped to educate children at a suitable quality. The PROBE survey of settlements in four traditionally underdeveloped states found a widespread absence of basic facilities like roofing, toilets, water supply, teaching kits and book resources. One third of the schools surveyed by PROBE were de facto single teacher schools, and the pupil-teacher ratio averaged 50:1.[60] The consequence of such resource shortages is that school facilities, while available, may be inadequate to enable learning.[61]

A major problem identified by numerous studies, and a strong disincentive to impoverished parents to bear the opportunity cost and the real cost of sending children to school, is the poor quality of schooling provided. Studies reveal not so much a lack of demand for education among the rural poor and so-called 'backward castes' and 'backward tribes,'[62] as a disaffection with the lack of learning that occurs after very considerable sacrifices are made to send children to school.[63] As one interviewee of a field study stated:

We are poor, but not so poor that we cannot send our children to school ... But how is it possible for them to continue? They don't learn anything here. We had to spend so much money on the books, and then the teacher is sitting so far away from the children that absolutely nothing is learned there. Everybody thinks so about the teachers. The only thing they can do is beat up the children. So when Raju came home, and I kept telling him everyday to go to school, he just burned his books.[64]

The quality problem identified in so many studies is in part a reflection of inadequate resources: it is hard for teachers to teach and students to learn in class sizes of fifty or more, in schools with no roof or without teaching aids. However, numerous authors[65] have suggested that complete indifference and inactivity on the part of teachers is to blame, and that this is a result not only of the difficult environment in which teachers must work but of a systematic institutional failure to produce and ensure good teaching through the provision of training, peer review and accountability to local communities.[66] Animating these general quality constraints in any specific case, and particularly in underdeveloped states and locales, are social hierarchies of caste, class and gender. From curricula that are completely unsuited to the educational needs and lived experience of first generation learners in rural areas or urban slums,[67] to discrimination against scheduled caste and scheduled tribe members in the location of schools and in the attitude of higher caste teachers, caste and class remain important determinants of access to and the quality of elementary education in India.[68] Likewise, important barriers remain to the education of girl-children from impoverished families.

This cursory overview of the obstacles to the provision of universal elementary education in India leaves out many important issues, such as the tendency toward the expansion of a 'two track' education system. But it does allow us to observe that the achievement of universal elementary education is not only a matter of the availability of resources or even just their distribution: it is a product of the interaction of social, political and institutional forces, of community mobilization and empowerment, and of challenging bureaucratic inertia and deeply embedded social hierarchies.

On the one hand, the complexity and durability of the social structures militating against the universalization of elementary education appears to be a strong argument against the proposition that litigation and court orders upholding the right to education could be effective. The American experience with court-ordered desegregation demonstrates the limitations of attempting to alter deep-seated social structures, such as race segregation, through case-by-case court orders that are ultimately unable to retrench the social forces which reproduce inequality of opportunity between black and white Americans. The prospect of having to try to reengineer the United States' schools and school districts, one by one, perhaps led the Supreme Court of this country to narrow its jurisprudence on desegregation.[69] While the Supreme Court of India has shown itself to be more willing to undertake Olympian tasks of investigation and supervision of government conduct, the record of government compliance with the Court's sweeping orders concerning social problems, such as bonded labour,[70] is not encouraging: 'a judge can only give directions: and in regard to many of the gravest problems these directions have to be given to the very institutions whose negligence has compounded the malady in the first place.'[71]

Indeed, in the first budget after the passage of the constitutional amendment establishing the fundamental right to education, the Central government ignored the expert committee report and failed to allocate the amount deemed necessary to universalize elementary education; in fact, the amount allocated was less than 50 percent of the estimated requirement of Rs 140,000,000,000 per annum[72] and less even than the Rs 98,000,000,000 recommended in the Financial Memorandum to the constitutional amendment bill.[73] The Central government has commenced preparation of a Free and Compulsory Education Bill to provide legislative machinery for the constitutional right, but a noted expert on education India comments that administrative structure envisaged by the act describes 'a mechanism of abdication of responsibilities by higher levels of authorities in favour of lower levels; and not a method of devolution of powers and resources, but a mechanism of mobilization of non-governmental resources.'[74]

But to accept that courts can't do everything does not imply acceptance of the opposite view, that they can do nothing at all. The last decade has seen a number of innovative responses to the problems of elementary education in India, and an important part of these innovations has been the embrace of education as a site of community mobilization and popular struggle.[75] The notion of education as a fundamental right has the potential to operate at a number of different levels to assist these kinds of innovations. First, the diffusion of' rights consciousness' could provide a basis for political organization within communities against discrimination and division on the basis of caste and gender, and thus be an instrument towards the creation of a 'social consensus' on the entitlement of equal access to quality elementary education. Articulating education in terms of a constitutional and human right, with reference to the content of that term as it has evolved at the international level, may be a useful and effective argumentative strategy within 'public spheres' at the local and national level. A 2001 review of a Kenyan access to justice projects supported by the United Kingdom Department for International Development concluded, 'the empowering influence of rights awareness is a catalyst for social organization and community-driven development. The activist function recognizes that legal rights ... can [best] be achieved ... through articulation of rights using advocacy and lobbying in an activist manner.'[76]

Second, litigation or the threat of litigation may greatly enhance the bargaining power of local communities vis-à-vis state and national bureaucracies and other centers of political power. Because the fundamental rights provisions of the Constitution apply to both state and central governments, villages and communities have the potential to build state-specific campaigns and cases that concern the specific needs of their locales, and to present these claims in the state courts. Of course, the realization of the opportunities presented by strategic litigation depends heavily upon effective, accessible and carefully conducted community lawyering (which is far from alien to India). As examples from the South African context illustrate, constitutional rights litigation can be a powerful process for community mobilization and the assertion of a hitherto latent political subjectivity by the disenfranchised and the oppressed.[77] As Stephen Golub argues the very process of preparing litigation through consultations with and education of the affected community enhances rights awareness, strengthens knowledge of government processes and gives decision-makers the sense that they are under scrutiny from those affected by their actions - even if the litigation itself is unsuccessful: 'A value of legal empowerment is that it can constitute a feedback loop, through which grass roots experience feeds legal and regulatory change, which further grassroots work in turn converts from reform on paper to reform in practice.' [78]

Third, successful litigation may help to change the budgeting priorities of the state, and start a process towards a more authentic institutional commitment toward education. Thus, for example, this commitment has been a decisive factor in the success of educational achievement in the state of Himachal Pradesh.[79]

Drawing Conclusions from the Indian Experience

While we have accorded considerable attention to the distinctive role played by the courts in India in the struggle to recognize and give effect to the right to education, it would be a mistake to focus only, or even primarily, on litigation as the key to promoting the realization of this right. While the Indian Supreme Court has certainly played an important catalytic role, the key ingredients of the Indian case study include the formal constitutional recognition of the right in the 1949 Constitution, the role of civil society in insisting that substance be given to that commitment, the contribution of sustained analytical critiques of the state of education, and the political salience of these demands.

The emphasis on treating education as a right brings two important dimensions which are all too often downplayed in the context of other approaches to education policy. They are empowerment and accountability. While each of these terms has been overused in the social science and development literature in recent years, their significance in this context is nonetheless considerable.

In terms of empowerment, the recognition of a right to education, and the adoption of an approach to education policy which accords some prominence to that dimension, serves to emphasize that the individual holder of the right is entitled to make certain demands, not only upon a government, but perhaps more importantly upon the right-holder's immediate community. The responsibilities which attach to human rights apply not only to governments in accordance with the traditional state-centric analysis of the functioning of international human rights norms. They also encapsulate and help to inform community expectations. In the context of the right to education for example this will play out as much at the family and village levels as it will in any of the more routine bureaucratic levels. Where a child is being denied educational opportunities, whether for reasons of gender, disability, caste, race, order in the family or whatever, a community which has come internalize a sensibility to, and set of expectations about, every child's inherent right to education will react to the perceived deprivation. The same applies at the village or community level where a right to education based obligation of those in charge will have an impact regardless of the insistence of those responsible that there are simply no available resources.

In the longer term the objective of rights such as the right to education is to internalize a value assumption to the point where a sense of injustice or even outrage follows automatically from any denial of access to primary education. Just as we respond instinctively against arbitrary physical violence exerted against another person, so too would a fully-internalized sense of the right to education lead to an instinctive reaction against a government, a community, or parents or guardians denying a child access to that right.

Closely linked to the concept of empowerment is the sense that the demand for education, by both parents and students, will be enhanced and legitimated by the deeper inculcation of the notion that every individual has not just an opportunity or a duty to learn but a right to education. While this demand-side effect cannot be taken for granted, nor should it be viewed only in terms of rational economic decision making. As Lant Pritchett has observed, there may well be economic conditions that are sufficiently stagnant as to warrant considering a decision not to attend school as 'the *optimal* decision from a narrowly drawn economic calculation.' But, as he notes:

> I would never recommend adopting this narrow view [because] the view that basic education is a human right and an essential element of well-being in the modern world is pretty compelling. But it is worth pointing out that when returns are low the economic calculation and the human rights desire may be at odds.[80]

This dimension of empowering the individual to put forward justified and internationally and constitutionally legitimated claims is a vital part of the human rights paradigm. It is also directly related to the notion of accountability which is an essential part of the human rights concept. As noted in the *Human Development Report 2000,* in asserting that there is a human right to primary education it follows that 'if some persons avoidably lack access to it, there must be some culpability somewhere in the social system.'[81] As the Report explains:

> This focus on locating accountability for failures within a social system can be a powerful tool in seeking remedy. It certainly broadens the outlook beyond the minimal claims of human development, and the analysis of human development can profit from it. The effect of a broader outlook is to focus on the actions, strategies and efforts that different duty bearers undertake to contribute to the fulfilment of specified human rights and to the advancement of the corresponding human development. It also leads to an analysis of the responsibilities of different actors and institutions when rights go unfulfilled.

The importance of these elements of empowerment and accountability which flow from treating education as a human right also serve to underscore the importance of distinguishing those policy approaches which are premised, to a greater or lesser degree, upon the recognition of the right to education, from those that set broader development goals relating to education. Michael Clemens, for example, has been highly critical of the practice of 'a succession of international meetings' of adopting 'a litany of utopian international goals' which inevitably fail to be realized.[83] He lists 18 occasions between 1934 and 2001 when governments explicitly approved the goal of universal primary education. They range from the 1934 International Conference on Public Education to the adoption of the Universal Declaration of Human Rights in 1948, and a succession of UNESCO Regional Conferences in the 1950s and 1960s, through the 1990 World Conference on Education for All and the 2000 Dakar World Education Forum to the Millennium Development Goals.

From a human rights perspective, his list is significantly incomplete since he lists only the Universal Declaration of 1948 and manifests no awareness of the more substantive commitments undertaken in a variety of specific international and regional-level treaties, such as the International Covenant on Economic, Social and Cultural Rights of 1966, and the Convention on the Rights of the Child of 1989. Of course, Clemens might well respond that the substantial lengthening of his list which would result from the addition of all of the relevant undertakings made in the human rights context only serves to reinforce his argument that repeated invocations of principle make little if any difference on their own. But there is a qualitative difference between treaty-based human rights commitments which give rise to binding legal obligations and undertakings given at regional conferences or in other context in which governments are convinced that they are making general policy statements which will have no direct domestic consequences and no sustained or obligatory international follow-up. The human rights undertakings, by contrast, import an obligation to take a variety of specific steps at the national level, and to acknowledge various forms of accountability at the international level.

While this is not the place in which to explore in detail the ways in which these international accountability mechanisms do or should function, it is appropriate to note that in 2003 the Indian Government prepared a very detailed report to the UN Committee on the Rights of the Child, including over 80 pages of detailed statistical and other information on the strengths and weaknesses of the system designed to give effect to the child's right to education.[84] This report was the occasion for the preparation of a range of 'alternative' reports prepared by civil society groups and also submitted to the UN Committee.[85] While the 'concluding observations' adopted by the Committee were very general in nature[86] and likely to be of little specific import, the process as a whole was clearly an important one.[87] Its capacity to provoke the Government to undertake a systematic inventory, its involvement of civil society both at the domestic and international level, its garnering of extensive domestic press coverage, and its formal evaluation of India's performance in relation to its obligations, all contribute to promoting an element of accountability which is almost entirely absent in the case of other international undertakings relating to education.

REFERENCES

1. Alfredo Sfeir-Younis, 'Human Rights Day Interview: How may 'human rights' enhance our development mission?
2. Committee on Economic, Social and Cultural Rights, General Comment No. 13 (Twenty-first session, 1999), 'The right to education (article 13 of the Covenant)', UN doc. HRI/GEN/1/Rev.6 (2003), p. 70, see paras. 31,43, 45 and 50.
3. *Investing in Every Child: An Economic Study of the Costs and Benefits of Eliminating Child Labour* (Geneva, ILO, 2003). In fairness it should be noted that a companion ILO study entitled *Every Child Counts* (Geneva, ILO, 2002) adopts more of a human rights type approach but the separation of the two approaches nevertheless confirms the point being argued here.

4. *Ibid.*, p. 15.
5. *Ibid.*, p. 3.
6. *Ibid.*, p. 1.
7. A. Hillman and E. Jenkner, User Payments for Basic Education in Low-Income Countries, IMF Working Paper WP/02/182 (2002), p. 1.
8. *Ibid.*, p.3.
9. *Ibid.*, p. 24.
10. *Ibid.*, p. 25.
11. *Ibid.*, pp. 25-26.
12. *Primary Education in India* (Washington DC, World Bank, 1997) p. 14.
13. *Ibid.*, p. 72. The demand-side factors identified are 'the poor quality of much schooling, weak implementation of compulsory schooling laws, grade repetition, and high demand for child labor.'
14. *2003 State Department Country Reports on Human Rights Practices* (Washington DC, 2004).
15. For a review of the arguments concerning public provision of education, see J B G Tilak, 'Public Subsidies in Education in India', *Economic and Political Weekly*, January 24, 2004, pp.343-359, at p.344-5.
16. A Sen, 'Basic Education and Human Security', paper delivered at workshop on 'Basic Education and Human Security' in Kolkata, India, 2-4 January 2002.
17. J. Drèze and A Sen, *India: Economic Development and Social Opportunity* (New Delhi, Oxford University Press, 1996), pp.14-15.
18. *Ibid* p.109.
19. One study lists over 40 international conventions and declarations that refer to education as a human right. See A

Fernandez and S Jenkner, eds, *International Declarations and Conventions on the Right to Education and the Freedom of Education* (Frankfurt, Info-3 Verlag, 1995).

20. See e.g. Manfred Nowak, 'The Right to Education', in Eide, Krause & Rosas (eds.), *Economic, Social and Cultural Rights: A Textbook* (The Hague, Kluwer, 2nd. ed., 2001) pp. 245-72.

21. For a cross-section of the literature see R. Levesque, 'The Right to Education in the United States: Beyond the Limits of the Lore and the Lure of the Law', 4 *Annual Survey of International and Comparative Law* (1997) 205; S. Steinke, 'The Exception to the Rule: Wisconsin's Fundamental Right to Education and Public School Financing', [1995] *Wisconsin Law Review* 1387; and M. Mills and W. Quin II, 'The Right to a "Minimally Adequate Education" as Guaranteed by the Mississippi Constitution', 61 *Albany Law Review* (1998) 1521.

22. K. Tomaševski, Free and Compulsory Education for all Children: The Gap between Promise and Performance (Lund, 2001), p. 19, available at http://www.right-to-education.org/

23. For background to this case see H. Hershkoff and B. Kingsbury, 'Crisis, Community, and Courts in Network Governance: A Response to Liebman and Sabel's Approach to Reform of Public Education', 28 *N.Y.U. Rev. of Law & Soc. Change* (2003) 319.

24. Greg Winter, 'Judge Orders Billions in Aid to City Schools', *New York Times*, 15 Feb. 2005, p.1.

25. For a brief history of constitutional litigation, see Burt Neuborne, 'The Supreme Court of India', 1 *International Journal of Constitutional Law* (2003) 476.

26. R Banerji, 'Poverty and Primary Schooling: Field Studies from Mumbai and Delhi', *Economic and Political Weekly*, March 4, 2000 p.795 (citing data from the 50th National Sample Survey).

27. Report of India to the Committee on the Rights of the Child, UN doc. CRC/C/93/Add.5 (2003), para. 801.
28. Government of India, Department of Education, *Selected Educational Statistics,* Constitutional Amendment making the right to Education a Fundamental Right', *International Journal of Constitutional Law* (2003) 149, 151.
29. A Shariff and P K Ghosh, 'Indian Education Scene and the Public Gap', *Economic and Political Weekly*, April 15, 2000, pp.1396-1406.
30. World Bank, *Primary Education in India* (1997) p.219.
31. Shariff and Ghosh, above n 29, 1399.
32. See *Human Development Report 2004* (New York, Oxford University Press, 2004).
33. *Frontline* (Madras), Vol. 17, No. 4, Feb 19 – March 03, 2000,
34. Neuborne, above n. 25, p. 503.
35. Constitution of India, Part IV, art 45.
36. Constitution of India, Part IV, art 37.
37. *Mohini Jain v State of Karnataka*, AIR 1992 SC 1858; *Unni Krishnan J.P. v State of Andhra Pradesh*, AIR 1993 SC 2178.
38. *Unni Krishnan*, at 2232.
39. Sripati and Thiruvengadam, above n 28, 153.
40. Available at http://arunmehta.freeyellow.com/page144.html.
41. Myron Weiner, 'Child Labour in Developing Countries: The Indian Case', 2 *International Journal of Children's Rights* (1994) 121.
42. R Wazir, 'Profiling the Problem' in Wazir, ed, *The Gender Gap in Basic Education: NGOs as Change Agents* (New Delhi, Sage Publications, 2000), p.18.
43. PROBE Team, *Public Report on Basic Education in India* (New Delhi, Oxford University Press, 1999).

44. *Ibid.*, p. 2.
45. *Ibid.*, pp. 4-5.
46. *Ibid.*, p.141.
47. Anil Sadgopal, 'A Convenient Consensus', *Frontline* (Madras), Dec 22, 2001 – Jan 04, 2002,
48. National Commission to Review the Working of the Constitution, *Final Report*, vol.1, ch.3 (2002) para 3.20.2, recommending that every child have the right to free education until he completes the age of fourteen years, and that girls and members of the Scheduled castes and the Scheduled tribes benefit from the right until the age of eighteen years.
49. Sadgopal, n. 47 above.
50. Drèze and Sen, above n 17, 114.
51. Banerji, above n. 26 above, p.795 (citing data from the 50th National Sample Survey).
52. Drèze and Sen, above n 17, 113.
53. PROBE Report, above n. 43; World Bank, *India: Primary Education: Achievements and Challenges* (1997); Banerji, above n 26, 799.
54. See, inter alia, Wazir, above n 42; PROBE Report, above n. 43; Drèze and Sen, above n 17; S Shukla and R Kaul, eds, *Education, Development and Underdevelopment* (New Delhi, Sage Publications, 1998); A Vaidyanathan and P R Gopinathan Nair, eds, *Elementary Education in Rural India* (New Delhi, Sage Publications, 2001); R Govinda, ed, *India Education Report* (New Delhi, Oxford University Press, 2002).
55. See notes 26-31 and text.
56. B. J. Tilak, 'Five Decades of Underinvestment in Education', *Economic and Political Weekly*, September 6-12, 1997; see also PROBE report, above n 43, p.134.
57. Shariff and Ghosh, above n. 29, p.1403.

58. *Ibid* 1405.
59. Drèze and Sen, above n 17, p.123.
60. PROBE Report, above n 43, ch.4
61. See also Vaidyanathan, above n 54, p.43-4.
62. An important exception to this result is the attitude towards the education of girl-children, which is more consistently negative.
63. *Ibid*, pp.26-7; Banerji, above n 26; G K Lieten, 'Children, Work and Education – I', *Economic and Political Weekly*, June 10, 2000, p.2037.
64. *Ibid.*, p.2175.
65. For an overview, see G Kingdon and M Muzammil, *The Political Economy of Education in India: Teacher Politics in Uttar Pradesh* (New Delhi, Oxford University Press, 2003), Ch 1.
66. R Sudarshan, 'Educational Status of Girls and Women: The Emerging Scenario' in Wazir, ed , above n 42, p.64; Vaidyanathan, above n 54, p.44-5; Govinda, above n 54, p.11.
67. See, eg, M Talib, 'Observations from a School in a Working Class Settlement in Delhi' in Shukla et al, eds, above n 54, pp. 189-199; PROBE Report, above n 43, pp. 68-75; Anita Rampal, 'Texts in Context: Development of Curricula, Textbooks, and Teaching Learning Materials' in Govinda, ed, above n 54, pp.154-166.
68. G Nambissan and M Sedwal, 'Education for all: The Situation of Dalit Children in India' in Govinda, ed, above n 54, 72-86; K Sujatha, 'Education Among Scheduled Tribes', pp.87-95; Banerji, above n. 26; Vaidyanathan, above n 54, pp.27-29.
69. James Liebman and Charles Sabel, 'A Public Laboratory Dewey Barely Imagined: The Emerging Model of School Governance and Legal Reform', 28 *New York University Review of Law and Social Change* (2003) 183, 192-201.

70. A Shourie, *Courts and Their Judgments* (New Delhi, Rupa, 2001), Ch. 3.

71. *Ibid* p.400.

72. At 2005 exchange rates this would be equivalent to around US$3.2 billion.

73. Azim Premji Foundation, 'Union Budget 2003-4 in the context of Elementary Education' (on file with authors); A Sadgopal, 'Education for Too Few', *Frontline* (Madras), Dec. 5, 2003.

74. J B Tilak, 'Free and Compulsory Education – Legislative Intervention', *Economic and Political Weekly*, February 14, 2004.

75. See, eg, R Govinda and R Diwan, *Community Participation and Empowerment in Primary Education*, Sage Publications, New Delhi, 2003; S Chowdhury, 'Universal Elementary Education in Rajasthan: A Study with Focus on Innovative Strategies' in Govinda, ed, above n 54, p.346; P Clarke, 'Education Reform in the Education Guarantee Scheme in Madhya Pradesh, India and the Fundescola Program in Brazil', March 2003, World Bank.

76. S Golub, *Beyond the Rule of Law Orthodoxy*, Carnegie Endowment for International Peace, Rule of Law Working Paper No. 41 (Oct 2003).

77. See Desai, *We are the Poors* (2002).

78. Golub, above n. 76.

79. J Drèze and A Sen, n. 17 above, p. 129; and Report of India, above n. 27, p. 248.

80. Lant Pritchett, 'Towards A New Consensus for Addressing the Global Challenge of the Lack of Education', Center for Global Development, Working Paper No. 43, June 2004.

81. *Human Rights and Human Development, Human Development Report 2000* (New York, Oxford University Press for UNDP, 2000) p. 21.

82. *Ibid.*, p. 22.
83. Michael Clemens, *The Long Walk to School: International Education Goals in Historical Perspective*, Center for Global Development Working Paper No 37, March 2004.
84. Report of India, above n. 27, pp. 232-314.
85. E.g. 'The Alternate Report by the National Movement of Working Children, India, submitted to the Committee on the Rights of the Child, July 2003'.
86. 'Concluding Observations: India', UN doc. CRC/C/15/Add.228 (2004).
87. The extent to which the process is relevant, despite its shortcomings, is well illustrated by a highly critical assessment published in one of India's leading weekly magazines immediately after the Committee had reported: The reporting process is like a diplomatic ritual .... Even a cursory look at the concluding observations made by the same committee in 2000 on the basis of the earlier report indicates that the committee has mechanically repeated this part of the observations and identified the same set of factors responsible for the poor status of children in India as it had last time. This highly limited level of analysis indicates a lack of engagement with the ground realities on part of the official delegation as well as the committee. The committee also played friendly by not listing 'lack of political will' and 'poor allocation of resources' as reasons for the dismal record. .. Some observations are stale, and have been rendered over and over again; some are new and have been keenly awaited; and some are completely missing ...

7

Public Administration and Human Rights

The 21st Century has witnessed tremendous changes in our country as in the world in general. Although the attainment of freedom on August 15, 1947 was by itself a landmark in history. The struggle for freedom in India was multidimensional. In later stages, it was Mahatma Gandhi who came to symbolize, despite many diversities and differing opinions, view points and the aspirations of the people and the freedom movement itself; the hopes, aspirations and ideals of the Freedom Movement are even today embodied in the Constitution that the people of India gave unto themselves for peace, prosperity and progress.

There have been regular attempts at administrative reforms and innovation, both at the Centre and in the States, including starting new institutions and systems in India since 1947. Although the results have been strong on assurances and weak on performance. Thus the results have not been commensurate with our hopes and needs. Further, besides persistence of problems of administration with increasing severity, we have also witnessed in succeeding decades acceleration in the process of degeneration in our socio-economic-political and administrative scenario. Today the situation has become so alarming now that even the law and order situation in many parts of the country, rural as well as urban, presents a depressing picture. There are many other burning issues also such as like propriety in the exercise of administrative discretion; paralysis of political will and capacity for decision making; mounting administrative corruption and political venality, leading to erosion in the credibility and effectiveness of democratic institutions. Today people expect a prompt and effective response to their problems and concerns in this Information Technology era.

In this paper an attempt would be made to focus on issues such as accountability, Indian administrative culture and trust with special reference to India. As the Public Administration machinery expands and becomes more complex, the need for holding it properly accountable is more acutely felt. Today there has been substantial agreement among writers of public administration that the principal problem of governmental administration today is not one of securing efficiency but one of insuring accountability; some scholars view it as the classic problem of public administration.[1]

In India the assumption in the context of democracy, is that the civil servants work for the people. But the problem of locating accountability therefore becomes acute because of the nature of the job performed and power exercised by the civil servants. Today they are no longer confined to the job of implementing the policies and executing the laws framed by the legislature. Now they consciously make laws and even adjudicate laws. In fact the laws made by the legislature lay down only the broad objectives, and the task of providing the details of making rules, regulations and bye-laws for filling up the gaps left in the legislation, is given to the administrators in order to facilitate the process of executing the laws. Thus, "the problem of keeping watch over the execution of laws has today grown into the more complex task of exercising control over policy formulation and policy implementation. The meaning of the concept of administrative accountability has, therefore, been expanded and consequently its dimensions have increased."[2] These days various expressions like responsiveness, responsibility, accountability and control are used to ensure the subservience of public servants.

The word Responsiveness means "the state of being responsive" i.e. answering or replying. In Indian democracy the citizens expect civil servants to be responsive to their requests and demands. A citizen who asks something of a government has the right to expect a response and to be treated as a legitimate source of demands. In fact responsiveness is a procedural requirement for good government.

The other word Responsibility implies that the civil servants will adhere to the explicit and implicit values of proper administration and policy. Responsible public servants know the law and have convictions about the proper administration of their programmes. Expertise and law thus become central to the working of civil service.

Responsibility and accountability are often used inter changeably. But the two can also be distinguished as accountability may refer to the legal and hierarchical locus of responsibility, where as responsibility has ethical and normative connotations. The word accountable seems to have come into usage in the English language for the first time in the year 1583, and the context was financial. Accountable means liable to be called to account. Accountability related to administration therefore means that the administration has to be accountable for the exercise of authority which it possesses. Now an important question is -accountability for what? In fact it is linked with performance and it is goal and achievement oriented. Accountability of administration has rightly been called the 'Kingpin' of democratic administration. Thus it becomes another facet of administrative performance, which evidently is the culmination of both policy making and its implementation. It is not merely regulatory and punitive in its purpose and contents, though occasionally regulation and punishment do become the necessary elements of administrative accountability.

The evolution of the concept of administrative accountability is a modern development. In England, a beginning in this direction was made by the restoration of monarchy in 1660. Later efforts were made to evolve in India, under British rule, a concept of administrative accountability to law and procedure under the limitations imposed by imperial interests and the peculiar conditions of Indian Society. Later on, after independence in 1947, the transfer of power from London to New Delhi signified no change in administrative terms. The political system introduced in 1950 was itself not free from ambiguity in so far as the location of sovereignty was concerned. Yet another significant development of post independence period is the increasing infiltration of politics into administration. Under the pressure of politics, an irrational category, the conceptual rationality of public administration trends to get blurred but continues nonetheless.

Tools of Administrative Accountability

It is necessary and essential in the interest of democracy as well as efficiency and effectiveness that good and proper tools or controls to check civil servants must be devised, generally controls are of two types - external and internal. According to Prof. Finer, the best way to enforce accountability is to develop institutions that vigorously monitor the actions of public bureaucracy and punish those guilty of maladministration. In the absence of other controls, such as profit motive, policy makers must monitor the performance of public administrators via formal mechanisms.[3]

Among the two controls executives responsibility to the legislature, legislative surveillance, judicial review, audit system, financial advisory system in ministries, judicial system, ombudsman etc. are examples of external formal controls. The internal controls of formal type are secured through organizational devices like hierarchy supervision, control, span of control, unity of command, inspection, tours etc. These are in practice, reinforced and supplemented by informal external devices such as mass media, political parties, interest groups, political and electoral process, Comptroller and Auditor General (CAG) etc. existing in the society. Beside this on the other hand, Carl Friedrich opines that inculcation of appropriate values among administrators serves as the major check on the bureaucracy.[4]

Forms of accountability : Accountability although has many facets but they are inter-related. It may be formal i.e. institutionalized or informal i.e. democratic and ethical. Accountability may also take the forms like political accountability, administrative accountability, legislative accountability, judicial accountability etc.

Ways to ensure accountability : In addition to the formal structures and informal modes prevalent in different nations to enforce accountability in public service, a few more are suggested by scholars. Some of them are as follows :

1. *Representative Bureaucracy* : In order to ensure that administrators remain responsive to the needs of the people, some scholars have pointed to the potential importance of representative bureaucracy. In fact this view holds that democracy will be served if bureaucrats mirror certain key characteristics of society. This view was first developed by Kingsley[5] which grew out of recognition of the inadequacy of the traditional legal institutional controls for insuring administrative accountability in a modern state.
2. *Positive Content* : Administrative accountability must be imparted positive content. In India at present accountability is devalued. It must become sensitive to reward and punishment and must not remain one-sided as it is now.
3. *Administrative reforms* : Administrative accountability is performance and efficiency based and result oriented,

so in a responsible system of government rules and procedures must be simplified to enable public servants to avoid delays caused by unnecessary procedures. Thus delegation, decentralization, devolution and deconcentration are vital to accountability. So is the need for reform in personnel administration, especially training, placement, promotion, performance appraisal etc. Infact administrative reform is among the pre-requisites to a system of effective accountability.

4. *Innovative Practices* : Today innovative practices like sun-set legislation, zero-base budgeting, social audit, freedom of Information Act, Sun-shine legislation, Citizens Charter etc. should be adopted to enhance accountability. In brief the concept of sun-set legislation implies that rules and regulations should be made for limited periods, and after the expiry of that period the laws or rules should cease to operate unless renewed. This will also necessitate review of rules and regulations periodically to check their continued validity. On the other side the sun-shine legislation, implies that legislation is intended to let the sun-shine on all government deliberations. Zero-base budgeting means a process of review, analysis and 3 .evaluation of each budget request in order to justify its inclusion or exclusion from the budget finally approved. Social Audit means an examination of social accounts (like education, health etc.) with a view to determine the correctness of these accounts and of the transactions they embody. Freedom of Information Act as passed in the U.S.A., gives citizens the right to see most records that the Government maintains. Accountability demands openness in the conduct of public business. The citizen charters are not expounding new legal rights or obligations but rather stipulating existing rights and detailing good practice, which

exists in some cases and should, in the government's view be the norm.

5. *Public Participation* : The direct involvement of public in the administrative process constitutes one of the major efforts to enforce administrative accountability. Generally in developing countries like India public participation consists of three ways that is :

(a) Consultation throughout the planning process,

(b) Public representation on decision-making boards; and

(c) Community control over funds and expenditure.

However, it would fail to ensure administrative accountability unless such participation educates the citizens and be informed about the broader socio-economic characteristics of the society itself. The idea of public participation is to expand the democratic basis of administrative action. Therefore the desire for accountability must be weighed against responsiveness and the ability to achieve policy ends efficiently and effectively.

Methods of Accountabiligy

Control over public administration is an essential feature of accountable and responsible administration. Lord Acton's insightful remark "Power corrupts and absolute power tends to corrupt absolutely" appears to have universal validity. Now to check it and make it accountable, certain safeguards are needed to make the administration accountable to the people through some specific devices and methods. Here in brief we shall discuss some of the methods of accountability as follows :

(1) *Legislative accountability* : The Legislature or Parliament plays an important role in making administration accountable. In parliamentary countries of which India is one, the executive is responsible to the legislature. It can hold office only so long as it enjoys the confidence, i.e.,

the majority support of the legislature. There are several means through which legislature exercises control over public administration. Some of the important means of this method are such as questions, discussions and debates, motions and resolutions on specific administrative actions and matter of grave concern. There are financial control through budget and parliamentary committees.

In India members of parliament also get opportunity to hold administration accountable through budgetary process at the time of general discussion on the budget, discussion and voting of demands for grants and consideration and passing of both the Appropriation Bill and the Finance Bill. Besides the standing committees such as public accounts committee, estimate committee, assurances committee, public undertaking committee etc. also play significant role. There are consultative committees attached to the ministries and parliamentary committees of investigations such as the Joint Parliamentary Committee for the investigation of security scam under the chairmanship of R. N. Mirdha, M.P. and a former Minister of India. Two other means of control available to the legislature are its power to pass laws and vote supplies. By detailed legislation and voting of supplies the legislature can control the activities of administration to any extent. But ultimately the success of the legislative methods for ensuring administrative accountability largely depends upon intelligence and enlightment of legislators.

(2) *Executive accountability* : Executive control is an internal control over administration exercised either by the superior over the subordinate within the chain of administrative hierarchy or by other parallel agencies in the executive branch of the government. Administrative structure is hierarchical in nature and so one level controls the other and none is outside the chain of command. The executive accountability and control is exercised in many ways. Most

of them are formal provided by the laws of the country but some of them are informal depending upon the good sense of the civil servants. The method of internal control is different such as Political or Ministerial control is the cardinal principle of Parliamentary democracy. There are number of techniques and devices such as inspection, supervision, reports etc. through which the head quarters administration controls the field agencies. An important means of control is the centralization of establishment or personnel functions. The chief executive is responsible for personnel management control which includes the methods of recruitment, salaries, promotion, conditions of service etc. The public servants if are not working in a proper way then they can be reprimanded, censured, removed and dismissed from the service. Beside it to carry out the functions of the government the budget provides necessary finances. Their activities can be controlled by controlling the finances made available to them through budget.

(3) *Electorate accountability* : As we all know that every popular government is ultimately responsible to the people or, to be more precise, the electorate which by its votes can make and unmake it. Apart from the general mass of voters, the various organized interests like industrialists, associations, religious groups etc. constantly exert pressure on government and administration to mould their policies and acts in their favour. Thus, in those countries where institutions of direct democracy exist, popular control manifests itself directly through initiative, referendum direct elections of officials, and recall.

(4) *Professional bodies accountability* : In every country officials of professional categories such as doctors, engineers, lawyers, teachers, computer analysts etc. are also responsible to their professional bodies like the bar

councils or medical councils for maintaining the minimum standards of these professions. And if they are guilty of unprofessional conduct, even their names may be removed by these professional bodies from their approved lists or register, thus disqualifying them (persons) from engaging in that profession any longer.

(5) *Judicial accountability* : In a democratic country, the judicial accountability through Judiciary restricts the discretion and arbitrariness of both the executive and administrative agencies; safe guards of rights and liberty of the citizens; helps in redressal of the grievances of the citizens; curbs corruption in government and administration and can declare ultra-virus the acts of the government and administration is case they exceed their jurisdiction. So, if some administrative action causes loss to the citizen, he may knock at the door of the Judiciary for redressal of his grievances. Finally, administration is subject to judicial control exercised by the Courts. Looked at from the point of view of the citizens whose liberties and rights they are intended to protect, the controls exercised by the courts are called judicial remedies for the citizens against official excesses or abuse of power, are the two faces of the same coin.

(6) *Ombudsman-lokpal and lokayukta accountability* : As a good government must provide a citizen an opportunity of seeking redress from arbitrary actions of civil servants, to look into the problems of individual citizens who feel aggrieved by the decisions of civil servants. India has made attempts to institute the office of ombudsman to give the citizen an independent hearing about his grief; and to remove inefficiency and mal practices pervading in the administration. On the recommendation of the Administrative Reforms Commission (ARC), 1966, a Bill

providing for Ombudsman-Lokpal was introduced in the Lok Sabha (House of People) on May 9, 1968 but due to political changes and other reasons it is yet to be passed by Parliament. However, states like Maharashtra, Madhya Pradesh, Karnataka, Bihar, Orissa, Himachal Pradesh, and Rajasthan have appointed Lokayuktas.[6]

(7) Political Parties, Interest Groups, Press and Public

Accountability

In the Parliamentary democracy, political parties and interest groups too play an important role in expressing public opinion and they check the arbitrary use of powers and actions of the executive along with administrative executive. Press also plays an important role to enforce administrative accountability through editorials, news regarding administrative irregularities, mismanagement, inefficiency, delays and corrupt practices of the civil servants. Even public get their grievances ventilated through columns of newspapers.

Limitations of Accountability

Public servants feel primarily accountable to their agencies or superiors, whereas the public's problem is to hold them accountable. Now to what extent and in what ways administrative accountability would be achieved is a matter of legal-institutional arrangements as well as political and social culture. As we all know the working of the process of accountability is not simple and easy, there are, however, some limitations to administrative accountability :

- First of all, accountability, being culture oriented operates withinthe cultural atmosphere of a political system. The nature and meaning of administrative accountability, to a large extent, are therefore, defined by it.
- Secondly, administrative accountability is conditioned by

the political structure of a country. Here for example, the nature and extent of administrative accountability will be different in the unitary system from that in a federal system. In India the problem is more complicated where personnel of the All India Services (IAS/IPS/IFS) are recruited and regulated by the Union Government but work under State Governments, Corporation, autonomous agencies etc. So they cannot be held fully accountable to the latter because they remain under the disciplinary power of the former.

- Thirdly, when government enters into business or manufacturing i.e. public enterprises and undertakes some commercial activities, new problems of administrative accountability of the managers arise. Infact administrative accountability needs to be specially defined as the pattern and practices of management have to be different from those of a typical government department.
- Fourthly, sometimes administrative accountability is limited in situations which may be called 'non-administration'. In fact, it is really very hard to insure administrative accountability where there is hardly any administration worth the name. In those administrative systems where decisions are taken by bypassing the formal administrative institutions and procedures, it is almost next to impossible to expect proper kind of administrative accountability.
- Fifthly, trade unions activities too sometimes set a limit of accountability to the departmental rules and the regulations or even budgetary norms.
- Lastly, sometimes even professional ethics of a person may come into conflict with his administrative ethics. This is particularly so where technical specialists or professionals are employed in government services. To conclude, it may be stressed that government and

administrative accountability in a democratic country like India is of great significance. Administrative accountability has to be insured through dynamic role of legislature, executive, electorates, professional bodies, judiciary, political parties, press and the public. Therefore making administration honest, accountable and responsive, public should not only be aware of policies but should also be active, aware, vigilant, intelligent, enthusiastic and cooperative. Beside administrative accountability also depends on the administrative culture of the country.

The Concept of Indian Administrative Culture

In India public service is generally viewed as a high and a noble calling. It is service in the cause of the nation and there can be no service higher than that of the sovereign state. People who join it do not anticipate becoming rich and famous, but majority of them feel a basic commitment to the values of public service; others develop such a commitment after working in the government for some time.

No administrator functions in a vacuum. As one is influenced heavily by the current cultural milieu : i.e. values, belief and attitude prevalent in society, as well as the culture unique to the organization. Culture basically represents a pattern of values and behaviour, where response pattern persists over a period of time and gets institutionalized. Due to these patterns there are different Agrarian, Industrial and Transitia societies with sala model bureaucracies.[7]

Every country whether under-developed, developing and developed has its own administrative culture. The overall socio-economic and political environment in which the administration works has a direct bearing upon its functionaries, and goes to mould their manner, style and behaviour pattern; their aspirations, ethos and values are shaped by them. These, in combination, constitute what many are called the Administrative Culture. The administrative culture is a complex phenomenon. Today it is not easy to identify the parameters and dimensions that constitute administrative culture. It is difficult even to say whether administrative culture is something distinct or it is only a subsystem of the culture of a country. Nevertheless, it is realized that the administrator and his outlook or world view, his perception of the natural goals and functional purposes, politico-administrative environment, the socio-cultural norms and ideals of the society, his perception and the response of the citizens help in understanding as well as determining the administrative culture of any society.

The administrative culture of India, as well as of many other Third World nations, has drawn on two basic foundations: (a) the colonial heritage, and (b) the traditional influences.[8] these two have greatly shaped the character of the prevailing administrative culture of these countries.[9]

The administrator, as an individual and as part of the system, through his manners, behaviour, ways and style, influences the formation of an administrative personality which also shapes the attitude and motivations of that individual. The shaping of his personality is affected by time. It may still persist or even change over time. The overall impact of personality and time is on the situation in which the administration functions. Whether it functions effectively and efficiently or ineffective and inefficiently, depend upon the administrative culture which has a direct reference to the laws of the land, rules, regulations, procedures, norms, manners etc. Beside it the style of administration, on the one hand, depends upon social economic and political environment, and the public of that nation. Thus culture is the man-made part of the environment. It is the totality of belief, norms and values related to the regulatory pattern in administrator's behaviour.

Carl Friedrich opines that inculcation of appropriate values among administrators serves as the major check on the bureaucracy. This view holds that formal institutional checks will usually fail if officials do not have sound democratic and administrative values.[10] In essence, administrators must have an internal compass i.e. values to point them in the appropriate direction and way.

The view as given above led by Carl Friedrich brings us to the question of integrity, ethics and values in Civil service. Indeed in the world of today we need such men in public service who have strong minds, great hearts, true faith and ready hands. The administrators have to exhibit own "integration of universal values, such as wisdom and reverence, honesty and integrity, devotion to human interests as well as those traditions which are favoured in the cultural stream of a particular civilization. Administrators have to develop as sense of mission, an understanding of inter-relations and a compelling sense of overall objectives and values".[11]

The maintenance of moral standards and norms in the conduct of public affairs in a democratic country India tends to become major problems for the people. These days we hear and read a lot about various kinds' scams and lack of integrity in public life. The dictionary meaning of world integrity is soundness of moral principles, character of uncorrupted virtue, uprightness, honesty, sincerity etc. Infact the concept of integrity is an outcome of modern legal system of rule of law. Integrity is, indeed, the most essential attribute of a welfare and democratic state.[12]

Today "Speed money" is reported to have become a fairly common type of corrupt practice, particularly in matters relating to grant of licenses, permit, revenue, police etc. Now a question arises has corruption become a part of the Indian DNA ? Here the answer is no as ordinary Indians are as honest as people anywhere in the world, Indians by nature are not corrupt but it cannot be denied that the Sanskrit word 'bhrasht' (corrupt) conveys the sense of corruption better for us. It means fallen or dropped, strayed or deviated from, separated from, deprived of, expelled or turned our from, decayed, lost, vicious, deprived. We are all this and much more. Abuse of authority is a natural propensity in all societies. And people submit to such abuse because they have no realistic option. Here yes generally it is seen our irresponsibility and "Chalta hai'[13] (OK) approach to things make us more corrupt India.

In area of technology we think machines will minimize corruption i.e. "Computerization' will solve all our problems. What could be a greater instance of corruption than trusting a machine more than a fellow human being? Today it is a disease of the soul; it is a character flaw, an imaginative shortcoming. At present from santri (policeman) to mantri (minister) all are corrupt. Thus, we need to increase the risks of corruption to unacceptably high levels, and enhance rewards for good conduct. Comprehensive electoral reform including proportional representation and funding reform, substantial decentralization and empowerment of local governments, measures for efficient justice will radically alter the risks and rewards and promote honesty.

Ethics has several attributes, some of which are universalistic in nature, while others are also bound by time and place. It may be specific to a particular task, situation, profession or area of responsibility, e.g., ethics of a doctor, a chartered accountant, a teacher or an administrator. Certain things are expected from everyone while there may be a few specific things expected according to the nature of groups or responsibilities. Ethics is something related to a state of mind, a way of looking at things which may develop into a pattern of behaviour or way of life and social conduct.

According to O. Glenn Stahl "the problem of ethical conduct of public officials arises by virtue of the power and influence that he commands and the commitment that he undertakes of loyal and disinterested service to the public".[14] another view has been articulated by Carl Friedrich[15] when he argues that the responsibility of the official is moral responsibility. The quality of administration and policy making depends upon the official's sense of responsibility of the standards of his profession, a sense of duty to the public that is entirely inward, and adherence to the technological basis of his particular job or the branch of the service in which he works. Infact administrator is responsible to two dominant factors : technical knowledge and popular sentiment. With regard to personal control, education and training programmes are very important in enhancing administrative ethics. But such programmes should be designed to challenge people's imagination about values and help them to think clearly about principles and how to apply these principles to the real world of government.

Values play significant role in administrative ethics. We all know values are the driving force of human behaviour. What a man does, can be explained in terms of this value structure. They help to determine one's norms, standards and goals and to select the means to realize chosen goals or ends of action. A value has been defined as "a conception, explicit or implicit, distinctive of an individual or characteristics of a group of the desirable which influences the selection from available modes, means and ends of action."[16]. Values differ from individual to individual, group to group and community to community, they are closely related to culture and change with time. Values are of different kinds such as social values, historical values, structural values, political values, institutional values, professional values, personal values, etc. Generally, every individual builds up his value system on cultural influences, religion, science, innovation, ethical influence, life experience etc.

Now a question arises will one adhere to a personal code which upholds obligations to self, family and friends ? And this could clash with the public interest or professional obligations. Infact what is required in public service is the conciliation of personal and the professional or institutional values. To quote Peter Drucker, "the blending of institutional and individual values becomes the ultimate principle in administration."[17] Values more than techniques, are the eventual determinants of the actions of the administrators.

Factors Affecting Indian Adminstrative Culture

In India there are various factors affecting Indian Administrative Culture. Every administrative culture system is built upon the following factors which influences and affects it. Some of the factors are as follows :

(1) *Individual Value System* : All administrators have. a philosophy; that is, an individual value system which prioritizes basic convictions. A review of the literature concludes that an individual's value system is determined by cultural norms, education and experience that he or she has been exposed to. This individual value system, when combined with the unique history of an organization, determines an administrator's behaviour.

We all know that no administrator functions in a vacuum as one is influenced heavily by his surroundings i.e. cultural values, beliefs, attitude prevalent in society, as well as the culture unique to the organization. A fact often overlooked however, is that the present has been determined by the past. Beside it an individual is influenced by the education. Here education is the understanding and interpretation of knowledge. After education comes the experience gained by working in any organization for a long period.

(2) *Family* : We know family plays an important role in the society. Every administrator is a part of a family which in turn is a part of society. It is the family where a person learns his first lesson of life about what is bad and what is good; etc. The good qualities and behaviour which an administrator gets from his or her family helps them in work process also. Due to family impact Indians are more gods fearing than most other cultures, and we still have strong families and peer pressure to moderate our behaviour.

(3) *Socio-cultural dimension (Society)* : Every administrator is a part of society. Indian society is a stratified one, both vertically and horizontally. The Hindus are divided into four major castes i.e. Brahmins, Vaishya, Kshatriya and Sudras and each caste has numerous subcastes. This has, in its turn, influenced the stratification process among Muslims and Christians too. In modern times although the caste system is gradually shedding its traditional purpose, under the impact of universal suffrage, it evokes new meaning and serves other purposes.

Horizontally, Indian society is divided along regional, districts, states, linguistic, and religious lines and these have varying degrees of influence on the civil service. Although Weberian model would expect the civil servants to be objective and impersonal in their administrative actions but we have seen that they are continually exposed to forces drawing sustenance from caste, community, religion, region, language etc. and some succumb to these forces and their demands. The impact of socio-cultural environment on the theory and practice of government is felt in other ways as well. Society in India still remains feudal and the public officials come from this feudal stock that belongs to urban elitist families. This introduces contradictions and conflicts of varying magnitude in the structure and patterns of inter action in society. Formally, administrators are objective and impartial but society expects them to safeguard the interests of their kith and kin.

(4) *Education* : Education is very essential for mankind. Infact education is the understanding and interpretation of knowledge. Education tries to mould and help in developing the aptitude of person and aim at increasing administrator's personnel skill. Formal and informal both type of education is essential for public. These days the Indian Administrative Services are joined not only by man and woman having degree of arts, social science,

commerce and science but technocrats with B. Tech., B.E. and M.B.B.S. degree. Thus after joining the service when decisions are taken by them they are influenced by the education which they have received.

(5) *Religion* : Administrative culture of any country is influenced by its religion. Although India is a secular nation but majority of people is Hindus. The Hindu religion is rooted in a very powerful ideological system with unification of a divided society. In India there are religious foundations of administrative culture.[18]

(6) *Political System* : For the developing nations like India where speedy socio- economic development has to be steadily pushed through, the nature, character and culture of civil services assume special significance. The first problem is how to declass the civil service that culturally belonged the colonial era and served the imperial interest. As the Indian experience shows, the colonial administrative system was allowed to continue even after independence and it was thought that the changed political leadership and institutional framework coupled with proper training and motivation would bring about desired 'cultural' changes in the Administrative Service. The result of all this was neutral, representative and politicized administrator a political.

Today political system is not wholly segregated from social milieu, but together they provide the settings for functioning of public administration. In India loyalty to the nation, equality and a written constitution influences the administrative culture. The most important influence on the nature, structure and functioning of Indian Administrative System is that of the Indian Constitution. The influence of the Constitution on administration is broadly of two types : the formal or discernible influences that prescribe the configuration of the administrative system and the informal influences which determine the role, responsibility and responsiveness of the administrative system, the character of governance and the behaviour of administrators in our country. Beside all this administrative culture is influenced by different political parties, pressure groups, interest groups etc.

(7) *Mass Media* : We all know mass media like Radio, films; Television, Newspapers, books etc. play an important role in the administrative system. When Late Shree Rajiv Gandhi became Prime Minister in year 1984 promised, among other things, to revamp the public administration of the country. In 1985, a number of programmes began on the Indian Television under private initiative and these brought within their ambit the pathological problems of administration. Here mention many particularly be made of television serials like 'Panorama', 'Sach Ki Parchhayian' (In the shadow of Truth), 'Aaihna' (Mirror), 'Chaupal' (related to villagers and farmers), 'Rajni' (related to administrative problems faced by common man), 'Janvani' (the voice of people), 'Police Public', 'Ankhon Dekhi' (Eye Seen), etc. Mass Media always served a useful purpose, in the sense of instilling a sense of accountability in the administration and so improving its efficiency.

(8) *Economic dimension* : Among economic factors poverty, hunger, unemployment, general scarcities are the chief features of the Indian economy. Some of these themselves being the direct outcome of the economic plans, policies and strategies of development followed over the decades. Beside all this the rapidly growing population has partly wiped out the economic gains achieved by the country through planning. Due to this there is disequilibrium between the public and administration. The problem of poverty and unemployment in society results in intense pressures on government jobs and even overstaffing

government offices. Shortages, compounded by government interferenc , breed pressures for supply and consequent corruption. The administrator, since he controls the distribution of essential commodities to the public, finds himself subjected to heavy pressures. Thus, the prevailing political atmosphere, the falling standards of public life and the loss of moral values among the politicians have bred a corresponding insensitivity, demoralize and unresponsiveness among administrators.

The public administration constitutes merely an aspect of the social system. As other aspects such as value system, economic, social, political, cultural and educational, constantly interact with the administrative system. Hence enhancement of the administrative capability requires changes in the social environment i.e. development of the society. So long as the majority of the public remain poor, uneducated and unaware of their rights and duties, they cannot properly participate in programs of development. Import of high technology can not deliver the goods in the situation of general economic and social backwardness. So if the data received from the field are defective, the processing of the data on a computer by highly trained specialist is of no use. Enhancement of administrative capability, therefore, requires development of the society generally, even as administrative development helps all round development. In the end we come to conclusion that administrative culture is not just a function of the training environment and the value systems of civil service. Infact, it reflects the changing values in the social environment itself.

The people in developing countries suffer from a number of problems, such as poverty, hunger unemployment, bad health, illiteracy, corruption and authoritarianism. The state is responsible for bringing about development. Hence the state has to shoulder more and more responsibility. Since the state functions through the government, and the government, in turn depends to a large extent upon the administration, the administrator's role also keeps expanding. The Indian administration during the course of its evolution has acquired quite a few aberrations and irregularities in its functioning. As per K.V.V. Subramanyam,[19] some of the major afflictions are :

(i) Chronic and almost incurable delays at all levels;

(ii) Equally chronic habit of evading decision making;

(iii) Non-availability or inaccessibility of officials at all levels to individual citizen;

(iv) Singular lack of courtesy, consideration and concern to the grievances of individual citizens or groups;

(v) Lack of a humane approach to the visitor in any government office;

(vi) Failure and indifference of officials to bend their energies to issues affecting common man;

(vii) Time consuming meetings and discussions with ministers and high officials which are mostly unproductive and which eat into administrative time;

(viii) Spectacular schemes from political leadership which are mostly populist and fail to touch the grassroot;

(ix) Failure of system of inspection and controls which are time honoured tools of gauging the work and efficiency at all levels; and (x) Consequently corruption in the form of 'speed money' for getting irregular things done.

Due to above problems people have no trust in administration. Trust in administration is very significant and essential for developing country like India. In simple words Trust means faith and belief in your administrative system. Public can only have trust when administration is open transparent, efficient, responsive, sensitive, accountable and responsible.

Public Administration for the 21st Century has endured by conceding and adapting to the changing times. It has risen to the challenges of modern times, state has not been static and has metamorphosed from a Political State to the Administrative State and to the Bureaucratic State and is today on the threshold of becoming a Cybernetic State.[20] In this state, "government functions as a servo-mechanism, conjoining the polity and economy to achieve public objectives,"[21] and distinction between public and private disappears. Even the decision making is likely to be more efficient and rational due to easy accessibility of information through computers. Besides; it new concept of man i.e. the highly educated (urban class), complex, violent, over ambitions new man replaces the simple, innocent, submissive and contended man. So now it is not easy that public can accept maladministration which is corrupt, unaccountable, unresponsive, insensitive, time consuming, inefficient, etc. Now for faith and belief in administration some tools of trust are essential for present modern times. Some such tools are such as :

(1) *Open and Transparent Administration* : Public can easily have trust and faith in administration if it is open and transparent. In India in order to achieve open and transparent administration, the Government instituted an Inter-ministerial working Group under the Chairmanship of H.D.Shourie, Director, Common Cause to examine the feasibility and need of introducing a full fledged Right to Information Act so as to meet the needs of an open, transparent and responsive government. Based on its recommendation, a bill was introduced and passed in one of the session of the Parliament, which ensured transparency in government operations, and every department now have an information officer to provide information. Some other administrative reforms are also being undertaken by the Government as creation of

facilitation counters, establishing a code of ethics for Public Services tackling corruption and cleansing the administration, and ensuring the stability of tenure and a scheme for Civil Service Boards etc.

(2) *Citizens Charter* : For trust in government now even government's accountability syndrome has been changing. Today we talk about citizen's Charter introduced for the first time by the British Government in year 1991. The key aspects of the charter are the requirements that public agencies publish commitments to standards of service, that there be independent monitoring and publication of standards achieved, and that mechanism be established through which the 'customer' can achieve satisfaction when standards are not met.[22] It included various forms of compensation and alternative arrangements for service provision where agencies do not live up to their promises.

In India, the then Prime Minister, had inaugurated a conference of Chief Secretaries in 1996, called to develop "An Agenda for an Effective and Responsive Administration" to make the public services more efficient, clean, transparent, accountable and citizen friendly. The conference recommended that accountability should be interpreted in a larger sense in relation to public satisfaction and responsive delivery of services, and a phased introduction of Citizen's Charter for as many service institutions as possible. Later on the Department of Administrative Reforms and Public Services in 1997 evolved an "Action Plan on Effective and Responsive Administration", based on the responses and reactions received from officials, experts, voluntary agencies, citizen's groups, media etc. The three main areas of Action Plan that were discussed in the Conference of Chief Ministers on May 24, 1997 were :[23]

(i) Making administration accountable and citizen-friendly,

(ii) Ensuring transparency and right to information, and

(iii) Taking measures to cleanse and motivate civil services.

The State Governments and the Ministries / Departments at the Centre are all involved, in some manner or the other, in providing public services. Government of India has directed them and other agencies with public interface to formulate a citizen's charter, lay down time-limits and standards for services, avenues of grievance redressal and put in place monitoring systems and independent scrutiny to ensure implementation of the charter.

(3) *Right to Information* : Right to Information is not a new one for developed countries like U.S.A. (1964), Germany, U.K., Australia etc. In developing countries like India this new concept became popular in recent years. On 6 August, 2002 the Central Cabinet decided to give acceptance to the laws related to right to information. Under this act the citizens will have right to have any information related to government procedures and their life. Beside it there is a provision if government's procedure is affecting freedom of any citizen then in that case government will have to inform him within 48 hours. Infact one bill related to it was presented in Lok Sabha on July 2002, on which one parliamentary committee was established and on its recommendations only the bill was finalized and later on accepted. In India for the first time there was a case in the Supreme Court, Uttar Pradesh Government v/s Raj Narain then it was said that every citizen of India has right to get information regarding public works. Before this in year 1960 also there was a case on Humdard Dawakhana V/S Government of India. At that time also some comments regarding right to information for citizens was given by the Supreme Court. In India our state Rajasthan is the first state to give legal status to right to information.

Due to Right to Information Act, all government offices at centre and state level have computerized facilitation/information counter so that information and assistances is available to the public on various essential services and approvals. Public facilitation centre provide information regarding services, schemes, procedures through brochures, booklets, reports, position of waiting list and applications through computers, screens updated every day, and through websites, utilizing Interactive Voice system where feasible for enquiry response etc.

(4) *Responsive Administration* : For trust in administration the citizens expect civil servants to be responsive to their requests and demands. A citizen who asks some thing of a government has the right to expect a response i.e. answering and replying and to be treated as a legitimate source of demands. Responsive administration is that which identifies the needs and requirements of the people and formulates plans and programmes in accordance with those needs. It even evaluates development programmes in order to ascertain that people have been benefited and develops procedures for future improvements. For campaigning transparency in administration there are examples such as Ajmer experience in Rajasthan state of India where to check corruption in Panchayat System the Mazdoor Kisan Shakti Sangathan (people's association) gave slogan 'Hamare Paise Hamara Hisab' (Our money our accounts), in Jaipur, Beawar and Alwar districts there were dharana (agitations) against corruption and in Bilaspur Experience (Madhya Pradesh) here Divisional Commissioner (i.e. Civil Servant) decided to provide to the people the right to information about the public distribution system and other government programmes.

(5) *Sensitive Administration and Administrative Accountability* : People trust sensitive administration. As

we all know every government is ultimately responsible to the people that are the electorate which by its votes can make and unmake it. Holders of public office are accountable for their decisions and actions to the public. So if power is not to be abused, it must be accompanied by responsibility. For the proper exercise of the powers vested in them the administrative offices and officials have, therefore, to be made responsible to appropriate authorities.

(6) *Redress of Public Grievances* : Redress of public grievances also plays a significant role in modern administration. The objective of redressal machinery has been not only to provide speedy and effective redresses of grievances, but also to smooth the relationship between public and government. For public trust government even tries to utilize the media for transmission of information on various innovative measures taken by it and for creating awareness among the people about their rights and privileges and the services, including grievance redress and arrangements available to them. The machinery includes police, anti-corruption departments, CID, CBI, Lokpal (not yet), Lokayukta (States), Central Vigilance Commission etc. To supplement the governmental effort in the sphere of public grievances, voluntary agencies are being involved like the Standing Committees of - Voluntary Agencies (SCOVA) in the ministry of Health, Department of Women and Child Development, Department of Youth Affairs & Sports, Department of Electronics, Department of Pensions and Pensioner's Welfare etc. Beside it with a view to bringing, face to face, the aggrieved with the department concerned for on the spot redress of public grievances, the concept of Shikayat Adalat[24] (Grievances Court) has been introduced as an innovative scheme. The

scheme has been tried out in the Department of Tele Communications, Delhi Development Authority etc. and has evoked good response.

(7) *Client-Oriented Administration* : In developing countries like India development administration is positively oriented towards meeting the needs of the specific target groups, like small and marginal farmers of landless agricultural labourers and rural artisans. Many target groups centered or beneficiary-group oriented organizations have to be created so as to provide these under-privileged sections the requisite goods and services. It has been suggested that today development administration is 'people-oriented' administration which gives priority to the needs of its beneficiaries by preparing, reviewing, and if necessary, changing the policies, programmes and activities aimed at the satisfaction of the needs of people in question. The welfare of the weaker sections (S.C. & S.T.) is a part of the administrative values. This feature points out the 'humane' character of administration.

(8) *Participation-Oriented Administration* : Administration accepts for its purposes the principle of associative and participative system. Here, people are not treated as mere passive recipients of benefits or goods and services. Now they are taken as active participants in the formulation and implementation of development plans, policies and programmes. It is recognized that centralized administration will not only be unable to take cognizance of local problems in a realistic frame, but it would also be deprived of the use of local initiatives, energies and resources. Hence, effective formulation of programmes (adult education programme, women development, family welfare etc.) and their implementation with the help and association of the local people is now a well recognized principle of

administration by giving people an increasing share in the governance and management of developmental affairs of the government.

(9) *Efficient Administration* : The activities of administration are directed towards two ends - provision of certain services for the benefit of the people such as transport, education, health, welfare, etc. and regulation of the individual's conduct in the interest of the public good. The former kind of activity is beneficial and does not present, except in rare cases, any serious problems of enforcement, but latter i.e., regulatory activity is often onerous and restrictive in relation to the individual and often produces clashes between him and the administrative authorities. So Administration has to be efficient and effective which people can trust. There is, however considerable frustration and dissatisfaction amongst the public, especially the weaker sections of society, about the apathy, inefficiency, irresponsiveness, corrupt, and lack of accountability of public servants.

(10) *Code of Ethics for Public Services* : People trust administration if it is responsive and clean. This depends, inter alia, on adherence of the employees in public services to ethical standards and the basic principles of the constitution, such as secularism, social and economic justice, attention to the needs of weaker sections and vulnerable groups, equality and rule of law. It is the obligation of every employee in the public service to uphold the Rule of law and respect for human rights, and to act solely in the public interest while making recommendations or exercising administrative authority. Administrators must maintain the highest standards of probity and integrity. The efforts could be centered on immediate and exemplary prosecution and removal of corrupt officials without any

political protection, while supporting honest and competent employees. Even in States the Lok Ayuktas could be adequately empowered and resourced to deal effectively with all cases or allegation of corruption.

Thus we come to conclusion that if above given tools of trust in administration are followed public we will have faith, belief in government as well as administration. The element of accountability, administrative culture and trust in administration all three together can lead nation to progress and development. Regarding administrative accountability Prof. Dwivedi rightly says : "In general, an overall environment of responsible behaviour must emerge if a country wished to sustain an accountable administration."[25]

Since the search for good administration dynamic and sensitive, clean, open and transparent, responsive and responsible, efficient and effective, accountable and consequently, the need for its restructuring and remodeling not necessarily its reinventing is something of a moving equilibrium of human affairs is an unstable and uncertain world. Hence, the paramount need for, and sustained interest and attention to, 'matters administrative' which are dismissed lightly, at considerable cost to society later on. Beside it the search for administrative accountability in terms of effectiveness as well as responsiveness is a continuing process because it is full of human dilemmas.

Thus the issues of accountability, culture and trust are mutually interrelated and interdependent. The accountability of public servants depends on the culture of the society to which they belong as well as the amount of trust citizens repose in their ability and competence. The public in turn must device methods to ensure the proper accountability of its administrative system which alone can ensure their trust in both.

In the era of globalization, liberalization, privatization and human security there is no doubt that the accountability of administration with good values among administrators and trust of people in administration along with its tools, if formulated and implemented in an objective, conscious, moral and committed manner to give the public their due can lead us Towards Good Governance in India.

REFERENCES

1. Asokh Mukhopadhyay, *Administrative Accountability : A conceptual Analysis;* Indian Journal of Public Administration, Vol. XXIX; No. 3, July- Sept., 1983, I.I.P.A., New Delhi; p. 473
2. *Ibid*, p.474
3. Charles H. Levine, B. Guy Peters and Frank J. Thompson; *Public Administration Challenges Choices, Consequences;* Scott, Foresman and Co., Glen view Illinois; 1990, p. 191-192.
4. Ibid.
5. Asokh Mukhopadhyay; *op. cit.;* p. 481.
6. See, *Annual Report* of the Lokayukta of Rajasthan State, Jaipur, 1975-76, p.10-11.
7. F.W.Riggs, *Administration in developing Countries : The Theory of Prismatic Society,* Boston, Houghton Mifflin, 1964, p. 162.
8. O.P.Dwivedi, *Administrative Theology : Dharma of Public Officials;* I.J.P.A., Vol. XXXVI; No. 3; July-September, 1990, I.I.P.A., New Delhi; p. 406.
9. R.N. Thakur, *Contemporary administrative culture and Indian social reality* : towards a model building; I.J.P.A., Vol. XXXVI; No. 3; July- September, 1990, I.I.P.A., New Delhi; p. 480-481.
10. Charles H. Levine : *op. cit;* p. 191.

11. Marina R. Pinto; *Values in Public Services; Indian Journal of Public Administration;* Vol. XXXV; No. 1; Jan-March, 1989, I.I.P.A. Delhi, p.61-62

12. *Ibid.,* p.70-72

13. 'Chalta hai' common hindi language word used for work O.K.

14. O. Glenn Stahl, *Public Personnel Administration,* New York, Harper & Row, 1976, p.271

15. Charles H. Levine; *op. cit.* p. 197

16. M.R. Pinto; *op. cit.* p.60

17. Peter F. Drucker, *The Practice of Management,* New York, Harper, 1965, p. 185

18. O.P.Dwivedi; op. cit.; p. 408-409

19. K.V.V. Subramanyam; *"Administration in Crisis : Time for Soul-Searching",* The Hindu (News Paper), Delhi, April 23, 1996.

20. Allen Shick, *"Toward the Cybernetic State",* Transaction, Vol.7, February, 1970

21. *Ibid.*

22. *R.B.Jain; Public Administration in India;* New Delhi, Deep & Deep Publications Pvt. Ltd., 2002, p. 208-209.

23. Action Plan for an effective and responsive Government Department of Administrative Reforms and Public Grievances, Ministry of Personnel & Public Grievances, New Delhi, Government of India.

24. *Ibid.* 25. O. P. Dwivedi, *Reflections on moral Government and Public Service as a Vocation;* The Indian Journal of Public Administration, July-September 1995, I.J.P.A., Vol. XLI; No. 3; I.I.P.A., New Delhi; p. 297.

8

Democratic Citizenship and Human Rights

Defining Democratic Citizenship

Democratic citizenship has been described as a 'polysemous and ontested concept'. At the core, however, citizenship 'is always a matter of belonging to a community, which entrains politics and rights'. Citizenship always has a political dimension, because citizens have the capacity to determine the law (Audigier, 1998). In Europe, citizenship is based on respect for justice, human rights, fundamental freedoms and the rule of law.

Citizens belong to communities, defined as groupings of people who recognise that they have something in common. What unites them may simply be an acceptance of the legitimacy of the state within which they live. It may also be a strong affective bond based on shared history, ethnicity, religion or common purpose. States are internationally recognised entities with governments which have the power to confer nationality or the right to residence in the state's territory. In Europe, states have the obligation to respect the rights of all those who come under their jurisdiction. This means that, in theory, nationals and non-nationals living within a state can exercise citizenship. That means that they can participate in the economic, social and political life of their community.

Thus, although citizenship is often closely associated with nationality, it is a freestanding and independent concept. The nation is only one possible (imagined) community within which citizenship is exercised . Citizenship is most commonly experienced at local levels and it exists at supranational levels such as Europe. Recent discussions on citizenship posit a new term 'world citizenship' or 'global citizenship' reflecting the new context of the communications age.

Diverse language communities can live together harmoniously within a state or a wider political entity such as Europe. However different language communities may not have equal power. Citizenship stresses the notion of equal respect and dignity even where there is inequality of power. It also acknowledges the right of individuals to group together and engage in political and cultural activity to assert their rights. Such non-violent democratic activity, is one legitimate, even exemplary expression of citizenship.

Citizenship in the member states of the Council of Europe is based on a commitment to fundamental freedoms. The liberal democracies of Europe are founded on principles first proclaimed in the eighteenth century in such documents as the American Declaration of Independence and the French Declaration of the Rights of Man and the Citizen. The principles were re-defined in the aftermath of the Second World War in the United Nations Charter and the Universal Declaration of Human Rights. The European Convention on Human Rights transformed the principles into legally enforceable guarantees. The twin pillars of European political values are 'an effective political democracy' on the one hand and 'a common understanding and observance of [...] human rights'.

The Committee of Ministers of the Council of Europe, in their Declaration and Programme of Education for Democratic Citizenship of 7 May 1999, at the time of the 50th anniversary of the Council of Europe reaffirmed their vision of building Europe as:

a freer, more tolerant and just society based on solidarity, common values and a cultural heritage enriched by its diversity (Council of Europe, 1999).

Languages are a particularly important component of this cultural heritage. The diversity of languages contributes to the richness of Europe's culture. Their preservation and development depend on common understandings of citizenship.

For the ministers, education for democratic citizenship, based on the rights and responsibilities of citizenship is a lifelong learning experience and a participative process developed in various contexts which, *inter alia:*

- Equips men and women to play an active part in public life and to shape in a responsible way their own destiny and that of their society.
- Aims to instil a culture of human rights.
- Prepares people to live in a multicultural society and to deal with difference knowledgeably, sensibly, tolerantly and morally.
- Strengthens social cohesion, mutual understanding and solidarity.

A further definition of democratic citizenship, as understood by the Council of Europe is:

About greater participation, social cohesion, access, equity and solidarity. Democratic citizenship is about inclusion rather than exclusion, participation rather than marginalisation, culture and values rather than simple procedural issues (such as voting) and E about being active in shaping understandings and practices of citizenship.

In terms of education for democratic citizenship, it is:

All those practices and activities aimed at making young people and adults better equipped to participate actively in democratic life by assuming and exercising their rights and responsibilities in society.

This expresses what is sometimes referred to as 'political literacy'. Citizens need to know about the institutions, problems and practices of a democracy and require skills and values which enable them to be effective and exercise influence locally, regionally and nationally.

Democratic Citizenship and Languages

Citizens are able to participate in the life of their communities when they have rights, fundamental freedoms, legal and political equality and protection from discrimination. All of these are guaranteed within the member states of the Council of Europe by national laws and the ECHR. Several of the articles of this Convention refer to language or have particular relevance.

Article 10 guarantees freedom of expression. Within Europe there is the right to speak, broadcast and publish in any language, so long as the content is respectful of the rights, privacy and dignity of others. Freedom of association (article 11) allows meetings for cultural, political, religious or educational purposes and the creation of trade unions, political parties and pressure groups. Discrimination on the basis of language is specifically outlawed in article 14. As one example, an individual charged with a criminal offence is required to be kept informed 'in a language which he understands'.

Communities, particularly the political communities that are member states, are therefore expected to be multilingual entities in which freedom of expression is not constrained, insofar as it remains respectful of human rights, and freedom of association is guaranteed. Healthy democracies are composed of individuals who are able to communicate with their fellow citizens and use their linguistic skills to participate actively in, for instance, associations, movements, cultural groups and political parties.

Issues of language, identities and participation are common to policies for the teaching and learning both of languages and of democratic citizenship. Central to both is an awareness of and concern for human rights as a legal and an ethical basis for citizenship and for education.

Language Rights

Language is one of the most important social and cultural markers of identity and the international community in its essence is multilingual. Although relations between language communities can be a source of tension within and between nations, the achievement of equality of citizenship in multilingual communities is a demonstration of the possibility of success of democracy and may be considered exemplary of the very essence of democracy. Although language is sometimes perceived as a marker of difference, the linguistic capacities of human beings are a unifying feature, distinguishing humans from other species and bringing with them an automatic entitlement to human rights.

Article 2 of the Universal Declaration of Human Rights and the International Covenant on Civil and Political Rights as well as Article 14 of the European Convention on Human Rights (1950) protect individuals against discrimination in their entitlement to rights and specifically mention language in this respect. The International Covenant, in its Article 27 refers to linguistic minorities within states and affirms:

Persons belonging to such minorities shall not be denied the right, in community with the other members of their group, to enjoy their own culture, to profess and practise their own religion, or to use their own language.

Although human rights apply to individuals, this formulation starts to approach the concept of group rights. Communication between individuals is by definition a group phenomenon. Languages die if there are insufficient social contexts in which they can be used. The use of a minority language is sometimes perceived as a threat by members of other language groups. As the European Language Council points out in its Policy Paper on *Multilingualism and the less widely used and less taught languages,* the most likely impediment to the right to communicate in one's own language is the possible inability of others to comprehend, not to say the possible hostility users of minority languages may face. Education for linguistic pluralism and tolerance can start to remove obstacles to the full democratic participation of individuals from different language communities.

Within international law, the main instrument covering Europe is the European Charter for Regional or Minority Languages of 1992. Its purpose is partly to protect minority languages as part of 'Europe's cultural wealth and traditions'. More positively it stresses 'the value of interculturalism and multilingualism' which are essential elements of the Council of Europe's project to build a continent-wide democratic space:

> the protection and promotion of regional or minority languages in the different countries and regions of Europe represent an important contribution to the building of a Europe based on the principles of democracy and cultural diversity within the framework of national sovereignty and territorial integrity;
>
> It is confirmed in the Charter that:
>
> the protection and encouragement of regional or minority languages should not be to the detriment of the official languages and the need to learn them.

At a global level, the World Federation of Modern Language Teaching Associations (FIPLV) and UNESCO's Linguapax Committee have been active in drafting further instruments and recommendations such as the Pecs principles (FIPLV, 1991), which informed the Universal Declaration of Linguistic Rights.

This was adopted at the World Conference of Linguistic Rights held in Barcelona 6 - 8 June 1996. It is a comprehensive document with over 50 articles. It is based on the concept of equality for languages and therefore avoids the terms regional or minority languages which have been used to restrict the rights of language communities. Currently the Declaration has no legal force, but it sets out an agenda for policy and legislation.

Its starting point is that 'linguistic rights are individual and collective rights at one and the same time'. It lists five 'inalienable personal rights which may be exercised in any situation' namely:

- To be recognised as a member of a language community.
- To the use of one's own language both in private and in public.
- To the use of one's own name.
- To interrelate and associate with other members of one's language community of origin.
- To maintain and develop one's own culture.

There follow four 'collective rights of language groups', which are:

- For their own language and culture to be taught.
- Access to cultural services.
- An equitable presence of their language and culture in the communications media.
- To receive attention in their own language from government bodies and in socio-economic relations.

Some of these rights are already covered by the ECHR. However, those making policy in the area of language teaching and learning will wish to be sensitive to all these demands, even if they are not in a position to guarantee the full range of linguistic rights.

One right of particular relevance to teachers is the use of one's own name, which is expanded in articles 31 - 34 of the Declaration. The right to a name is also guaranteed under the UN Convention on the Rights of the Child. Schools are still not always respectful of the names of their pupils, particularly where teachers are unfamiliar with naming conventions or pronunciation. Employers too, within Europe, have been known to ask workers, particularly Muslims, to change their name. Education about names, their importance in identity formation and their cultural significance should be part of the curriculum for teachers and for pupils.

The right to attention in one's own language from government bodies implies both that members of a variety of linguistic groups be employed in government service and that some government employees be recruited on the basis of their linguistic skills.

Articles 23 - 30 concern education. Of particular relevance to citizenship is article 23.3:

Education must always be at the service of linguistic and cultural diversity and of harmonious relations between different language communities throughout the world.

In particular language education should be committed to helping to overcome prejudices about the relative value of languages.

Languages and Antiracism

Education for democratic citizenship and human rights is a policy priority in Europe. In May 1999 the Committee of Ministers affirmed: the urgency of strengthening individuals' awareness and understanding of their rights and responsibilities so that they develop a capacity to exercise these rights and respect the rights of others;

The context of this is the continued presence in Europe of ideologies and political parties which are not respectful of diversity. The ministers are:

Concerned by the development of violence, xenophobia, racism, aggressive nationalism and religious intolerance, which constitutes a major threat to the reinforcement of peace and democracy both at national and international level .

The teaching and learning of languages has an important part to play as an element of an interdisciplinary approach to a positive culture of antiracism. Whilst language learning by itself does not necessarily reduce or remove prejudices, when accompanied by other well-conceived educational experiences it can be a powerful contributor to a culture of human rights and equity. This perspective underpins the Common European Framework of Reference.

Negative stereotypes can be played upon by the unscrupulous and dangerous as well as unpleasant forms of inter-community fears and hatreds can be built up into violent backlash against closer European and global co-operation. The best protection against all such forms of racism and xenophobia is provided by knowledge and direct experience of the foreign reality and improved life and communication skills.

The need for mobility and access to information taken together with the importance of mutual understanding and tolerance establish effective communication skills across language boundaries as an indispensable part of the equipment of tomorrow's citizens facing the challenges and opportunities of a transformed European society.

Education for and about human rights and its corollary the refusal to accept racism is potentially a powerful means to strengthen democracy. Such education can make a significant contribution to removing obstacles to the democratic participation of citizens.

The reduction of obstacles to participation, in particular socio-economic obstacles, is an integral part of any strategy aimed at strengthening democratic citizenship.

Language education can help learners acquire an understanding of the, often subtle, mechanisms of racism. One requirement is the preparation and production of appropriate materials. A second is that authentic texts be subject to critical study. A combination of these might be particularly effective.

Those preparing materials for language learning often try to engage students in study and debate of socially and politically controversial issues. Many courses contain a unit on questions of demographic diversity, including immigration. The following guidelines may help writers of materials to avoid reinforcing stereotypes and promote positive intercultural perspectives:

- Acknowledge racism as an explanatory factor of the situation of ethnic minorities in Europe and explore the concept.
- Include oral and written material produced by members of minority communities as well as material from institutional sources such as the press.
- Ensure that the minority perspective includes a political dimension of organisation and struggle as citizens, as well as a cultural dimension.
- Show minority witnesses as dignified human beings with complex identities.
- Include ethnic minority voices and experts in a number of units (e. g. politics, media, history, environment, science) not just the unit on immigration.
- Have an interdisciplinary team approach to producing materials. Work with sociologists, political scientists, specialists in pedagogy.
- Integrate specifically language exercises to reinforce rather than vitiate the antiracist and human rights perspective.

Another promising development is that of *critical discourse analysis* (CDA) which 'is a type of discourse analytical research that primarily studies the way social power abuse, dominance and inequality are enacted, reproduced and resisted by text and talk in the social and political context'. CDA can provide a set of guidelines for interrogating an authentic text, so that students engage with the content critically at the same time as they attempt to understand other more superficial aspects of the text. In this way learners may confront texts of a possibly xenophobic nature to explore the discourse mechanisms of racism.

As an example, students of Spanish at an Irish university studied newspaper articles on the theme of immigration. They closely examined the texts looking for discourse features such as: sources, perspectives, arguments; rhetorical devices such as metaphors and similes. Having made this critical analysis of the linguistic and stylistic features of the press coverage of immigration, students felt confident to discuss the issue and to make comparisons with coverage in the Irish press. They then wrote an account of their findings and their feelings about them .

A related approach, *critical cultural awareness* (Byram, 1997) is described in section 10 below.

Languages and Peace Education

Linguapax, which started in 1987, is an international project for teaching foreign languages and literature fostered by UNESCO to:

- promote the culture of peace through plurilingual education
- protect linguistic heritage
- and understanding and co-operation between peoples (Cunningham and Candelier, 1995).

It is co-ordinated by UNESCO's Language Division and the UNESCO Centre of Catalonia. The project considers that:

Education is a fundamental part of the process by which

individuals are socialised, thereby acquiring values, attitudes and behavioural patterns. By presenting the learner with communicative practices different from his/her own, language teaching offers an excellent means of promoting values and representations favouring the development of a culture of peace.

A Special Symposium on *The Contribution of Modern Language Teaching to the Promotion of Peace* was held at the European Centre for Modern Languages, Graz, (Austria) September 30 - October 3, 1998. It drafted a series of statements and recommendations including the following:

- With the aim of enabling individuals and groups to live together in plurilingual and pluricultural societies which need to develop all kinds of contacts with their international environment (immediate or distant), school plays an essential role in ensuring a pacific climate of inter-individual and inter-community relations.
- Modern language teaching must take on a prime responsibility in the achievement of this task, insofar as communication constitutes both one of its essential objectives and its preferred means; language is also closely linked to the cultural aspects of communities and the study of language is able to demonstrate the relative nature of the interpretation schemas of each community.
- In order for this responsibility to be completely fulfilled, certain restraints or obstacles need to be removed. States and local authorities are asked:
- to take all necessary measures to improve the status of the various languages present in their territories, in accordance with the guidelines laid down in the Charter for Regional and Minority Languages of the Council of Europe, also taking into account the languages of migrants;

to take all necessary measures likely to favour the development of a positive collective attitude towards these languages and towards linguistic diversity in general;

- to promote reflection on the means of evaluation of attitudes and competencies developed within the framework of language teaching which contribute to the promotion of peace, and to raise questions about the often exclusively linguistic orientation of examinations;
- to encourage collective reflection by teachers and educational specialists on the content of a professional ethics relative to the teaching of modern languages which takes account of the responsibilities towards individuals and societies of this teaching and those to whom it is entrusted.

Participants were provided with a set of materials (Candelier,1998) which include the following statement in the introduction:

> Knowing another's language may, because it entails communication, be a definitive step towards tolerance. ... One of the fundamental objectives of language teaching... is to develop the learners' communicative ability. The language class becomes the environment in which are exercised and developed the ability to listen to others, the place where learners become aware of how mutually enriching a sharing of perspectives can be. Experiencing a tolerant approach in the language class prepares learners to extend this beyond the school environment.

In a society where numerous cultural factors increasingly coexist, language teaching (...) can (thus) contribute to the development of a solidly responsible society which is respectful of individual identities... It is no longer sufficient simply to ask how to develop the mechanisms of comprehension and expression.

The cultural dimension and the demands implied therein at the level of what is known and accepted in others - a necessarily reciprocal process - are inextricably linked to communication. A particularly active network of language teachers working broadly within a framework of peace education and concern to promote global citizenship is co-ordinated by the National Special Interest Group of the Japan Association for Language Teaching (JALT) which produces a Global Issues in Language Education Newsletter. A project on English for World Citizenship, which used materials produced for world studies and citizenship education in the context of a language class is described by Cates (1995).

Core Competencies and skills for Democratic Citizenship

The Council of Europe's project on Education for Democratic Citizenship produced a statement of core competencies:

> Thus the core competencies associated with democratic citizenship are those called for by the construction of a free and autonomous person, aware of his rights and duties in a society where the power to establish the law, i.e. the rules of community life which define the framework in which the freedom of each is exercised, and where the appointment and control of the people who exercise this power are under the supervision of all the citizens.

Three broad categories are distinguished: cognitive competencies; affective competencies and those connected with the choice of values; those connected with action. These are described as follows.

Cognitive Competencies

- competencies of a legal and political nature, i.e. knowledge concerning the rules of collective life.
- knowledge of the present world including a historical dimension and a cultural dimension.

- competencies of a procedural nature,: the ability to speak and argue, connected with the debate, and the ability to reflect,
- knowledge of the principles and values of human rights and democratic citizenship.

Affective Competencies and Choice of Values

Citizenship cannot be reduced to a catalogue of rights and duties, it is also belonging to a group or to groups. It thus requires a personal and collective affective dimension.

- the capacity to live with others, to co-operate, to construct and implement joint projects, to take on responsibilities,
- the capacity to resolve conflicts in accordance with the principles of democratic law,
- the capacity to take part in public debate, to argue and choose in a real-life situation.

These broad educational aims can be complemented by a list of more precise outcomes and key skills, taken from the Recommendation No. R(85)7 of the Council of Europe's Committee of Ministers to Member States on *Teaching and learning about Human Rights in schools.* Since human rights underpin democracy, these are by definition also key skills for democratic citizenship.

The skills associated with understanding and supporting human rights include:

Intellectual Skills, in particular:

o skills involving judgement, such as:

the collection and examination of material from various sources, including the mass media, and the ability to analyse it and to arrive at fair and balanced conclusions; the identification of bias, prejudice, stereotypes and discrimination;

social skills, in particular:

- recognising and accepting differences;
- establishing positive and non-oppressive personal relationships o resolving conflict in a non-violent way o taking responsibility o participating in decisions
- understanding the use of the mechanisms for the protection of human rights at local, regional, European and world levels.

All these competencies and skills can be developed through the study of languages. Indeed, many of them are listed in the *Common European Framework of Reference for languages.*

Sociocultural competencies and skills in the *Common European Framework of Reference for Languages*

One area for possible future revision is the Table 1 giving an External Context for Use. In the Public domain, although political parties and public meetings are included, other sites of citizenship are severely under-represented.

All these competencies and skills can be mapped onto a model of citizenship education which draws on the Council of Europe's work in human rights education and which has been successfully applied to a study for the European Commission analysing the contribution of its mobility and curriculum development programmes to citizenship education. It is also possible to map onto it policies for language teaching and learning.

The model uses the distinction between a 'minimal' and a 'maximal' approach and a further distinction between the 'civic education' element of education for citizenship, and the 'personal, social and moral education' dimension. The former is here characterised as being about the structural and the political, the latter as the personal and the cultural. The former is more likely to emphasise the cognitive, whereas the latter gives expression to the affective and develops the active.

The model proposes that the basis of citizenship is, on the one hand structural and political and on the other cultural and personal. The structural and political dimensions are concerned with, at a minimal level, the human rights recognised by states as the entitlement of citizens. In practice, economic, social and cultural factors may combine to deny some citizens their basic rights and so to exclude them from society. The realisation of this denial of rights demands a political response intended to ensure the inclusion of citizens. As mechanisms of exclusion are not fully under the control of political and structural processes, but also depend on individual agency, policies and regulations will always be to some extent inadequate. Thus the concern for inclusion and community is described in the model as 'maximal', recognising that, whereas the guarantee of rights is a basic minimum, their realisation is likely to be a goal or aspiration.

One important potential site for the realisation of political and structural equality and inclusion is the learning communities themselves, whether schools, universities, adult learning centres or virtual learning centres. All, ideally, will be based on human rights, in other words equality of dignity for individuals and fundamental freedoms for individuals including freedom of expression and association. They can be, in some respects, models of democratic societies. The Council of Europe's Education for Democratic Citizenship Project is developing the concept of 'sites of citizenship', which are projects creating communities which develop both learning and participation.

The right hand side of the model is about the cultural and personal dimensions of citizenship. This corresponds to the affective dimension in Audigier's classification. The model suggests that identities are no longer able to be imposed by a national, even nationalist education, but are culturally and personally defined and increasingly multiple. In other words, in European liberal democracies citizens recognise that, as well as exclusive notions of identity (e.g. French or British; British or Irish) which produce tensions and social and cultural exclusion, processes of education enable them to feel at ease with notions of multiple identities. Thus citizenship may be constructed on the basis of multiply situated selves rather than exclusivity.

Language learning is an important component of constructing such complex identities. Guilherme and Byram apply the insights of critical pedagogy, developed from the work of Freire by writers such as Giroux, to the teaching of languages. Critical pedagogy: has been influenced... by a post-modern conception of identity that emphasises hybridity - the treatment of identity as contingent, temporary, and disruptive of oppositional categories.

Byram and Guilherme argue that it is not paradoxical for this post-modern view, that can tend towards relativism, to be tempered by a modernist commitment to universal human rights. The model above is one means of expressing this duality.

Whereas each citizen is socialised into cultures and identities, the full realisation of citizenship (the maximal dimension in the model) implies the capacity to influence one's environment at whatever level. This requires a set of competencies which develop throughout life and which, too, are therefore goals and aspirations. Amongst the most important of these competencies for action are linguistic competencies, including skills involving oral expression, such as making a case, discussing and negotiating, as well as the critical comprehension skills of understanding written and media documents. The development of co-operation skills is another area where language education can make a significant contribution.

Language education as a site of learning for democratic citizenship: knowledge Language teaching is potentially a most important site of learning for democratic citizenship. Even where citizenship education is a formal curriculum requirement, which is increasingly the case, the relatively small amount of time allotted and the prestige of more traditional, examined disciplines tends to minimise its impact. Language teaching, on the other hand, requires and is given substantial curriculum time and benefits from the prestige of an established university discipline. Moreover, the content of language teaching has for long been flexible, including literature, cultural awareness, media studies and debates of topical issues. Whereas not all teachers of languages are aware of their potential contribution to education for citizenship, including human rights education, many, often inspired by participation in European projects and meetings, have pioneered citizenship education through language teaching.

The development of policy in the area of the language curriculum might include a revision of the taxonomies that are the Threshold, Way stage and Vantage level documents. Currently these specifications, which are widely used in Europe in the construction of teaching and assessment syllabuses, have a distinct emphasis on the transactional and the institutional. The dimension of capacities for action is less well represented.

The *Vantage* level specification (B2 level) is aimed at:

Those who want to use another language for communication with persons who speak it, both for transacting the business of everyday life and for exchanging information and opinions on private life and public affairs (van Ek & Trim, 1996:5).

However the emphasis on acting together as well as speaking together could be developed. Personal interaction and social contact, for example, is exemplified as 'to engage in meaningful relations in various domains of public life (e.g. business, education, welfare, entertainment)' *(Vantage,* chapter 2). Whereas this

20

does not exclude working with others to promote democratic citizenship, this element could be more strongly represented in the taxonomy. For instance, whereas a page is devoted to the vocabulary of specifically British political institutions, including titles of nobility and a further page to war and peace, including the names of military ranks and types of weapons the section on social affairs is limited to six terms. This is one area for possible expansion with a more international dimension.

In many educational systems, the programme of study for languages is determined more by process and linguistic concerns than by a specific content. There is therefore potentially scope within the languages curriculum to cover three of the cognitive competencies for citizenship which are explicitly or implicitly included in the Common European Framework, namely:

- knowledge of the law and political systems;
- knowledge of the present world;
- knowledge of the principles and values of human rights and democratic citizenship.

This could include specific reference to human rights instruments and the discussion of case studies in the light of this knowledge and awareness.

Indeed, the 1998 Council of Europe Recommendation of the Committee of Ministers on *Linguistic Diversity* seeks to 'encourage the use of foreign languages in the teaching of non-linguistic subjects'. Non-linguistic subjects include citizenship and human rights, which make excellent material for Culture and Language Integrated Learning .

That said, current approaches to syllabus construction are often weak on including such potentially interesting questions in the lower secondary school. Learners may be faced with topics well below the interest level of those encountered elsewhere in the curriculum. One consequence is that the learning of languages may be more attractive to some groups than to others. Boys, for instance, are in some cases more reluctant learners than girls.

An analysis of an examination syllabus studied by 15 - 16 year old students in England found that six topics were girl-centred, three were boy-centred, four were equally appreciated by both sexes and three were equally disliked by both. As examples, House and Home was enjoyed by girls who liked to describe room furnishings in detail. However, the boys tended merely to list items of electrical equipment. Family and Daily Routine includes descriptions of household tasks. However, girls are much more likely to have experience of these tasks than boys. If the teaching was re-structured to include a debate on the gendering of household tasks, this could include both groups more equally and promote some awareness of equality issues.

None of the topics in this syllabus involves the public domain, apart from school itself. Its potential as a vehicle for citizenship education is therefore severely limited. Nonetheless, the same topics addressed critically and problematised could contribute to citizenship. There is certainly scope for development and synergy in syllabus construction for citizenship and languages in the lower secondary school.

Expressed positively, Citizenship and Languages can have a significant reciprocal relationship. When topics from the public domain, such as questions of peace, gender relations, racism, social and cultural movements become part of the curriculum for languages, and simultaneously the skills of debate and of critical analysis are taught, motivation for many students is likely to increase. Affective barriers to learning languages may be removed. Attitudes to language and languages and their speakers are likely to improve if learners have a more rewarding experience.

Language Education as a Site of Learning for Democratic Citizenship: Skills

A second area of contribution of languages to citizenship is that of the pedagogy associated with language learning since the development of communicative methods is in itself democratic. The skills developed in language classes are directly transferable to citizenship education.

The communicative language classroom implies that priority is given to speech acts. The role of the teacher is to guide pupils in their use of the new communicative tool, the second language. Teachers will be concerned not just with linguistic achievements but with communicative competence as an end in itself. Skills *(savoir faire)* such as ability to listen, to reformulate the words of another the better to understand them, put a different point of view, produce a valid argument, conceding are all life skills *(savoir être)* with applicability elsewhere in school and in the outside world.

When the requirement is for advanced, complex communication, such as a formal debate, the learner has to draw on knowledge *(savoirs)* (culture, lexis, grammar), skills *(savoir faire)* (function of arguments, agreements and disagreements, riposte etc) and life skills *(savoir être)* such as listening, making eye-contact, using persuasive intonation, reformulating an opposing view before modifying or refuting it, remaining calm and polite etc. We can see that the language class is a site where education for dialogue is especially developed.

In the communicative language classroom learners are often required to speak and discuss in pairs and groups, having the freedom to express their own opinions and develop ideas and new ways of thinking. This contribution to the overall project of democratic citizenship can also be recognised and developed. In particular it can help develop 'competencies of a procedural nature'. What is more, since the topics chosen may involve personal choices and require a consideration of values, there is much scope for work on the affective dimension of citizenship. Further, since discussion and debate require working with others, taking part in public discourse and working to resolve conflicts, language teaching can contribute substantially to capacities for action and social competencies. Language teachers will recognise the assertion that:

Argumentation and debate call for a knowledge of the subject under discussion, the capacity to listen to the other and acknowledgement of his (sic) point of view, as well as the application of these capacities to the precise situation in which the people find themselves.

Language Education as a Site of Learning for Democratic Citizenship: Culture

A third and equally important dimension of language teaching is the consideration of culture. The Parliamentary Assembly's Recommendation 1383 on Linguistic Diversification calls for:

> the promotion of a type of education which gives greater emphasis to the culture and society of the countries concerned.

Studying other cultures enables learners to decentre from their own world-view, accept relativities and develop multiple identities. To acquire the ability to communicate in a new language is the first step to identifying with other speakers of that language community. This intercultural dimension of language learning has the potential to promote antiracism as a positive principle of democratic citizenship. As the rapporteur to the Parliamentary Assembly's Committee on Culture, Science and Education puts it:

> Beyond this utilitarian aspect, however, language learning has a strong socio-cultural component. In an increasingly uniform world, cultural diversity will become ever more important as a means of preserving human values. Learning a language means learning to be closer to others. Learning a foreign language means equipping oneself with intellectual tools for confronting the real and the unknown, as well as personal enrichment through a knowledge of other cultures and other views of the world. Learning also means combating the ignorance that lies at the root of intolerance and racism.

There are a number of approaches to learning about cultures, one of them being *critical cultural awareness* which is an ability to evaluate critically and on the basis of explicit criteria, perspectives, practices and products in one's own and other cultures and countries. This involves the ability to:

- Identify and interpret explicit or implicit values in documents and events in one's own and other cultures, using a range of analytical approaches to place a document or event in context and be aware of the ideological dimension.
- Make an evaluative analysis of the documents and events by reference to an explicit perspective and criteria such as human rights, liberal democracy, religion, political ideology.
- Interact and mediate in intercultural exchanges, being aware of potential conflict between one's own and other ideological positions and attempting to find common criteria. Where this is not possible, to negotiate agreement on places of conflict and acceptance of difference.

Cultural Studies is an academic discipline with its roots in Britain in the 1950s and 1960s but acknowledging the intellectual contribution of French academics such as Barthes, Bourdieu and Foucault. It can be focused on cultural forms found within particular national communities, such as British Cultural Studies or French Cultural Studies. In essence culture is conceptualised as 'neither aesthetic nor humanist in emphasis, but political'.

The introduction to a textbook on British Cultural Studies produced in Romania describes the expectations of the authors for the learner:

> This book is less concerned about making you learn information by heart than with encouraging you to *process* the information contained here. For example, in the class on Scotland you are asked to *compare* what a Scottish person says about Scotland and what a compilation from reference books says about Scotland. You do not have to learn one or the other, but you do have to learn the process of comparison. The same process of comparison of different kinds of information takes place in many classes. In others, you are

asked to *apply* concepts such as 'gender' or 'nation as imagined community' in your analyses of society. In short, what we want E to provide you with the skills to *argue* . .. not learn by heart.

Sources of information used in this approach are authentic texts, including audio recordings and a variety of written documents and visuals such as maps, photographs, diagrams and cartoons. The setting is a language class and the activities involve understanding, discussing and writing in the target language. The approach to the materials is always critical.

The study of literature and media such as film and television is often a central aspect of the language education curriculum. Texts are often chosen for their social as well as their aesthetic importance. The critical study and discussion of such texts, including a perspective of human rights and citizenship, can also contribute to the goals of education for democratic citizenship.

Intercultural Education and Intercultural Communication

In the 1970s Intercultural education was essentially based on the teaching of languages to newly arrived communities in Europe. In the 1980s, with the slowing down of immigration in some parts of Europe, attention turned to broader educational objectives and there was considerable identification of intercultural education with human rights education.

The socio-cultural competencies included in the *Common European Framework of Reference for languages* have been re-defined by Byram as elements of 'intercultural communicative competence'. The European Language Council produced a policy paper on Intercultural Communication which provides the following definition:

All communication is fundamentally intercultural, in the sense that each participant in an act of communication brings to it a specific repertoire of identities, positions and expectations formed through complex relationships with their own and other cultures. Here, culture is understood in the widest sense as an acquired or constructed pattern of values, beliefs, skills and knowledge, which shapes and is shaped by its participants. Effective communication is closely related to the participants' understanding and management of these different cultural identities and positions. Social progress and the building of relations of peace and equality between people in Europe depend on the development of awareness of such cultural variety and difference.

In the context of European integration, the national dimension is often perceived as the most salient, but it is not the only significant determinant of different cultural identities. Important determinants lie, for example, in class, gender, ethnicity, language, education, political or religious affiliation, and individual dispositions.

The Policy Document then Specifies Three Levels or Dimensions of which the Second is Citizenship

At this level, the focus is on communication between individuals as active members of society, with a need to participate in social and political developments, and to work towards shared approaches to issues arising from them. Participants need to be reciprocally aware of the knowledge and values shared, or not shared, by members of particular cultural groupings, and must be able to situate their own knowledge and values in relation to those of others, identifying both differences and common points of reference. In this context, citizenship is to an important extent mediated by institutions .

One development with further potential for language learning and intercultural communication is specific work on identity.

The purpose of identity work is to establish which communicative features should be acknowledged by the group or audience as constitutive of its collective identity (however transitory or unstable the group as such may be), and which should be socially acknowledged as tokens of individuality. Three processes are seen as essential for the negotiation of social identities: sharing codes, sharing topics, and sharing assumptions. In a series of recordings involving native and non-native speakers of Spanish in two different activity types, including discussions and interviews, the identity work which takes place between the interactants has been studied from various angles. A programme for the application of the analyses to language training has been elaborated at the Department of Spanish and Portuguese in Stockholm University. A basic assumption of the programme is that the intercultural skills of language students can be successfully improved, if the students become aware of the various mechanisms of identity work with regard to how codes are shared, and which kind of topics and assumptions tend to be preferred, both in the home and the foreign language/culture community. Such awareness should be accomplished not only by means of data analysis but also through role play.

Culture and Language Integrated Learning

This movement, also known as CLIC (culture and language integrated classrooms), promotes formalised attempts to acquire simultaneously language competence and curricular skills, values and knowledge traditionally viewed as separate disciplines. In linguistic terms it derives from the view that form can be learnt whilst the user's attention is on content. It takes advantage of the extra time that can be gained for language learning if time for other disciplines is appropriated and joint curricular outcomes are achieved. Amongst other sources of inspiration is the Canadian immersion programme. Other parallel developments have been called Content Based Language Teaching or Content Based Language Learning.

Such projects are developing new pedagogies involving interactivity between different types of language use.

The learners participate in the classroom by exposure to and usage of three interlocking types of language use: medium-oriented (communication about language), message-oriented (communication in which content is transmitted) and socially oriented (interpersonally meaningful communication). It is the chemistry between these three elements which is the goal of many of the more interesting methodologies used.

Any subject can be taught in this way, though often history and geography are chosen. Citizenship is a logical partner and there are some reports of, for instance, road safety education and environmental education taught through CLIL.

Although the potential range of subjects to be taught through a CLIL approach is limitless, human rights education might be a particularly appropriate field for further experimentation. In terms of knowledge, the following content was recommended in 1985 by the Committee of Ministers of the Council of Europe:

"Topics to be covered in learning about human rights could include:

(i) the main categories of human rights, duties, obligations and responsibilities

(ii) the various forms of injustice, inequality and discrimination, including sexism and racism;

(iii) people, movements and key events, both successes and failures, in the historical and continuing struggle for human rights;

(iv) the main international declarations and conventions on human rights, such as the Universal Declaration of Human Rights and the Convention for the Protection of Human Rights and Fundamental Freedoms" (Council of Europe, 1985 - Recommendation R (85) 7).

Developments in CLIL throw up a number of issues that remain to be resolved, particularly in relation to resources and the training of teachers. Amongst other questions, commentators have noted that CLIL experiments have tended to be small scale and therefore potentially elitist. Learners in the early stages are unlikely to have the linguistic resources to participate as they might in other lessons and may become frustrated at the passive role they have to adopt.

One suggestion is to use specially produced simplified materials and that would constitute a radical break with the assumption that the use of authentic materials is always best. Furthermore, this form of language education has brought into sharp focus questions of code-switching and achievement of partial competence.

Real and Virtual Visits and Exchanges

The advent of widespread access to Information and Communications Technology has considerable implications for language learning and for citizenship. The web is in many respects a democratic medium, allowing for increased exchange of information and ideas. Individual learners can have access to innumerable authentic documents in any written language.

Exchanges, visits and residence in another community are the ways in which the claims of language learning as a means to develop broader notions of community and citizenship are both developed and tested.

The physical movement of students can be usefully prepared through contacts with the host institution provided through websites. Reflection on the experience of residence in another community can also be facilitated through web-based guidance provided on the web by the host institution.

Multilingual websites for school-age learners of languages have been developed. One of these, http://www.darespeak.org/ provides texts and questions in several languages, links to the press, songs, travel tips, dictionaries on-line and other incentives for young language learners. The focus on news is a particularly striking example of a synergy with education for democratic citizenship.

The practice of correspondence with a pen pal in another language has been refined and up-dated through e-mail. Bilingual partnerships for communication, known as tandem links, are increasingly encouraged by universities. Guidelines for sensitive and reciprocally effective communication are provided. Participants agree to support each other in their learning. Topics of current interest falling within the domain of citizenship provide incentives to develop conversation and communication.

One important potential development for learners and speakers of less widely taught and used languages is that discussion lists can be created to bring together learners who might otherwise be dispersed and have little opportunity for real contact. For instance an American university hosts an open discussion list for learners of Welsh.

Whereas current technologies support asynchronous written communication, developing technologies can support synchronous audio, written and visual communication. Teachers can create a virtual language laboratory linking widely dispersed learners in a network where they can communicate orally and in writing. They can work in a large group or in pairs or smaller groups within the conference and the teacher can monitor all the communication and intervene where appropriate.

CONCLUSION

This study demonstrates and illustrates the many opportunities available to language teachers to contribute to education for democratic citizenship. Language teaching in Europe, particularly at school level, has been heavily influenced by considerations of how to communicate, often at the expense of what to communicate about or for. A concern for intercultural communication within Europe has recently placed language teaching and learning at the heart of a humanistic curriculum.

Citizens in a democracy need intercultural skills for living in communities where cultural diversity is the norm. They need critical cultural awareness to understand the world around them and challenge injustice, complacency, social exclusion and unwarranted discrimination. The construction of a peaceful, democratic and multicultural Europe requires plurilingual citizens.

REFERENCES

Anderson, B. 1991, *Imagined Communities: Reflections on the Origin and Spread of Nationalism.* London: Verso.

Audigier, F. 1998, *Basic concepts and core competencies of education for democratic citizenship; an initial consolidated report.* [DECS/CIT (98) 35] Strasbourg: Council of Europe.

Audigier, F. 1999, *L'éducation à la citoyenneté.* Paris: INRP.

Bassnett, S. (ed.) 1997, *Studying British Cultures: an Introduction.* London: Routledge.

Beheydt, L. 1999, Preliminaries to material development for content and language integrated learning. In D. Marsh, and B. Marsland (eds.) *CLIL Initiatives for the Millenium: Report on the CEILINK Think-Tank.* Jyväskylä: University of Jyväskylä, Continuing Education Centre pp57-61.

Byram, M. 1997, *Teaching and Assessing Intercultural Communicative Competence.* Clevedon: Multilingual Matters.

Byram, M. 1999, Foreign Language Education for Critical Cultural Awareness and Democratic Citizenship. In D. Killick and M. Parry (eds.) *Languages for Cross-Cultural Capability.* Proceedings of the conference at Leeds Metropolitan University. 12 - 14 December 1998. LMU: Centre for Language Study pp53-68.

Byram, M. and M. Guilherme (2000). Human Rights, Cultures and Language Teaching. In A. Osler *Citizenship and Democracy in Schools: Diversity, Identity, Equality..* Stoke-on-Trent: Trentham Books: 63-78.

Callahan, M. 1998, An investigation into the causes of boys' underachievement in French. *Language Learning Journal* 17.

Candelier, M. 1998, *Language Teaching and Tolerance : Collection of Materials for Teachers.* Graz ECML: Council of Europe.

Carlson, D. and Apple, M. (eds.) 1998, *Power/Knowledge/ Pedagogy.* Oxford: Westview Press.

Cates, K. 1995, Language Teaching for World Citizenship. In D. Cunningham and M. Candelier (eds.) *Linguapax V Melbourne, Australia June 30 - July 2 1995.* AFMLTA, FIPLV, UNESCO: Belgrave, Australia.

Chichirdan, A. et al. 1998, *Crossing Cultures. British Cultural Studies for 12th Grade Romanian Students.* Bucharest: The British Council.

Council of Europe, 2001, *Common European Framework of Reference for Languages: Learning, teaching, assessment.* Cambridge: Cambridge University Press.

Council of Europe, 2002, *A Common European Framework of Reference - A General Guide for Users.* Strasbourg: Council of Europe

Council of Europe, 1985, Recommendation No. R(85)7 of the Committee of Ministers on *Teaching and learning about Human Rights in schools.*

Council of Europe, 1998, Recommendation 98(6) of the Committee of Ministers on *Linguistic Diversity* .

Council of Europe, 1999, Declaration and Programme of Action 99(76) of the Committee of Ministers on *Education for Democratic Citizenship based on the Rights and Responsibilities of Citizens,* Strasbourg: Council of Europe.

Crick, B. 1998, *Education for Citizenship and the Teaching of Democracy in Schools.* Final report of the Advisory Group on Citizenship (the Crick Report). London: QCA/98/245.

Cunningham, D. and Candelier, M. (eds.) 1995, *Linguapax V Melbourne, Australia June 30 - July 2 1995.* AFMLTA, FIPLV, UNESCO: Belgrave, Australia.

European Language Council, 1997, Intercultural Communication Group - Policy Paper http://www.fu-berlin.de/elc

European Language Council, 1999, *Bulletin* 5 http://www.fu-berlin.de/elc

FIPLV, 1991, *Fundamental Principles for a Universal Declaration on Language Rights.* Document approved by the General Assembly of FIPLV(International Federation of Teachers of Living Languages) Pecs, Hungary, August 1991.

Fiske, J. 1987, 'British Cultural Studies and Television'. In Allen, R. (ed.) *Channels of Discourse: Television and Contemporary Criticism.* Chapel Hill, NC: University of North Carolina Press.

Forbes, J. and Kelly, M. 1995, *French Cultural Studies.* Oxford: Oxford University Press.

Forrester, K. 1999, *Guidelines for a Site Report.* Strasbourg: Council of Europe DECS/EDU/CIT (99)6.

Guilherme, M. 1999, The Political Challenge of Teaching a Foreign Culture. In D. Killick and M. Parry (eds.) *Languages for Cross-Cultural Capability.* Proceedings of the conference at Leeds Metropolitan University. 12 - 14 December 1998. LMU: Centre for Language Study pp123-128.

Kötter, M., Shield, L. and Stevens, A. 1999, Real-time audio and email for fluency: promoting distance language learners' aural and oral skills via the internet. *ReCall* 11.2. http://www.hull.ac.uk/cti/eurocall/recall/rvol1 1no2.pdf

Krashen, S. 1985, *The Input Hypothesis:Issues and Implications.* London: Longman.

Legendre, J. 1998, *Explanatory memorandum to report on Linguistic Diversification.* http://stars.coe.fr/doc/doc98/EDOC8173.htm

Marsh, D. and Marsland, B. (eds.) 1999, *CLIL Initiatives for the Millenium: Report on the CEILINK Think-Tank.* Jyväskylä: University of Jyväskylä, Continuing Education Centre.

Marsh, D., Marsland, B. and Nikula, T. 1999, Position Statement. CLIL a review of current thinking. In D. Marsh and B. Marsland (eds.) *CLIL Initiatives for the Millenium: Report on the CEILINK Think-Tank.* Jyväskylä: University of Jyväskylä, Continuing Education Centre pp. 35-45.

McLaughlin, T. 1992, Citizenship, Diversity and Education. *Journal of Moral Education* 21, 3, 235-250.

Osler, A. and Starkey, H. 1996, *Teacher Education and Human Rights.* London: Fulton.

Osler, A. and Starkey, H. 1999, Rights, Identities and Inclusion: European action programmes as political education. *Oxford Review of Education* 25, 1&2.

Osler, A. and Starkey, H. 2000, Intercultural Education and Foreign Language Learning: Issues of Racism, Identity and Modernity. *Race, Ethnicity and Education* 3 (2).

Osler, A. and Starkey, H., 2001 ,Antiracisme et enseignement des langues: quels matériels et quelle pédagogie? In Zarate, G. (ed.) *Langues, xénophobie, xénophilie dans une Europe multiculturelle* CRDP de Basse-Normandie pp203 - 215

Perotti, A. 1989, *Action to Combat Intolerance and Xenophobia in the Activities of the Council of Europe's Council for Cultural Co-operation 1969 - 1989.* Strasbourg: Council of Europe.

Perotti, A. 1994, *Plaidoyer pour Vinterculturel* Strasbourg: Council of Europe.

Ramos, F. P. (2001a). 'Why Do They Hit the Headlines?': Critical Media Literacy in the Foreign Language Class. *Journal of Intercultural Studies* Vol 22(1) pp. 33-49.

Ramos, F. P. (2001b). Pour un enseignement contre le préjugé ethnoculturel: l'analyse du discours journalistique sur l'immigration dans la classe de langue étrangère. In G. Zarate *Langues, Xénophobie, Xénophilie Dans Une Europe Multiculturelle.* CRDP de Basse-Normandie pp. 181-192.

Richardson, R. 1996, The Terrestrial Teacher. In M. Steiner (ed.) *Developing the Global Teacher.* Stoke-on-Trent: Trentham Books.

Soetaert, R. and Bonamie, B. 1999, New Rules for the Language and Content Game. From CBLT/CALL to CLIL/TILL. http://www.euroclic.net/english/bulletin/e12.pdf

Starkey, H. 1990, World studies and foreign language teaching: converging approaches in textbook writing. In D. Buttjes and M. Byram, (eds.) *Mediating Languages and Cultures.* Clevedon: Multilingual Matters, pp. 209-227.

Starkey, H. 1996, Intercultural education through foreign language learning: a human rights approach. In A. Osler, H. Rathenow, and H. Starkey (eds.) *Teaching for Citizenship in Europe* Stoke: Trentham, pp. 103-16.

Starkey, H. 1997, Foreign language learning and citizenship: issues for lifelong learning. In I. Davies and A. Sobisch, (eds.) *Developing European Citizens,* Sheffield: Sheffield Hallam University Press, pp. 187 - 208.

Starkey, H. 1999, Foreign language teaching to adults: implicit and explicit political education. *Oxford Review of Education* 25, No.1&2, pp. 155-169.

Starkey, H. and Osler, A. (2001). Language Learning and Antiracism: Some Pedagogical Challenges. *The Curriculum Journal* Vol 12(3) pp. 313-329.

Storey, J. (ed.) 1996, *What is Cultural Studies? A reader.* London: Arnold. Tardieu, C. 1999, *Le Professeur Citoyen.* Bourg-la-Reine: Editions M.T. Van Dijk, T. 1997 *(ed.) Discourse as Social Interaction.* London: Sage.

Van Ek, J. and Trim, J. 2000, *Vantage.* Strasbourg and Cambridge University Press.

9

Human Rights and Indian Democracy

Human Rights and Democracy in India's Emerging Role in Asia India is unique among post-Colonial states in successfully building a vibrant democracy that has withstood the test of time. It is not only the largest among world democracies - close to 600 million people go to polls since the 1990s - but also a very diverse one with deep-seated differences of religion, ethnicity and regional identities. The rapid and sustained growth of the Indian economy during the last two decades has made the Indian experiment even more significant for the international community.

Almost all recent discussions about international security or economics have focused on the rise of China and India as the future agents of change in Asia. This is largely because economic expansion is rapidly translating into military power and the ability to shape events. How do India's expanding capabilities affect the ability to exercise soft power? How does a rising India balance democracy, its most significant soft power asset, against imperatives of security? As a representative of successful democracy in the third world, India should be in the forefront of promoting political rights, freedom, and justice. But Indian policies have been ambivalent on this score. Why? What has been the Indian perspective on this issue? How do recent developments, the danger from Jihadi Islam to its west and the rise of China in the east, shape India's security? What changes in its own expanded capabilities affect the emerging balance of democracy and security in India policy, particularly in Asia? The following paper outlines ways in which we might think about these questions and identify directions in India's Asia policy.

Why Do Normative Constructions Matter?

The exercising of soft power requires an agreement among a significant number of powerful states on the larger frame of collective norms. Normative orders provide the grand narrative to explain the past and legitimize the future. The grand narrative of nineteenth century Europe was premised on the "balance of power," which was believed to preserve peace by deterring overly ambitious European states from taking aggressive action. Between the two world wars, President Woodrow Wilson sought to create a peaceful and just order based on norms of self-determination and democracy. It gave the victors in the First World War the power to redraw the map of Europe. The narrative of historic contradiction between socialism and capitalism shaped the Cold War and legitimized the bipolar world.

As the leaders of the two rival camps, the United States and the Soviet Union competed for influence but observed tacit rules of conduct that avoided mutual destruction. History then tells us that any state (or group of states) that can build a widely accepted normative frame for collective policies and root these in a set of institutionalized relationships is likely to wield power over future developments. Grand narratives strengthen proponents to structure inter-state relations and justify actions to punish and isolate, or do its opposite, reward and befriend those excluded from the core cluster of sponsors.

Such a grand conceptual narrative is yet to evolve in the post-Cold War era although several have vied for attention. Francis

Fukuyama in his famous essay heralded the "end of history" and the triumph of Western values of democracy and market economics. He claimed that individual rights, civil liberties, property rights, and freedom to profit had proved their superiority over state-led growth, collective rights, and hierarchical order. But lurking in the shadows of this triumphalism were challenges that had already surfaced to undermine his argument. Impressive growth of Asia's smaller economies - Taiwan, Singapore, South Korea, and Malaysia - within a frame of soft authoritarianism raised doubts about Fukuyama's thesis. The spectacular rise of China, occurring as it has within a harder authoritarian system, undermined even more the economic claims on behalf of liberal democracy. Kishore Mahbubani in Singapore and Mahathir Mohamad in Malaysia have proposed a counter narrative based on the merits of 'Asian Values' in contrast to the Fukuyama's argument. They suggest that these values were the true engine of Asian growth.

India in the Emerging International Context

It is in this context that democratic India, Asia's "second country," the seat of a great world civilization, and growth rates to match those of China, assumes critical weight. We might look at India's soft power asset - liberal democracy - in at least two ways: as a model or an example (although perhaps not exemplary) of a viable federal, liberal, secular democracy and as a promoter of international democracy. India's political path proves that a liberal democracy is possible in a tradition-bound, multi-ethnic, and poor society can be a solution to the problem of modernization and growth. The second perspective is to see India's democratic identity as a stepping stone to international alliances and collective diplomatic engagement. A cluster of democracies can come together to create a common formula to exclude the politically incorrect, impose sanctions, or to deny recognition. A democratic coalition will not only enable its sponsors to capture the moral high ground and shape international discourse but also bring collective power to bear on recalcitrant regimes.

India's liberal, democratic, and market-oriented economy offers an alternative to the hard authoritarian growth model of East Asia. Furthermore, India's democratic path is arguably more relevant to the developing countries of Asia, Africa, and Middle East than the European road to modernization and democracy. India has developed a unique formula to balance individual and group rights, devolve federal power down to the village-level (Panchayet Raj), and use its multiparty system as a grand bargain to reconcile differences over identities, interests, and office. In this sense, India's democratic experiment is one of the greatest political experiments of our time.

However, India has been generally reluctant to export democracy or engage in policies of regime change for at least three reasons. First, protection of its 'strategic autonomy' has compelled India to reject attempts to set any general precedent of collective intervention on behalf of intervention in the domestic affairs of other states; it does not wish to set a precedent of intervention in the name of normative principles. Second, pro-democracy coalitions (for much of the Cold War period) were military alliances in disguise led by the United States to promote U.S. interests. India was reluctant to participate in these. Third, challenges arising from ethnic demography in Punjab, Indian Kashmir, and many parts of the Northeast have made India vulnerable to charges of human rights violations. India has therefore been reluctant to support any blanket endorsement of international human rights regimes. India's policy objective is to retain maximum freedom of action so that it can consolidate its own periphery and incorporate hitherto loosely integrated communities into the Indian Union. These structural problems explain India's ambivalence regarding the promotion of democracy and human rights. While India has the military power to affect regime change in smaller neighboring states, overlapping communities, disputed borders, and fear of domestic repercussions limit India's options.

The 1971 intervention in East Pakistan and the 1987 dispatch of peacekeeping forces to Sri Lanka are two outstanding examples of interventions on behalf of democracy and human rights. But these were never guided entirely or even largely by altruistic motives. Critical security interests were at stake in each case. Indian policymakers continue to remain averse to exporting ideology and prefer to conduct foreign relations guided by pragmatic considerations. It is the ghost of Lord Curzon and not Mahatma Gandhi that haunts the halls of the South Bloc.

One might argue that the policy of nonalignment pursued in the early years after Independence was an expression of the second approach to soft power, namely the creation of a common platform for gaining leverage in international politics. As a leading nonaligned state, India was in the forefront of this effort. However, nonalignment was more about protecting the autonomy of newly independent countries then about promoting democracy. In fact, a large number in the nonaligned states were single party states or military juntas. They did not endorse promotion of democracy as a priority. We might then conclude that throughout the Cold War, India's ability to market its democracy as an example or as a common platform remained severely circumscribed by the distribution of global power -which was averse to India - and India's limited capabilities. The end of the Cold War, however, removed the rationale for nonalignment as it was defined in that period. The threat environment changed and India's economic and military capacities expanded. This required a different order of response to the equation between security and democracy in India's policy.

Balance of Security and Democracy in South and Southeast Asia: the Indian Perspective

While security has trumped democracy in India's foreign policy perspective, democracy has become increasingly important as an underpinning for an Asian security architecture that could be in India's interest. India's security pivots around two objectives: to make India an influential Asian power and to protect India's strategic autonomy. India's international perspective is intensely geopolitical and breaks down into series of concentric circles defined by influence, immediacy, and reach. The first order of concern is the region of South Asia; the second tier includes Central and Southwest Asian states such as Saudi Arabia and Iran and Southeast Asian states such as Myanmar, Thailand, Malaysia, and Indonesia. India's ability to ward off adverse developments in the first and second tier states are shaped by the United States, China, Pakistan, and Russia, whose interests cut through the tiers important to India. For instance, China and Pakistan have border disputes with India while India is vulnerable to separatist ethnic communities that spill over across the borders into Pakistan, Myanmar, and Nepal. Close strategic ties between China and Pakistan compound the problem of India's territorial defense. Differences also exist between India and the United States over Iran, Pakistan, and Myanmar despite a mutual interest in building a strategic relationship and concluding an agreement over India's nuclear program. The United States supports Pakistan with weapons and economic assistance to secure its cooperation in prosecuting the war on terrorism, eliminating l-Qaeda and obtaining a pro-American, stable Southwest Asia. But a militarily strong Pakistan undermines India's strategic security.

For India the first line of defense is South Asia, given its particular ethno demography and geopolitics. The overlapping nationalities in divided Kashmir and Punjab, Bengal, and the northeast - a legacy of colonial divisions has locked India and its neighboring states into perennial conflicts over peoples, territory, and bodies of waters. Ethnic overlap preoccupies India's defense strategy and demands resources, blood, and money. For instance, the Naga insurgency spills over into Bangladesh and Myanmar,

Gorkha separatism confounds relations with Nepal, and separatist violence in Punjab and Kashmir invites Pakistani interference in India's domestic affairs. Defense against China and Pakistan is made more complex by the ability of these two countries to sponsor proxies or offer sanctuaries to ethnic separatists from across the border in India.

The United States has come to occupy a central place in India's international security yet the Indian policy community cannot agree on how close it wants to be to the United States. India cannot play the role Great Britain or Canada play in U.S. global strategy; it can be neither ajunior partner nor a passive neutral state for the United States. At the same time, India has much to gain from close ties, which creates a dilemma for Indian leaders. A case in point is India-Iran ties. Iran has been an important supplier of oil for India and if the Indian economy is to grow, it must sustain and build a positive relationship. However, there is considerable pressure from the Bush administration for India to redefine its ties with Iran. Some in India argue that such a sacrifice is worth the returns from strategic support from the United States. Beyond containing China and Pakistan, the United States is important to the development of India's economy and military. Since 2001, India has opted for strategic cooperation including intelligence sharing, military training, joint exercises, purchases of weapons and technology and massive flows of investments from U.S.-based multinational corporations. The Bush administration has stated that the United States would like to see India become a great power. Obviously, it also sees India as a stabilizer in the region and as a hedge against an ambitious China. As Ashley Tellis argues, China is far more worried about the expansion of India's economic and military power than it is willing to acknowledge.

The rise of radical Islam in the areas stretching from Iraq through Central Asia to Indonesia complicates the security scenario for both the United States and India. It blocks India's easy access to the oil rich central Asian economies and endangers domestic peace by spreading religious radicalism to Indian Muslims. It undermines India's ability to control the course of the insurgency in Kashmir or to sustain progress in bilateral Indo-Pakistan negotiations. India's objective (to its northwest) is to secure steady energy supplies from Central Asia and Persian Gulf for its growing economy, deter Pakistan, protect Kashmir, and stop Jihadi infiltration into India. India also sees itself as a prominent South Asian state with strategic interests extending from eastern Persian Gulf States to the Strait of Malacca.

Whether it is Central Asia, Pakistan, Myanmar, Nepal, or Southeast Asian states, India is in competition with China for influence, markets, and security. Yet much uncertainty remains in India's assessment of China's future intentions. Indian policymakers are not sure whether to regard China as an aggressive, expansionist country, or a reasonable neighboring state amenable to talks and cooperation.

Recent Chinese actions have been disturbing to India. China has extended trade and security ties with the military junta in Myanmar, transferred weapons and missile technology to Pakistan, secured contracts to develop the port of Gawdar in the Arabian Sea, and obtained Central Asian cooperation via the Shanghai Cooperation Organization. India therefore perceives itself to be encircled by China. To compound the problem, the India-China border dispute remains unresolved and recently China has challenged India's jurisdiction over Sikkim and Arunachal Pradesh including the Tawang tract. India has sought to counter the Chinese "encirclement" using two broad policy thrusts: the Indo-U.S. Strategic Partnership and the development of a "Look East' policy. India has also made efforts to expand bilateral cooperation with China. This is more an exercise in buying time to prepare for a showdown should it ever become necessary. Meanwhile, India seeks to broaden China's stake in good relations with India. India's prime minister visited China in January 2008 and signed an agreement to expand trade to $60 billion by 2010. As a confidence building measure, China and India have agreed to hold joint military exercises. In short, India's approach is to cooperate and prepare; a tactic that both Japan and the United States share with India.

Indias Asian Initiatives

India's "Look East" policy is an important counterthrust to break through what it considers to be Chinese encirclement. Accordingly, India has reversed its policy in Myanmar and tilted in favor of the military junta, taken a proactive role in Nepal, opened talks with Pakistan over Kashmir, expanded economic ties with Central Asian states and strengthened its border defense. India has sought entry into the Shanghai Cooperation Organization and Asian economic and security forums. Additionally, it has augmented its naval reach and power with a view to participating in the collective security of the Indian Ocean and the international waters extending from the Strait of Malacca to the Arabian Sea.

The "Look East" policy suggests that New Delhi is actively globalizing its diplomatic leverage and deploying military power to buttress diplomacy. India is Asia's third largest economy after Japan and China and has entered into numerous free trade agreements with East Asian economies, including a comprehensive economic cooperation agreement with Singapore and an early harvest scheme with Thailand. It is also negotiating similar agreements with Japan, South Korea, and ASEAN. In turn, Japan, South Korea, and Singapore have invested large amounts of funds into India's infrastructure development. 28 What role can India's democratic credentials play in Asia's emerging security environment? While India is reluctant to promote democratic forces in Myanmar (for fear of losing advantage to China), it is willing to participate in constructing a grand narrative that will secure its forward thrust in Southeast Asia. In his speech before a joint session of India's parliament in August 2007, Japanese Prime

Minister Shinzo Abe talked about common interests among of democratic states such as India, Japan and the United States. He included India in a "broader Asia" that would span "the entirety of the Pacific Ocean, incorporating the United States and Australia." This was undoubtedly an invitation to India to participate in building a normative and security architecture for Asia but in its subtext it is also a subtle warning to Beijing that a China-centered Asia would not be countenanced by the "democratic" states in Asia. Abe noted that these states comprise as "Arc of Freedom and Prosperity" of "like-minded countries" that "share fundamental values such as freedom, democracy and respect for basic human rights as well as strategic interests." Shinzo Abe is the third successive Japanese prime minister to visit India after Yoshiro Mori in 2000 and Koizumi in 2005. Manmohan Singh's 2006 visit culminated in signing of the "joint statement Towards Japan-India strategic and Global Partnership."

India can make significant security contributions to the alliance of "democratic" states envisaged in Premier Abe's speech. This has been steadily demonstrated in the joint naval exercises with Singapore since 1993, with Vietnam in 2000, and with Indonesia in the Andaman Sea. The Malabar CY 07-2 naval exercises in the Bay of Bengal held in September 2007 brought the navies of Japan, United States, Australia, and India together in a well-advertised, large-scale exercise. The joint statement by the Japan, United States, and Australian governments spoke of "a partnership with India to advance areas of common interests and increase cooperation, recognizing that India's continued growth is inextricably tied to the prosperity, freedom and security of the region." Not coincidentally the first four power talks occurred at the same time that the ASEAN Regional Forum (ARF) meeting was held in Manila. Similar discussions about promoting India in regional forums were conducted when President Bush, Japanese Prime Minister Abe, and Australian Prime Minster Howard met at the 2007 APEC meeting in Sydney.

CONCLUSION

Asia's political alignments are in flux, but at least three broad security futures can be envisaged. Democratic India can play an important part in each future although each will engage India differently and to a different degree. The first is a region divided along an opposite axis, a kind of Asian bipolar order in which the United States and China constitute the opposing poles. This future assumes hardened Westphalian inter-state relations and a more blatant game of "real politick" in forging alignments. The second hypothetical future revolves around an entente of great powers, a group of leading states that strive to keep order and preserve peace by rewarding those who toe the line and punish those who deviate from it. Although the Concert of Europe (following the Congress in Vienna) comes to mind as a historic analogy, its applicability to contemporary Asia remains limited. The concert of Europe presumed an external state - England - could throw in its weight to restore balance and deter potential aggressors. No such power is on the horizon in Asia at least in the foreseeable future. Only the United States can balance a powerful China; and only China can challenge the United States in Asia. But both these states would also be the leaders of their respective clusters in the second scenario. The third future is akin to the order founded on the 1975 Helsinki agreement in Europe that established a normative consensus (claimed by 35 states in Europe as a universal guide to international relations). The Helsinki consensus does not legitimize an uneven distribution of power or at least it is not meant to do so. Nor is it a front to secure hegemony of any single state. It is meant to be an open-ended order admitting revisions, inclusion, amendment, and extension based on democratic consensus. The steady incorporation of Eastern European states to the European Union underscores the flexibility of the otherwise "value-based" Helsinki consensus.

India benefits least from the first scenario of a bipolar, divided Asia although it will be regarded an attractive prize by those competing for influence and markets in Asia. The objective of "strategic autonomy" will by definition confine India to the margins of a bipolar Asia. India's current dilemma in dealing with China can only worsen in a divided Asia. Joining an anti-China alliance is sure to provoke Beijing; not joining an alliance will mean isolation. As in the days of Cold War, India's democratic credentials will have a limited role to play in the first future. But the first future does not seem likely because neither Japan nor the United States wish to push China into a corner. In the second future, democracy and human rights do not become a means to exclude and punish recalcitrant regimes. Rather, it instead becomes instead an invitation to peacefully integrate into the new normative order and its rules of conduct. The Japanese proposal to build an "arc of freedom" or a "value-based alliance" is an attempt to construct a grand narrative for such a collective order. It has the immediate purpose of preempting the moral high ground and inviting China to join in the common platform, which automatically rules out expansionist or destabilizing policies. Supported by a strategic alliance, the "arc of freedom" would enable powerful democratic states - the United States, Japan, India, Australia - to define a common set of interests such as freedom of international seas, protection of the environment, the war against terrorism, and open access to Asian markets, but it would also seek to prevent domination of Asia by China. The fact that no country has yet acted on it forcefully is testimony to the power of China and the uncertainty it has sown about the goals it is meant to serve. But a multi-polar Asia best serves India's interests as long as it does not become blatantly anti-Chinese or a front for promoting exclusive U.S. interests.

The possibility of creating an Asian Helsinki is remote given the force of nationalism and spread of ethnic conflicts across Asia's borders. There is no regional consensus on how to deal with separatist nationalities nor is there a possibility of arriving at one in the near future. India would find it extremely difficult to accept external guidelines while it deals with its own ethnic separatism in its Northwest and Northeast. Should such an order ever become a reality, India's democratic voice would assume immense importance.

Among the three futures outlined above, the second future best fits India's current and midterm security concerns. During his recent visit to Japan, Prime Minister Manmohan Singh suggested that the time has come for Japan and India, "our two ancient civilizations to build a strong contemporary relationship involving strategic and global partnership" and the "most important area in which we can build this partnership is in the field of knowledge economy." He was less reticent in stressing India's exceptional achievement as a developing democracy. " If there is an "idea of India" by which India should be defined," he said, "it is the idea of an inclusive, open, multi-cultural, multi-ethnic, multi-lingual society...(we) have an obligation to history and mankind to show that pluralism worked. Liberal democracy is the natural order of political organization in today's world. All alternate systems, authoritarian and majoritarian in varying degree, are an aberration. "30 Prime Minister Singh explicitly linked for the first time the Indian model of democracy to an alliance of democratic states in Asia; he saw it as India's obligation to reject authoritarian alternatives to prosperity.

In diplomatic parlance, this was a pointed reference to India as the alternative to China. As an authoritarian state, China could not become a core country in the proposed order for Asia. India's preferred grand narrative is then distinctly different from the one China might construct. Indian leaders remain anxious not to get ahead of the current developments in this regard; they are keenly aware nevertheless of the advantages in establishing a loose alliance of democracies. What is more, their ability to back it up has expanded substantially with the rapid growth in India's economic and military power.

Bibliography

Abul Hasnat Monjurul Kabir (2001) 'Establishing National Human Rights Commissions in South Asia: A Critical Analysis of the Processes and the Prospects', Asia –Pacific journal of Human Rights and the Law, Volume 2,Number 1, 1-53.

Anne Gallagher (2000) 'Making Human Rights Treaty Obligations A Reality: Working with New Actors and Partners', in Alston Philip &Crawford James (eds.) 'The Future of Human Rights Treaty Monitoring', Cambridge: Cambridge University Press.

Aurora Sneh (2001) 'Balancing the Scales: Gender Composition of Commonwealth National Human Rights Institutions', Commonwealth Human Rights Initiative.

Banerjee Sumanta (, February 1, 2003)'Human Rights in India in the Global Context', Economic and Political Weekly.

Basnet Madhavi, 'South Asia's Regional Initiative on Human Rights', The Human Rights Brief, Washington College of Law, American University, Volume 4, Number.2 Winter 1997

Brian Burdekin and Anne Gallagher (Human Rights-2/1998) 'The United Nations and National Human Rights Institutions', in A Quarterly Review of the Office of the UN High Commissioner for Human Rights.

Burdekin Brian and Evans Christine (2000) 'A Global Trend', Canadian Human Rights Foundation Newsletter-VolumeXV.

C.Raj Kumar (September 2000) 'Role and Contribution of National

Human Rights Commissions in Promoting National and International Human Rights Norms in the National Context' unpublished LL.M paper, Harvard Law School.

Cardenas Sonia, 'Adaptive States: The Proliferation of National Human Rights Institutions', Carr Centre for Human Rights Policy Working Paper T-01-04.

Chapman Audrey R., 'Indicators and Standards for Monitoring Economic, Social and Cultural Rights', American Association for the Advancement of Science http://shr.aaas.org/pubs/title.php

Consultation on the Second Asia –Pacific Regional Workshop on National Human Rights Institutions New Delhi, India: SAHRDC.

David Feldman (2002)'Confrontation and Co-Operation between Institution in the Protection of Human Rights', in '*Human Rights Protection: The Role of National Human Rights Institutions*', Butler.F (ed.), Kluwer Law International and British Institute for Human Rights.

Dayal Virendra (2002) 'Evolution of the National Human Rights Commission, 1993- 2002:A Decennial View', in Journal of the National Human Rights Commission, India, Vol.1, 39-70.

Dickson Brice, (2003) 'The Contribution of Human Rights Commissions to the Protection of Human Rights', Public Law Summer, 272-285, Sweet and Maxwell and Contributors.

Epp Charles R, 'The Rights Revolution: Lawyers, Activists, and Supreme Courts in Comparative perspective ', The university of Chicago Press, Chicago and London, 1998.

Gomez Mario (2000) 'National Human Rights Commissions and Economic, Social and Cultural Rights' in 'Circle of Rights: Economic, Social and Cultural Rights Activism: A Training Resource', International Human Rights Internship Program and Asian Forum for Human Rights and Development.

Hucker John (2002) 'Bringing Rights Home: The Role of National

Human Rights Institutions' in Butler.F (ed.) '*Human Rights Protection: The Role of National Human Rights Institutions*', Kluwer Law International and British Institute for Human Rights.

Human Rights Watch report (April 2002) 'we have No Orders to Save You: State Participation and Complicity in Communal Violence in Gujarat', Vol.14, No.3(c).

Jeewan Reddy B.P and Rajeev Dhavan (1994) 'The Jurisprudence of Human Rights', pp.175-226 in Beatty David M. (ed.) 'Human Rights and Judicial Review: A Comparative Perspective', International Studies in Human Rights, Martinus Nijhoff Publishers.

Kaur Jaskaran, 'A Judicial Blackout: Judicial Impunity for Disappearances in Punjab', India, 15 Harvard Human Rights Journal 269 (Summer 2002)

Lindsnaes Birgit, Lindholt Lone & Yigen Kristine (eds.) (2001) '*National Human Rights Institutions-Articles and Working Papers*', The Danish Centre for Human Rights.

NHRC (2002)'Proceedings of the NHRC on the Situation in Gujarat: 1March-1July', National Human Rights Commission of India, New Delhi.

NHRC Annual Report 1999-2000. National Human Rights Commission of India, New Delhi.

Reif C.Linda (2000)'Building Democratic Institutions: The Role of National Human Rights Institutions in Good Governance and Human Rights Protection', Harvard Human Rights Journal, vol.13 spring, 1-70.

South Asia Human Rights Documentation Centre (SAHRDC) (March 1998) *National Human Rights Institutions in the Asia Pacific Region*, Report of the Alternate NGO

South Asia Human Rights Documentation Centre (SAHRDC) (September 2001)'*Judgement Reserved: The Case of the National Human Rights commission of India*', New Delhi: SAHRDC.

Sripati Vijayshri (2001) 'India's National Human Rights Commission: Strengths and Weaknesses', in Lindsnaes Birgit, Lindholt Lone & Yigen Kristine (edit.), *'National Human Rights Institutions-Articles and Working Papers'*, The Danish Centre for Human Rights.

Steiner H. & Alston P. (2000)'International Human Rights in Context', 2nd ed. Oxford: Clarendon Press.

T. Kammingo (1992) "Inter State Accountability for Violations of Human Rights', Philadelphia: University of Pennsylvania Press.

Tigerstorm Von Barbara (2001) 'Implementing Economic, Social and Cultural Rights: The Role of National Human Rights Institutions', in Merali Isfahan and Oosterveld (eds.) *'Giving Meaning to Economic, Social and Cultural Rights'*, PENN University of Pennsylvania Press, Philadelphia.

V.Vijayakumar (2000) 'The Working of the National Human Rights Commission: A Perspective' in C.J Nirmal, (ed.) *Human Rights in India: Historical, Social and Political Perspectives* Oxford :Oxford University Press, Chapter 12.